Ebla

Ebla

An Empire Rediscovered

Paolo Matthiae

Translated by Christopher Holme

HODDER AND STOUGHTON
LONDON SYDNEY AUCKLAND TORONTO

To the friends and colleagues of the
Directorate-General of Antiquities of
the Syrian Arab Republic

British Library Cataloguing in Publication Data

Matthiae, Paolo
  Ebla
  1. Ebla, Syria
  I. Title
  939'.4   DS99.E25

  ISBN 0 340 22974 8

Hodder and Stoughton Editorial Office: 47 Bedford Square, London WC1B 3DP

Preface

In the conviction that Near Eastern archaeology was, properly speaking, historical research, my first aim, when in 1964 I undertook the exploration of Tell Mardikh, was to contribute to the early history of the cultural traditions of Syria. The period when the Old Syrian culture was being formed in the age of Hammurabi of Babylon was still very obscure. To reconstruct this development of cultural traditions a new approach was needed. In Near Eastern archaeology, though the technical aspects of field research are quite advanced, too often chance elements void of a real historical perspective prevailed. The sort of prehistoric anthropology into which the archaeology of the ancient Near East had so often lapsed had now been rejected, since the cultures concerned were now fully historical. Thus the best inspiration for a coherent method of research, it seemed, must be that of classical archaeology. In Italy there were sound historical reasons which until recent years had prevented the formation of a tradition of Near Eastern archaeology. In the wider world of classical studies, moreover, the roots of the West were almost exclusively sought in the soil of Greek culture first and of Latin only second. In Italy itself it was almost impossible to understand how largely the West, until the Counter Reformation had been permeated with attitudes foreign to the classical world and special to the East.

The years of my training owed most to the teaching of R. Bianchi Bandinelli for his penetrating reflections about the history of archaeological research in its aims and trends, on the one side, and in the firm consideration of archaeology as a descipline with specific methods related with a definite level of evidence, on the other. I found there the most promising lines of speculation on Syrian history to be followed up not only in the study but also in the field. The historical approach was to be the element of renewal for the stylistic pseudo-critique which passed for classical studies. It was also the key to a new, all-embracing vision of archaeology as nothing but historical science. In this spirit I found there the essential conditions for a new attack on the problem of the formation and development of the Prehellensistic cultures of Syria.

It is typical of the contradictions of this situation that no less a person than Henri Frankfort, one of the great personalities of Near Eastern archaeology, fine critic, penetrating historian, talented excavator, was responsible for an authoritative synthesis in which were taken up and codified some of the most antihistorical judgments on the artistic civilisation of Syria. Yet at the same time, in the Fifties, he was the author of illuminating studies on the continuity of the Syrian tradition especially in architecture. Frankfort did have the great merit of rejecting the attempts to base Syrian cultures on racial or ethnic characters

and of concentrating his attention on more complex and highly developed historical realities. But at the same time he identified a
succession of external influences as the very rhythm of Syria's history,
instead of seeking to define the peculiarities of artistic style in each
individual centre at a given period.

Some useful contributions, notably from E. Porada, U. Moortgat-
Corens, and H. J. Kantor, had laid the groundwork for a revision of
particular but important chronological problems. But a fundamental
renewal of Syrian archaeology could only arise from new exploration in
the field. Here the first big moment was the beginning of the excavation
of Tell Khuera by A. Moortgat. The start of operations at Tell Mardikh
a few years later pursued for the North Syrian area aims similar to those
entertained for Northern Mesopotamia by the Head of the Berlin
School of Archaeology, in the tradition of the pioneering exploration of
Tell Halaf. In the University of Rome Expedition, however, which was
to lead to the identification and discovery of Ebla, it must be clearly
emphasised that there was a fundamental difference. Our work was not
attached to an established cultural tradition or a solid framework of
organisation but was to be thought of as a new starting point by a nation
building from the foundations its tradition of studies of the historical
civilisations of the ancient Near East.

The Italian Archaeological Expedition to Syria of the University of
Rome was constituted in 1964, on the initiative of the Institute of Near
East Studies, then directed by Sabatino Moscati, to whom the credit is
due for promoting Near Eastern archaeology in Italy. It was supported
by financial contributions from the University itself, from the Ministry
of Foreign Affairs, and the National Council of Research, which
guaranteed the yearly budget required by the Expedition for carrying
on the excavations. In more recent years the Ministry of Public
Education has also made a contribution of its own. I tender my
most profound personal thanks to all these bodies which have enabled
the archaeological exploration of Tell Mardikh-Ebla to be carried on.

The work of the Expedition has been made possible from the start
and with the utmost regularity as it went on by the fraternal and
whole-hearted collaboration of the friends and colleagues of the
Directorate-General of Antiquities of the Syrian Arab Republic, to
whom these pages are dedicated in token of a cordial and conscious
sympathy and sincere gratitude.

It is in this spirit that I wish to express my warmest thanks to doctor
Selim Abd-ul-Hak, the Director-General of Antiquities at Damascus at
the time when the Expedition was first set up, and among his successors, who always gave the Italian archaeologists every support, to
Ambassador Abd-ul-Hamid Darkal. Our deepest gratitude is tendered
to Doctor Afif Bahnassi, the present Director-General of Antiquities,

for the help he has given on every occasion with understanding and friendship. I express my warmest thanks to Adnan Bounni, Director of the Archaeological Excavation Service in Damascus, to whose attentive care and sympathy the Expedition is indebted for having been able to carry on its labours in an atmosphere of unfailing cordiality. With him I should like to mention with sincere gratitude the other archaeologists of the Directorate General of Antiquities in Damascus, in particular Kassem Toueir, for his fraternal devotion, and of the Directorate of Antiquities at Aleppo, in particular Mahmud Heretani, Director of Antiquities for Northern Syria, Wahid Khayata, Director of the Aleppo Museum, and Shawki Shaath. A grateful thought goes also to the representatives of the Directorate of Antiquities, who have succeeded one another at Tell Mardikh from 1964 to 1976, solving innumerable problems for the Expedition. Among them I would mention Abd-er-Razak Hayeni, responsible for Antiquities in the Mohafaza of Idlib.

The civil and military authorities of the Mohafaza of Idlib, in whose territory Tell Mardikh is, have given protection and support to the Italian Expedition from the very first years of the excavations, and this has always been most valuable. H. E. Abdallah Ahmar, at present Vice-Secretary General of the Baath Arab Socialist Party and former Mohafez of Idlib, who has several times visited the excavations, showing his high appreciation, and still follows with lively sympathy the successes of the University of Rome Expedition, is hereby thanked most cordially. My most grateful recognition is due also to H. E. Tawfik Salha, Mohafez of Idlib, wise and enthusiastic promoter of the region's cultural treasures and true friend.

For its very first setting-up the Expedition is indebted to the intelligent and untiring services of Carlo Perrone Capano, then Italian Ambassador in Damascus. It was due to his far-sighted effort that this Italian archaeological activity in Syria was launched, and from distant posts he has followed its progress with undiminished interest ever since. I offer him my most affectionate gratitude. The Expedition has enjoyed constant support from the Italian diplomatic Deputation in Damascus, and with sincere gratitude I record the names of the Ambassadors Roberto Riccardi, Uberto Bozzini, Maurizio Bucci. My most cordial thanks, too, to the present Ambassador of Italy in Damascus, Giorgio Giacomelli, for his active and understanding support of the Expedition; to Paolo Marcopoli, Consul of Italy at Aleppo, for his unfailing and valuable support; and to Bruno Cabras, Counsellor of the Italian Embassy in Damascus, for his friendly help over the past few years.

In a generally difficult and complex situation, the Expedition has had essential support from the academic authorities of the University of Rome. I have great personal satisfaction in expressing my deep obligation to Antonio Ruberti, Rector of the University, for his devoted and open support of the Expedition's scientific activities and his lively appreciation of its results. My most cordial thanks too to Luigi de Nardis, Head of the Faculty of Letters and Philosophy, for his continual and understanding attention to every problem of the Expedition.

In reaching preliminary interpretations of many aspects of the discoveries of Ebla, as they will be presented in the following pages and for which obviously the writer takes full responsibility, many colleagues have joined, often more than once, in exchanges of opinion with the writer. I should like to acknowledge a special debt of gratitude to Pierre Amiet, Paris; Robert J. Braidwood, Chicago; Pelio Fronzaroli, Florence; Ignace J. Gelb, Chicago; Donald P. Hansen, New York; Mario Liverani, Rome; Maurits N. van Loon, Amsterdam; Winfried Orthmann, Saarbrücken; Edith Porada, New York; Edmond Sollberger, London.

Last but not least, I want to record that the results so far achieved by the Expedition could not have been so without the collective efforts of a substantial group of fellow workers who have given their enthusiasm and effort on the Tell Mardikh site. Since it is impossible, however much their due, to enumerate all those — colleagues, fellow workers, students — who have contributed even for short periods to the discovery of Ebla, I should like, while remembering everyone with the liveliest gratitude, to record the names at least of my friends Pelio Fronzaroli, Mario Liverani, and Maria Squarciapino Floriani who put all their skills into planning the archaeological exploration of Tell Mardikh. To Giovanni Pettinato goes the credit for having read and interpreted the first documents of the Ebla State Archives and for having identified the North-West Semitic language in which they are written.

But those who together with the writer have borne the often heavy burden of the excavation in all its phases, contributing to make its interpretation possible by continual constructive discussion, are a group of students and fellow workers, both archaeologists and architects, without whose endeavours the major discoveries of Ebla would not have been made: Gabriella Scandone Matthiae, Carlo Cataldi Tassoni, Stefania Mazzoni, Alessandro de Maigret, Frances Pinnock, Francesca Baffi, Rita Dolce. In particular, it is with the greatest pleasure that I express my most affectionate and heart-felt thanks to my students Francesca Baffi, Rita Dolce, Stefania Mazzoni, and Frances Pinnock, who even in the most difficult moments have employed their best energies for the success of the Expedition.

Mardikh, October 1977

Ebla
Preface to the English Edition

The last pages of the original Italian edition of this book were completed in August 1977. Since then the archaeological exploration of
Ebla has continued year by year and produced results of great historical importance. The study of the texts in the State Archives has
been pursued through international collaboration, as a guarantee
against bias. The unscientific polemics about their contents, almost
always based on quite unfounded information, have sometimes
reached grotesque proportions.

The space of a preface is not the place to illustrate the recent
archaeological discoveries and new textual interpretations or to
reject the pseudo-historical speculations. But the author in present-
ing the English edition of this book does think the reader should now
have explained to him, though in very general terms at the current
level of research and study, what are the historical facts based on
documentary evidence and what is misunderstanding and speculation
distorted by the mass media.

The most recent archaeological investigations at Tell Mardikh not
only confirmed, enlarged and expanded in detail the data and documentation already obtained but opened entirely new horizons of
extraordinary interest. The north core of the Administrative
Quarters of the Royal Palace G of the third quarter of the Third
millennium B.C. has been uncovered completely. With its beautiful
colonnaded court and large south hall it was perhaps the centre of the
important political and cultural power that was Ebla in the Mature
Early Syrian Period. The unexpected extension of Royal Palace G to
the south of the Acropolis with its very well-preserved structures,
besides that to the west, is a current discovery at the time of writing
— the beginning of the 1979 season. The date of the destruction of
Royal Palace G and the end of the great culture of Mardikh IIB1 is
now determined with certainty by the discovery on the floor of the
inner court of the Administrative Quarters of several fragments of
stone vases imported from Egypt, two of which bear short hieroglyphic inscriptions with two names from the titles of Chefren, the
great pharaoh of the IVth Dynasty. A lid of an Egyptian alabaster
vase has a third hieroglyphic inscription with the complete titles of
Pepi I of the VIth Dynasty. While the first two inscriptions have
special historical significance, the third is a fundamental *terminus
post quem* for the destruction of Palace G. The Palace of the State
Archives cannot have been destroyed before Sargon of Akkad and
was most probably destroyed by Naram-Sin of Akkad. Any dating of
the destruction to the Early Dynastic Period of Mesopotamian chron-

ology, any date that is of the pre-Sargonid age, is therefore excluded.

In 1978 excavation was begun of a great palace complex, Building Q of Mardikh IIIA-B, founded probably around 1900 B.C., together with that of a princely necropolis stretching under the new palace. The two hypogea explored so far, the 'Tomb of the Princess' and the 'Tomb of the Lord of the Goats', explored in November 1978, probably belonged to very high-ranking personages of Mardikh IIIB, in the Mature Old Syrian Period. The rich furniture of these tombs and their certain connection with the monumental Building Q make it likely that the burial area was the royal necropolis of Amorite Ebla, contemporary with the royal tombs of Byblos. The development of current excavations leads us to believe that the 'Tomb of the Lord of the Goats' was violated at the same time as the final destruction of Mardikh IIIB around 1600 B.C. The disappearance of the body, and with it perhaps rich furniture, most probably taken by the Hittite conquerors, and two spearheads fixed in the wall of the funerary hypogeum are evidence of the profanation committed by the soldiers of Hattusilis I or Mursilis I.

The systematic study of the texts of the State Archives is in the hands of a group of Italian and foreign scholars, coordinated by the International Committee for the Study of Ebla Texts, which was appointed by the University of Rome on the proposal of the Directorate General of Antiquities at Damascus. The International Committee, which is the consultative organ of the Italian Expedition in epigraphic matters, plans, organises and coordinates the studies of the texts under the chairmanship and editorship of the author. The first volumes of the official final edition of the texts, dealing with administrative texts (*Archivi Reali de Ebla. Testi*), are now in an advanced stage of preparation.

Several articles have already appeared or are in print containing preliminary studies of the administrative texts (which deal with the distribution of textiles, the calendar, the system of weights and the breeding of cattle), of the 'historical' texts, of the literary texts and of the Sumerian and bilingual lexical texts. Studies have already been published and are now in print concerning the assessment of the Eblaite language and its position among the Semitic languages, with particular regard to its phonology, lexicology and aspects of its morphology. A collection of periodical studies concerning the archaeological and epigraphic discoveries at Ebla (*Annali di Ebla*) is now being published under the responsibility of the Italian Expedition, while systematic studies of the syllabary, the palaeography, the personal and place names, will be presented in a special series of monographs (*Archivi Reali de Ebla. Studi*). A programme of elaboration of the data by computer has been jointly worked out by the Expedition and Los Angeles University.

Further study of the texts of the Ebla State Archives will to some extent change the general picture we were able to present a few months after their discovery in October 1975.

Many elements of historical reconstruction are certain to emerge from the systematic study of the texts. The picture sketched some months ago looks valid and some doubtful data have now become clear. Akkad is not mentioned in Ebla texts, nor is Sargon of Akkad nor the legendary Dudiya of Assur. Iblul-Il of Mari certainly lived in the time of Enna-Dagan and therefore perhaps of Ar-Ennum of Ebla. Byblos most probably does not appear in the texts, for the place name initially identified with it now seems to be an upper Mesopotamian centre that must be read as Dulu.

Polemics, often harsh and always painful for the author, have arisen from individual speculations about presumed connections between the Ebla texts and Biblical characters, stories and episodes. The interest aroused among the public by these unfounded inferences of a relationship between Ebla and the Bible is understandable, but it must clearly be said that documentary evidence of them is effectively non-existent. The speculations had their origin in rash and inexplicable statements not authorised by the Italian Expedition.

It has been said and written that in the texts of the State Archives of Mature Early Syrian Ebla there is proof of the historical accuracy of the Bible patriarchs, news of a cult of Yahwe at Ebla, a mention of the cities of Sodom and Gomorrah and other cities of the plain, and a literary text with the story of the Flood. These are tales without foundation.

It has been said quite justifiably that the Ebla discoveries have revealed a new language, a new history and a new culture. The evidence already won and still emerging from these discoveries must be evaluated from a truly historical point of view. The Italian Expedition is morally and scientifically engaged in a wholehearted application of this principle.

Mardikh, September 1979

Contents

1
Archaeological Research in Syria and the Historical Problem of Prehellenistic Western Asia

The first steps towards a modern discipline of archaeology may be said to have been taken in the eighteenth century by the great German scholar and art historian J. J. Winckelmann. His concern with historical method in ordering the monuments of antiquity led gradually to their being regarded not only as aesthetic wonders but as sources of information. A way was marked for the random treasure-hunting of the first diggers to be replaced by a spirit of historical enquiry.

Yet when, well on into the nineteenth century, antiquarian interest began to move from ancient Greece and Rome to the lands further east, the new ideas might never have been heard of. They played almost no part in the first adventurous excavations begun at Khorsabad in 1842 by Paul Emile Botta, Italian-born French consul in Mosul, or by Sir Henry Layard a few months later at the not far distant tell of Nimrud. Both were looking for remains of the Assyrian splendours recorded in the Bible, and both found them. Botta in a few years uncovered 'Sargon's city', the short-lived Neo-Assyrian capital of Dur Sharrukin, while Layard found the ancient Kalhu. The sculptural decorations in both were so abundant and of such quality as to suggest the wealth of Nineveh itself. But neither of them was Nineveh, and only a few years later the tyrant city of Bible prophecy had itself been identified, with the two tells facing Mosul across the Tigris, Quyunjik and Nebi Yunus.

The excavation of the South-West Palace at Quyunjik with its reliefs, the vast epic cycles celebrating the exploits of Sennacherib (705–681 B.C.), the thousands of texts recovered from the famous library of Assurbanipal (668–627 B.C.) and the North Palace finds with their exquisite evocations of the King's hunts and wars completed the first phase in the rediscovery of the Assyrian civilisation.

These first archaeological researches in the northern part of the valley of the twin rivers yielded, right from the beginning, a wealth of evidence, both inscriptions and works of art, of the last great flowering of the Mesopotamian civilisation. They were followed in the southern area by explorations at first hasty and disorganised, but soon intensified, especially by J. E. Taylor, which led to the definite identification, from 1854 onward, of some of the great city centres of Babylonia. Thus Ur and Eridu, two of the most ancient Sumerian cities, were located.

Inscriptions were found in Southern Mesopotamia as abundantly as in the north. Even more extraordinary, however, seemed the reports about statues lying on the surface of one southern site, and these in 1877 led Ernest de Sarzec, French consul in Basrah, to Telloh, the ancient

Girsu, one of the greatest centres of the Sumerian civilisation of the third millennium B.C. The French authorities immediately recognised the importance of the discovery of Telloh and one result was the establishment of a department of oriental antiquities at the Louvre. Excavations on the site were continued for thirteen seasons, until 1900, and revealed to the West the language, art, and civilisation of the Sumerians. Following the discoveries at Telloh the site of Nippur was explored and proved exceptionally rich in inscriptions. Among these, besides a mass of economic documents, a large number of Sumerian literary and religious texts were brought to light.

An event of very different significance from the American Nippur expedition was the entry into Southern Mesopotamia of two German scholars. The work first of Robert Koldewey and then more especially of Walter Andrae on the fundamental sites of Babylonia and at Assur established Mesopotamian archaeology on a scientific footing. They laid down lines for the choice of sites and surveyed them with meticulous effort and tenacity. Their wide, global view, of real city centres to be explored, was combined with a technical accuracy that became a systematic rule of research. It was combined too with a feeling for the tangle of cultures out of which a historical approach to Mesopotamian archaeology might emerge. In his work at Assur Andrae never lost sight of the exact limits imposed by his method on the excavation of a Prehellenistic Mesopotamian site. In the years following the First World War the experience gained just before it by his co-workers on the site of the most ancient Assyrian capital was to prove a direct stimulus in the conduct of every major archaeological enterprise in the Mesopotamian area between the two wars. Foremost among these were the systematic excavation of Ur, with particular regard to its monumental centre, by Sir Leonard Woolley; the exploration of a complex of important historical sites in the area of the River Diyala under the direction of Henri Frankfort; the examination in depth of the two great cult centres at Uruk by J. Jordan, A. Nöldeke, E. Heinrich, and H. J. Lenzen.

1. The beginnings of archaeological exploration in Syria: the recovery of the 'Neo-Hittite' culture and art of the first millennium B.C.

The first important excavation in the Syrian area was that of the tell of Zinjirli, the ancient Sam'al. In 1888 Felix von Luschan, following the chance discovery of some partially exposed sculptures on this mound, uncovered an important city settlement of the Iron Age (c. 1200–535 B.C.). It belonged to the cultural complex which has been called, rather

Figure 1   The Major Archaeological Sites of Syria

loosely, 'Neo-Hittite' or Aramaean. Syria had not until then attracted much attention from archaeologists, chiefly because of its apparent poverty in written documents. The French 'Expedition to Phoenicia' of 1860 was an attempt of the second Napoleonic era to repeat the successes of Napoleon I's celebrated expedition to Egypt. Its leader, Ernest Renan, took numerous soundings at Byblos, Sidon, Tyre, and Arwad. But there were no sensational finds of early material, and it was only the richness of some late tombs in the necropolises of Sidon — Persian or Hellenistic at best — which, after Renan's return to Europe, induced the Imperial Museums of Constantinople to carry out excavations in the area of the great Phoenician cities. The historical interpretation of Phoenician civilisation, based reasonably enough in those early years by Count Charles Melchior de Vogüé on what little had been brought to light from the great centres of the Mediterranean coast, was soon overtaken by a more popular current of scholarly

opinion derived from the attribution to the Phoenicians of the splendid
ivories found at Nimrud.

The excavations of Zinjirli, in which Koldewey also collaborated
before his gigantic assignment in Babylonia, were relatively
methodical. A fairly complete picture of the lay-out of the city,
especially the citadel with its many typical palace units, was obtained.
An idea was also gained of the artistic achievement of this centre which
over a long period protected itself from Neo-Assyrian expansionism
through a skilful policy of vassalage. The size of the reliefs decorating
the gates and some of the palace buildings in the citadel for the first time
put back on show a substantial body of art from the Syrian area. Some
long inscriptions in Aramaic enabled the greater part of it to be dated to
the ninth to eighth centuries B.C. The only parallel to these first discoveries at Zinjirli were some scattered remains found a few years later
at Tell Tayanat and Marash. In accounting for the historical development of the civilisation thus brought to light scholars at that time
compared them, almost as a matter of course, with the huge contemporary Neo-Assyrian reliefs and supposed them to be a product of
Assyrian artistic influence.

A further important development in the exploration of the North
Syrian area was the chance discovery in 1899 by M. von Oppenheim of
the sculptures on the surface at Tell Halaf, a big tell near the source of
the Khabur, a left-bank tributary of the Euphrates. He was not able to
organise the excavations until 1911, when they lasted until 1914, with
resumptions in 1927 and 1929. Here as at Zinjirli a significant part was
played in the conduct of the dig by architects of the Koldewey school.
The successes of the Tell Halaf Expedition in bringing to light what is
now known to have been a capital of the Aramaean period were
overshadowed by a mistaken dating of the sculptures which were
re-used in the building of the so-called Temple-Palace. The hand of the
German school of architect-archaeologists in the Koldewey tradition
was evident in the meticulous care with which the architecture was
graphically recorded. But von Oppenheim insisted on dating a great
part of the reliefs to the fourth millennium B.C. and for a time secured
authoritative backing from E. Herzfeld. But it soon appeared to many
scholars that the whole complex of sculptures at Tell Halaf could not be
dated earlier than the twelfth century B.C. When it was finally decided,
many years after the excavation, to bring out a definitive, systematic
publication of the finds, an analytic study by A. Moortgat confirmed
that the most ancient works must in fact be of the tenth century.

Like the archaic reliefs of Zinjirli the small 'orthostats' of Tell Halaf
came to be regarded as specially 'primitive'. Aesthetic prejudices of this
kind were profoundly damaging to history and to the development of a
correct critical approach to the artistic achievements of Syria and

Northern Mesopotamia in the first millennium B.C. The relatively good preservation of the buildings in which this culture was now being revealed provided archaeological contexts well suited to a thorough investigation of its elements and character. And these discoveries at Zinjirli and Tell Halaf did indeed give rise, from the very first, to a serious debate on the cultural relations between Assyrian and Aramaean architecture. But in the case of monumental art the old attitudes persisted. This was seen as having undergone a purely evolutionary development, from a 'primitive' stage earlier than any Assyrian influence to a 'mature' stage under that influence. This ruled out in advance any proper understanding of the culture of the North Syrian area at the beginning of the first millennium, with historical roots so remote from those of the Neo-Assyrian culture. Thus all possibility was denied of piecing together the historical origins of this art and its earliest components — rather as if the whole civilisation had been outside history until Assyria came on the scene. A kind of pseudo-criticism grew up. In the historical assessment of the North Syrian culture only external influences were allowed to count, because only they, it was thought, could be exactly dated by criteria independent of the artistic quality of the works themselves. Thus from the very first disorganised and piecemeal assessments of these North Syrian art works, soon to be defined as Neo-Hittite, two of the most obstinate dogmas in the art history of the ancient East became established: they lacked all originality and were totally dependent on outside influences.

The third great centre of the first millennium to be brought to light was Carchemish, on the upper Euphrates. It was identified with great perspicacity by G. Smith in 1876 and excavations were begun in 1908 by D. G. Hogarth and C. L. (later Sir Leonard) Woolley. They were resumed in 1920 and then finally abandoned. The exploration of Carchemish, prompted once again by the presence on the surface of the citadel of remains of monumental sculpture, was undertaken essentially in order to permit the recovery of numerous reliefs of the Neo-Hittite period. At the time when the excavations were carried out, the written documentation in Middle Hittite from Hattusas and in Old Babylonian from Mari was not yet available to prove the important part played by Carchemish in the Hittite imperial period from the fourteenth century onward and in the period of the Amorite dynasties between the end of the nineteenth and middle of the eighteenth centuries B.C. Thus the investigations were limited to the recovery of numerous reliefs and of Luvian hieroglyphic inscriptions. They did not, except to a limited extent in the area of the main tell, back this up with a systematic study of levels earlier than the first millennium. The Carchemish excavations could not draw on the experience of a group of architects like those engaged during those same years at Tell Halaf and for this reason their interest in architectural problems was rather limited. But they did recover artistic material of the first importance both in the quality of the works and in the homogeneity of the context in which the reliefs were still preserved in their original positions.

Being so much older, the case of Carchemish was radically different from those of Sam'al in the west and Guzana, the ancient name of Tell Halaf, in the east. These two may be considered as new foundations of the Early Iron Age. It is moreover certain that there were no important settlements of the Late Bronze (c. 1600–1200 B.C.) at Zinjirli and Tell Halaf. But Carchemish was a very ancient centre of civilisation. Today it is clear that the 'Neo-Hittite' art which was brought to fruition there was the outcome of a long cultural process. The city played a leading part in the history of Northern Syria at least from the beginning of the second millennium, and indeed, as we now know from Ebla texts, even from the middle of the third. The mass of figurative objects from Carchemish have a definite stamp of individuality — a well-considered formal elaboration, and an evident regard for traditional values. Their internal chronology is complicated and the evidence from inscriptions often very doubtful. But it was quickly felt that they must be considered together with those of Sam'al and Guzana as expressions of a single artistic culture. A difficulty here was the contrast between the formal solidity of the Carchemish works and the apparently modest and popular tone of the more ancient pieces from Sam'al and Guzana. They were thus all given the composite and self-contradictory name of 'Syro-Hittite', to indicate a unity and apparent discordance which the un-historical critique of the day was quite incapable of explaining. Thus, though the first archaeological explorations of the Syrian area had already brought to light, before the First World War, the most significant architectural and artistic assemblages of Syrian culture in the first centuries of the first millennium B.C., it was already clear that critical judgment was handicapped by serious prejudices. These hindered not only the understanding of the artistic achievement of Syria in the Iron Age, but also the possible identification of an independent Syrian tradition in the preceding centuries.

At the end of the nineteenth century trial exploration carried out in the area of Southern Palestine, particularly at Tell el-Hesi, by W. F. (Sir Flinders) Petrie, with the collaboration of J. F. Bliss, prepared the ground for the development of a stratigraphic archaeology. The attention given to the registration of all finds, however minor, the systematic use of ceramics to set up a relative chronology, the graphical recording of the succession of levels in relation to the provenance of every find, were the cardinal points of the system which Petrie had been working out. They remained the fundamental ingredients of an operational method of excavation which, despite initial scepticism, rapidly assumed the character of a set of rules for general use. The archaeology of the Syrian area, however, remained apart from this significant advance in the rules and technique of investigation. Its links were with the prevailing tendencies of Mesopotamian archaeology, in which, as I have indicated, the architectural interest took priority over the stratigraphical.

	1920	1930	1940	1950	1960	1970
El-Mina						
Ugarit		Schaeffer (1929)				Margueron (1975)
Tell Sukas					Riis (1958)	
Tell Kazel					Bounni (1957)	
Byblos	Montet (1922) Dunand (1926)					
Sidon	Contenau (1920)					
Tyre	Le Lasseur (1921)					

Figure 2   Chronology of Archaeological Exploration in Coastal Syria

2. Excavations between the wars: the fundamental aspects of the Old Syrian and Middle Syrian cultures of the second millennium B.C.

There was a vigorous return to archaeological exploration in the Near East after the First World War. But it was conditioned by the profound political changes which had occurred there, a great part of the region being now under British and French Mandate. In Iraq the first important work to be resumed was that of the British expeditions to Kish and Ur, while in the Syrian area there were intensive efforts by France to locate the centres of special importance to be chosen as sites for long and successful programmes of field research. Excavations were at once launched at Sidon in 1920 under the direction of G. Contenau, at Tyre in 1921 under D. Le Lasseur. In 1922 P. Montet started the exploration of Byblos, which after four seasons under his leadership was taken over by M. Dunand. The French evidently felt it as their first need to take up where Renan had left off, and despite his relative lack of success, to lay the foundations of a deeper knowledge of the Phoenician world of the first millennium. Here were the great creative centres of a culture which had more immediate and conspicuous contacts with the world of the Bible and the West than with the East. Even the choice of sites — Sidon, Tyre, Byblos — seemed to be based on

Renan's well-known statement of method, according to which any definition of the Phoenician culture must be derived from archaeological elements originating in the four major Phoenician centres of Arwad, Byblos, Sidon and Tyre.

But these very intentions were largely disappointed. At Tyre results were limited to the exploration of tombs of the Roman period. At Sidon, apart from the excavation of late Persian and Hellenistic tombs, only one sounding in the area of the crusader castle seemed to have reached levels of Iron Age I and II, while the only monument of importance there on which study could begin was the largely late Phoenician temple of Eshmun. Only at Byblos did the results match expectations from the very start. King Ahiram's sarcophagus, which was found there, was the first outstanding monument of Phoenician art of assured date and provenance from the beginning of the tenth century B.C. The judgments of historians on Phoenician art could now be reassessed on a solid basis, as could the important survey by F. Poulsen in which the principal artistic material considered had been that reaching Kalhu, as tribute or loot of uncertain origin. Byblos under Dunand became a site of great importance. Abundant evidence of its time-honoured links with Egypt particularly under the Old Kingdom came to light. A great deal was done, too, to illustrate the characteristics of the Byblite culture, especially in architecture, during the last centuries of the third millennium and the first centuries of the second. The excavations are still in progress, and the widening of their area beyond the actual tell of Jebail has revealed much that was not represented including most of the Iron Age city. Probably at the beginning of the Late Bronze, and certainly by the beinning of the Iron Age, a little after 1200 B.C., the settlement must have been moved. The ancient residential area was abandoned, though not perhaps the sanctuaries. It seems probable that the properly Phoenician city of Byblos of the first millennium must lie under the modern town, rather as in the case of Arwad, Sidon, and Tyre.

It must be emphasised that the archaeological exploration of Syria in the Twenties was not according to a programme or system. There were no surface explorations to prepare archaeological maps of limited zones characterised by a certain ecological unity and record the sites of historical interest for the Prehellenistic periods. Quite the contrary, the excavations were always occasioned by chance finds or by presumed identifications with historical centres known from written sources.

As for the sites of the Syrian interior, the first case was that of Mishrife, an immense tell of regular shape a few kilometres from Homs, where the excavations, begun in 1926 by R. du Mesnil du Buisson and continued for four campaigns, led to the identification of the ancient Qatna. The second was Tell Nebi Mend, also in the Homs

region, which was identified with fair certainty as the ancient Qadesh
and explored from 1921 onwards under the directon of M. Pézard. The
results, however, were not very impressive, apart from a rather broad
definition of the periods represented on the site. Moreover, the tells
seem to have been chosen simply because they were near to modern city
centres and thus more accessible to excavation. Thus a variety of
miscellaneous reasons must have determined the excavation in 1926 of
Neyrab, a few kilometres east of Aleppo, by M. Abel and A. Barrois.
This site, so convenient from a logistic point of view, was wrongly
regarded as the find-spot of the Aramaean stelae described as 'from
Neyrab' in the Louvre. The name Neyrab is found in these inscriptions
and is today widespread among North Syrian place-names, so that the
site was identified with an ancient city of the same name, for which
there is no other evidence.

	1900	1910	1920	1930	1940	1950	1960	1970
Amuq				McEwan (1931)				
Tell Atchana					Woolley (1936)			
Ayn Dara							Seirafi (1956)	
Tell Rifaat								
Carchemish	Hogarth/ Woolley (1908)							
Arslan Tash				Thureau-Dangin (1928)				
Tell Ahmar				Thureau-Dangin (1929)				
Neyrab				Abel/Barrois (1926)				
Tell Afis								Matthiae (1970)
Tell Mardikh							Matthiae (1964)	
Hama					Ingholt (1932)			
Mishrife				du Mesnil du Buisson (1926)				
Tell Nebi Mend				Pezard (1921)				
Mari					Parrot (1933)			
Tell Ashara								Buccellati (1975)

Figure 3 Chronology of Archaeological Exploration of Inland Syria

No coherent picture could be given by such a fragmentary and
scattered pattern of research, nearly always of very brief duration. The
exceptional tell of Mishrife was identified as the ancient Qatna, and
the site was of evident importance as early as the end of the third
millennium, but more especially during the Middle Bronze and the first
part of the Late Bronze Ages. But the excavations were abandoned in
1929 after only four campaigns. The texts recovered there, especially

the Qatna temple inventories datable to the fifteenth century B.C.,
furnished a succession of kings of the great city. These must have
reigned several decades before its final destruction by Suppiluliumas, at
a time when Qatna was for a while in the area of Egyptian control and
thereafter at the limits first of the Mitannic and then of the Egyptian
spheres of influence. Tell Nebi Mend was another site which appeared
suitable to furnish a picture of the Middle Syrian culture in the Late
Bronze Age. But here too the opportunity was not fully grasped. In
fact, the beginnings of archaeological exploration in the region of Homs
in the Syrian interior were disappointing. Though they included the two
most important Late Bronze Age centres not obscured by subsequent
levels, they failed to realise their aim. There was no decisive advance in
knowledge of the Middle Syrian culture, and they missed the importance and wide range of the culture of Syria in the last centuries of the
third millennium. Yet the ceramic evidence for it was appearing everywhere in the Homs and Hama region. In fact it was the soundings made
by R. du Mesnil du Buisson in a series of tells north of Hama — Suran,
Tell As, Khan Sheykhun — which made known the ceramic culture,
later inappropriately called 'chalice culture', corresponding to Early
Bronze IVA-B.

The only important excavations of the immediate post-war period on
the major historical sites of the early first millennium were those led by
the great Assyriologist F. Thureau-Dangin, with the collaboration of
M. Dunand and G. Dossin, at Arslan Tash and Tell Ahmar.

At Arslan Tash, the ancient Hadatu, the excavations were completed
in two campaigns in 1928. The localities were already noted for having
provided the Imperial Museums of Constantinople with a group of
provincial Neo-Assyrian sculptures attributed to the reign of Tiglath-
pileser III (745–727 B.C.). The French explorations, though quite short,
brought to light structures of the Assyrian provincial residency and a
very important collection of ivories, almost certainly of the eighth
century, possibly of Phoenician manufacture, designed partly or wholly
to decorate furniture ordered by a king of Damascus. This noteworthy
series of ivories, today preserved partly in the Louvre and partly in the
Aleppo Museum, was not recovered intact, and a substantial number of
pieces, also in good condition, were filched during the excavation and
reappeared recently on the antique market, to end up mostly in the
Karlsruhe Museum. In the three seasons immediately following, from
1929 to 1931 at Tell Ahmar, the ancient Til Barsip, capital of the small
Aramaean kingdom of Bit Adini and afterwards seat of an Assyrian
prefecture, F. Thureau-Dangin recovered some interesting examples
of 'Neo-Hittite' sculpture earlier than the Assyrian conquest and to be
placed undoubtedly in the cultural and artistic context of near-by
Carchemish. But the most sensational of his discoveries were the

splendid Neo-Assyrian pictorial cycles dating from the time of Shamshi-ilu and Tiglat-pileser III.

For a history of the cultures of Syria in the ninth and eighth centuries B.C. the Arslan Tash and Tell Ahmar excavations are of particular significance. The arrays of sculpture and painting in the two centres have made it possible to see the form actually taken by the great Neo-Assyrian figurative tradition in an easily intelligible historical environment, as provided by these two provincial residencies. The sculptures of Arslan Tash are specially important in showing how the Assyrian tradition might mix with the 'Neo-Hittite' atmosphere in a centre of patronage closely linked with the court of Kalhu. On the other hand the extraordinary paintings of Til Barsip revealed that even in a 'Neo-Hittite' atmosphere the courtly style of the great Neo-Assyrian art might prevail. Here, in a provincial residency where the attractions of the central power were specially strong, it had been employed with unhesitating assurance. It had, moreover, the sort of classical taste which only a strong artistic guild can impose and which must certainly have come direct from Assur or Kalhu.

The decade of the Thirties opened with an event which was to have exceptional consequences in the history of Syrian archaeology. This was the excavation begun in 1929 of the tell of Ras Shamra, a short distance from Lattakia, on the Mediterranean coast, under the direction of C. F. A. Schaeffer. The discovery, in the very first season, of texts in alphabetic cuneiform of the fourteenth to thirteenth centuries B.C., expressing a North-Western Semitic language close to Phoenician, was an unexpected revelation which at once enabled the ancient site to be identified with the city of Ugarit. The continuation of the excavations regularly and systematically led to the recovery of a great number of administrative and literary texts and vocabularies in Ugaritic, of many documents, especially administrative and political, in Middle Babylonian and of texts, some very important, in Hittite and Hurrian. But it also gave a complete picture of an important centre of the Late Bronze Age which had been the capital of one of the kingdoms of the North Syrian coastal area. The excavations, interrupted in 1939 and resumed after the war under the leadership of C. F. A. Schaeffer, who was succeeded in 1975 by J. C. Margueron, yielded material of such abundance and variety that Ugarit in many minds came to stand for Late Bronze Age Syria. The speaking image which it had become possible to form of this city was seen as typical of those last two centuries.

Yet the cultural situation of Ugarit is far more complex. It becomes rash to assume any simple equivalence between the culture of Ugarit and that of inland or even coastal Syria at that period. Art work of such varied provenance is found there as to suggest a world without any easily identifiable mode of expression of its own. But at least we can say that in the architecture of Middle Syrian Ugarit and in artistic products such as the sculpture of the stelae and the carving of the ivories, we have a quite mature taste which can be called peculiarly Syrian. From the very beginning of the Ugarit discoveries the essential problem has been and today still is to identify an atmosphere, or historical reality, of taste, instead of simply isolating components in traditional terms of influences. In fact what is Egyptian or Anatolian in the bronzes, seals and gems of Ugarit is quite evident. For a correct historical setting something else is needed. The Ugarit figurative culture is all too frequently treated, with misleading simplifications, as a composite one. Instead, what is needed is to identify the chronological phases and technical forms of any possible influences and assign them to definite social environments.

The extraordinarily rich material from Middle Syrian Ugarit was soon supplemented by evidence for the Old Syrian Period which, though more fragmentary and less coherent in context, was of great importance. The consequent revolution in Syrian archaeology attracted, during the Thirties, energies which had until then been employed in Mesopotamia. In fact, after 1933, new legislation in Iraq had reformed the rules for assigning the finds of archaeological expeditions. As a result the Louvre and the British Museum jointly decided to leave Iraq and concentrate their efforts on Syria. This showed very clearly how archaeological exploration in the Near East between the two world wars was fundamentally concerned with the enrichment of museum collections rather than with increasing our knowledge of the past. The expeditions were still in large part financed by the great European and American museums rather than by institutions specifically devoted to archaeological research. It was in consequence of museum decisions that Sir Leonard Woolley moved from Ur to North Syria and began the excavation of Tell Atchana, while A. Parrot left Larsa and took over the exploration of Tell Hariri on the Euphrates, which W. F. Albright a few years earlier had proposed to identify with Mari. At the same time M. E. L. Mallowan began a vigorous and pertinacious field investigation of various centres of Upper Mesopotamia, in the basins of the Khabur and Balikh rivers, an area which had been almost completely abandoned since von Oppenheim's departure from Tell Halaf.

The exploration of Mari, begun in 1933, suspended by the war, was resumed after it. Still in progress under the directon of A. Parrot, it is a fundamental stage in the progress of our knowledge of the civilisation of the ancient Near East. Mari is today one of the best-known centres of Mesopotamian culture for the later phases of the Early Dynastic Period and the age of Hammurabi of Babylon, who took it and finally destroyed it towards the end of his reign, about 1760 B.C. The diplomatic archives of the royal palace of Mari, comprising texts dating for the most part from the reigns of Yasmah-Addu, son of Shamshi-Adad I of Assyria, and of Zimri-Lim, the last king of the city, provide a fine crop of data on the political history of Syria through the involved relations of Mari with the North Syrian kingdoms. And yet Mari is fundamentally a centre of Mesopotamian civilisation. It is thus the most western of Mesopotamian cities, laid open by its geographical position to frequent contacts with the worlds of North Syria and Anatolia. But at every period of its history its cultural features remained from any point of view Mesopotamian.

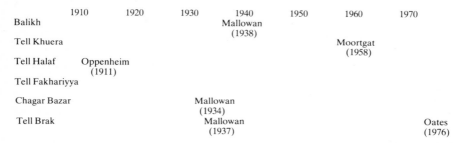

Figure 4 Chronology of Archaeological Exploration of Upper Mesopotamia

Of the very greatest importance were the investigations carried out in Upper Mesopotamia by M. E. L. (later Sir Max) Mallowan. They were profoundly innovative in spirit and concerned an extensive region which had been completely neglected archaeologically and in the Thirties was still largely unexplored. Now, for the first time, the North Syrian area was subjected to a systematic plan of research. Of the numerous centres which strew the basins of the Khabur and Balikh some were excavated while there was surface prospecting of others. The whole operation was governed by a clear appreciation of the significance of the area explored. In late prehistoric times and during the whole Protohistoric period, it must have been an important area of contact between regions of the north-west Iranian plateau, of eastern Mesopotamia, and of Northern Syria, while during a second period, at least from the beginning of the second millennium B.C., it must have been traversed by the roads connecting Assur with the centres of Cappadocia where the Old Assyrian trading colonies were established. There is no doubt that Mallowan's previous excavating experience was of special help in the complex requirements of this region. After having assisted Sir Leonard Woolley at Ur, he had directed the excavation of Tell Arpachiya in the Assyrian area. The first tell excavated, Chagar

Bazar, in the upper Khabur Basin, between 1934 and 1937, often mistakenly identified with the ancient Shubat Enlil, the capital of Shamshi-Adad I, provided noteworthy evidence of a centre important in the prehistoric periods, but more so in the protohistoric phase of Jemdet Nasr. The Chagar Bazar excavations revealed for more recent periods the historical context and absolute chronology of the important ceramic culture which has been called the 'Khabur Ware' culture. Its characteristic monochrome painted pottery with geometrical designs seems to have been established in Upper Mesopotamia during the development of the Middle Bronze Age culture.

The three seasons of excavation carried out in 1937 and 1938 at Tell Brak by the British School of Archaeology in Iraq, still under Mallowan's direction, were even more rewarding. The site, one of the largest of the whole region, situated on the west bank of the River Jaghjagha, proved to have been a flourishing centre of the Uruk period, with a typical 'Polished Red Ware' of local production but related to contemporary wares of Sumer and Elam. Tell Brak also yielded unexpected evidence of the following Jemdet Nasr period. This was a sacred building, the 'Eye Temple'. With certain variations it was in the characteristic tripartite form, on a high terrace, with a long central cella and a splendidly decorated podium on the short side opposite the entrance, typical of the mature architecture of the Uruk culture in Sumer. Unfortunately, although it was clear that the 'Eye Temple' had been reconstructed during the Protodynastic I Period and there were indications that Tell Brak had enjoyed considerable consequence during the whole Protodynastic Period, it proved impossible to explore the levels for this fundamental phase in the development of city civilisation. All the same, the excavation of the great Palace of Naram-Sin, the first certain example to this day of a palace structure built by the great king of Akkad, made a most important contribution to the history of the Khabur region. All the more so as proof was obtained of the destruction of the palace probably not long after its building, perhaps during the reign of Sharkalisharri, and its rebuilding, almost certainly in the time of Ur-Nammu, the founder of the Third Dynasty of Ur. Tell Brak thus turned out unexpectedly to have been closely linked throughout the whole third millennium B.C. with the more momentous upheavals in the history of Sumer.

At the end of the Thirties these findings, isolated as they still were, seemed astonishing. Though the inscriptions put them beyond doubt, many years had to pass before they could take their place in a solid historical framework, filled out with fuller, though not yet exhaustive, detail. In the second millennium Tell Brak lost a great deal of its importance, and a large part of the area occupied in the third millennium had to be abandoned. It did however yield an outstanding harvest of 'White Painted Ware', a sophisticated range of palace pottery characteristic of the fifteenth to fourteenth century, often attributed to the Mitanni kingdom and called Nuzi pottery from the place in Assyria where it was found in abundance. Tell Brak too, like most of the tells of the Balikh basin — Tell Jidle, Tell Hammam, Tell Sahlan — where Mallowan made useful investigations in 1938, was finally abandoned about 1400 B.C. or a little later. Of the other sites in the Balikh area where soundings were taken in 1938, Tell Aswad and Tell Mefesh are particularly important for an understanding of regional relations in the late prehistoric phases when the first experiments were started in advanced city life which were to become characteristic of the Protohistoric Period, as attested in the major centres of the Khabur basin like Tell Brak.

While the British School of Archaeology in Iraq was at work in Upper Mesopotamia discovering minor evidence of Late Bronze I in an area where it is certain that the major centres of Mitanni had flourished and where von Oppenheim was still hoping to discover the mysterious Wassukkanni, the unidentified Mitannian capital, Sir Leonard Woolley with his exploration of Tell Atchana in the lower Orontes valley for the first time obtained detailed information about a typical North Syrian centre of the Middle Bronze or Late Bronze. Excavations were begun in 1936, broken off for the duration of the war in 1939, and the exploration then completed in 1949. Tell Atchana was found to correspond with the ancient Alalakh on evidence from the archives discovered in the palaces at levels VII and IV, the first of Middle Bronze II and the second of Late Bronze I. Alalakh must have been quite an important centre during Middle Bronze I, to which the levels XVI–IX must be attributed at least in great part, though they were given a much earlier, absolutely untenable dating by the excavator. At the time of level VII, during Middle Bronze II, it was the seat of a small kingdom, a vassal of Yamhad (Aleppo) and governed by an Amorite dynasty related to its ruling family. Alalakh VII, with its palace, its palace temple, its private houses, its monumental gateway *à tenaille*, its splendid seal work, is excellently representative of the civilisation of the so-called Mature Old Syrian Period. The administrative archives, written in Old Babylonian, show the international diffusion of this language in the chanceries of all the Amorite kingdoms of the time, from Southern Mesopotamia to Assyria, Upper Mesopotamia, and North Syria. The Late Bronze material is also particularly important. Alalakh was then the capital of the small kingdom of Mukish, at first under Mitannian suzerainty and then under Hittite control. The palace of Level IV and the succession of temples up to Level I are particularly noteworthy. Mukish was destroyed, like Ugarit, in 1190 B.C. at the end of Late Bronze II, and never reoccupied. Together with Ugarit, though in a lesser degree, it is a major source of our knowledge of the Middle and Old Syrian worlds.

The inter-war period was that in which stratigraphic techniques, especially in Mesopotamia and Palestine, were brought to their highest perfection. In Mesopotamia the stratigraphic sequence established by the expedition of the Deutsche Orient-Gesellschaft at Uruk split the chronology of the Protohistoric Period into two phases, Uruk and Jemdet Nasr. Almost at the same time the Iraq Expedition of the Chicago Oriental Institute, under the direction of Henri Frankfort, on the basis of a comparative study of the sequences at Tell Asmar, Khafaje and Tell Agrab, laid down a first valid chronology for the Early Dynastic Period. This was no longer merely a theoretical succession of stylistic phases but based on archaeological fact as gathered over all from different historical centres. A little earlier W. F. Albright in Palestine, following an empirical method but making careful use of minute observations, at Tell Beit Mirsim laid the foundations for an archaeological chronology of the Palestine area from the last centuries of the third millennium B.C. down to the fall of the kingdom of Judah. Some years later the British expeditions to Lachish and Samaria perfected the technique of stratigraphic investigation, basing it on the minute study of deposits and the detection of ever smaller changes in pottery types. This method, deriving from the intuitions of Sir Flinders Petrie, was then elaborated into a precise synthesis of theoretical principles and practical applications by K. M. (later Dame Kathleen) Kenyon. In Near Eastern archaeology she may be regarded as the one who put the principles, methods and techniques of modern stratigraphic procedure in their final form.

The Syrian area, too, in the Thirties reflected the intensive experimentation going on in the Mesopotamian and Palestinian areas. There were two important expeditions: one in the Amuq, the region of Antioch in the lower valley of the Orontes; the other at Hama. The so-called Syro-Hittite Expedition of the Oriental Institute of Chicago, under the direction of C. McEwan, with unusually generous financial resources, worked in a series of tells of the Amuq Plain, Tell Tayanat, Tell Judaida and Chatal Huyuk, and put together a new stratigraphic profile applying to the whole Amuq region. For the most ancient phases this expedition received notable assistance from R. J. Braidwood. The Danish Expedition of the Carlsberg Foundation, under the direction of H. Ingholt, assisted in particular by P. J. Riis, from 1932 to 1939 worked on the tell of Hama citadel, defining for this important centre the cultural phases in stratigraphic succession. The excavations at Tell Tayanat and Hama added substantially to the finds made in the years previous to the First World War and datable to the beginning of the first millennium. But, from the point of view of the history of Syrian archaeology, the most important achievement of both expeditions was the abundant evidence produced by their stratigraphic researches.

The inter-war period, besides the memorable exploration of Ugarit, was characterised by the deeper, though still very limited, knowledge gained of the Middle Syrian cultures and to a lesser degree of the Mature Old Syrian. This phase of Syrian archaeology was concluded in the years of the Second World War with the resuscitation of an old project of von Oppenheim's. An expedition of the Oriental Institute of the University of Chicago excavated the great centre of Tell Fakhariyya in the Khabur region, in search of the Mitannian capital of Wassuk-kanni. With this brief and in part disappointing experiment, concluded in 1940, and aimed interestingly enough at the discovery of the most powerful capital of the Middle Syrian Period, a chapter in the archaeology of Syria was closed. It had its moments of brilliant illumination but on the whole left broad areas of thick shade in the cultures of the Old Syrian Period, and scarcely allowed even a glimpse of the great civilisations of the Protosyrian Period.

3. Exploration today: light on the formation of urban culture in Syria at the end of the fourth and during the third millennium B.C.

In the years following the Second World War the countries of the Near East gained their independence. The Arab countries thereafter were deeply occupied with organising their social, economic and political life on new principles, emerging slowly in accordance with the new realities. They began also to modernise the administration of their cultural heritage, often with inadequate staff and accommodation.

The cultural policies of the Syrian Arab Republic in the management of antiquities were quickly realigned according to three main principles. First, every chance was taken of improving the actual museum buildings so as to display the nation's artistic and historical heritage and give a clear impression of the contribution of the Syrian area to the early history of man, with emphasis on the more specific and significant aspects of this contribution. Secondly, by lengthy courses of study in the major centres of European oriental and archaeological studies, steps were taken to train a group of young scholars who could be directly employed, at the archaeological level especially, in the study of the ancient cultures of Syria. The purpose was thus to set up, and expand as need arose, a framework for the administration of cultural possessions, with decentralised control of the territory concerned. In the University of Damascus teaching facilities were to be established to educate staff in future to take over the supervision of these cultural possessions. Thirdly, an open policy was followed towards international collaboration in the prospecting, exploring and excavating of historic sites. The immediate, urgent aim was to reduce or eliminate clandestine excavation, and in the long run to enrich and complete the knowledge of Syria's past. By fruitful comparison of methods and techniques of investigation it was hoped to create an effective administration of the nation's cultural heritage.

These general lines of cultural policy were coordinated, with close and constant attention, by the Directorate-General of Antiquities in Damascus. It took personal charge of major excavations and even minor works, wherever there was good and urgent reason for its intervention. It also undertook a series of restoration programmes, to conserve or put to good use the nation's architectural and artistic heritage. Palmyra was systematically explored under the leadership of A. Bounni, side by side with the more particular investigations entrusted to the Polish and Swiss Expeditions directed by K. Michalowski and P. Collart. There were the excavations of Tell Kazel, directed by A. Bounni in collaboration with M. Dunand. Apart from these major archaeological enterprises, the restoration works at Palmyra, Apamea and Bosra were of the greatest importance for the preservation of outstanding monumental complexes of the classical period. Finally there was a most interesting exercise in restoration by N. Saliby of the splendid temple of Amrit, a picturesque and unique survival of Phoenician architecture of the Persian Period.

Thus the foundations were laid for a modern museum organisation. The results are the present arrangement of the National Museum of Damascus and of the Aleppo Archaeological Museum, together with the establishment of smaller museums at Hama, Tartus and Homs. Excavations were resumed at Ugarit and Mari, once more on the initiative of C. F. A. Schaeffer and A. Parrot. The first new undertaking of importance after the Second World War was a surface exploration of the Khabur region in an attempt to solve the problem of identifying and excavating Wassukkanni. Surface exploration was among the most conspicuous gaps in Syrian archaeology. There had been only two important attempts of this kind, a little before and during the Second World War. First, R. J. Braidwood had compiled a most useful catalogue of the tells of the Amuq. Secondly, a group of British archaeologists made a more summary list of the tells in the region of the Jabbul salt lake east of Aleppo. A third survey, by J. Lassus, in the region north of Hama, had merely indicated some tells without giving any chronological indications at all. In 1955 A. Moortgat, with funds provided by the M. von Oppenheim Foundation for archaeological research in Upper Mesopotamia, while completing the final publication of the Tell Halaf excavations with R. Naumann and B. Hrouda, revived an ancient project of the great German explorer. He took soundings at Tell Fakhariyya, examining a series of big tells and finally choosing for future excavation the site of Tell Khuera.

Although some important excavations of the Sixties had returned essentially to exploring centres of the Iron and Late Bronze Ages, there was in the end a rather unexpected development among the cultures of Northern Syria and Upper Mesopotamia. Here the greatest revelations concerned the third millennium and beginning of the second. A Syrian expedition from the Aleppo Museum brought to light an important group of 'Neo-Hittite' sculptures on the Acropolis of Tell Ayn Dara, probably to be identified with the ancient Kinalua, capital of the kingdom of Hattina. A British expedition under M. V. Seton-Williams took on the excavation of Tell Rifaat, at a short distance from Aleppo and almost certainly the ancient Arpad, the major centre of the Aramaean kingdom of Bit Agushi. The work on this last site was broken off all too soon, without furnishing indications of any importance on the Aramaean stronghold. On the coast a Danish expedition led by P. J. Riis carried out important investigations at Tell Sukas, certainly the Shuksu of Ugaritic texts. The stratigraphic results were good and important evidence was gained of the settlements of Iron Age II and III. They found useful traces of the presence of Greek imports, corresponding to that obtained by Woolley at El-Mina. Here, at the mouth of the Orontes, excavated at the time of the Tell Atchana campaigns, a Greek trading centre of the Archaic Period must have been established. Further to the south, still in the coastal plain, A. Bounni, with a Syrian expedition of the Damascus Archaeological Excavation Service, undertook the excavation of Tell Kazel which it was hoped to identify with the ancient Simira. This had been one of the Egyptian seats of government in Asia during the New Kingdom, and had been mistakenly proposed before the war as identifiable with the not far distant Tell Simiriyan. The Syrian Expedition obtained enough stratigraphic information to confirm that Tell Kazel had been the site of an important Late Bronze settlement, and even to make probable its identification with Simira.

But as I have said, the biggest results that began to arrive related to the third millennium and the first half of the second. The sources were Ugarit, Mari, Tell Khuera and Tell Mardikh. A succession of prehistoric cultures was established in particular at Ugarit, where stratigraphic soundings were more and more intensified. There C. F. A. Schaeffer and others, particularly H. de Contenson, tried to obtain information about the most ancient origins of the coastal city culture. They obtained an important set of stratigraphic sequences from the

Neolithic age up to the third millennium. At Mari the excavation of the great Palace of Zimri-Lim, as it was called, had already been completed before the war. Since then A. Parrot had for several years been excavating the Early Dynastic levels, uncovering first a temple of Ishtar and then temples of Ishtarat and Ninnizaza. In more recent years, by means of soundings in the area of the Palace of the Old Babylonian Period, he identified and began to uncover the so-called Pre-Sargonic Palace, an extraordinary monument in an exceptional state of preservation. The later Palace, whose original construction has recently been dated by A. Moortgat to the Neo-Sumerian Period, was founded on its ruins.

The researches initiated at Tell Khuera by the M. von Oppenheim Foundation revealed an important third millennium centre with several noteworthy monuments. Among these was a small temple of which several phases could be identified and which must have been founded in the first half of the third millennium. This yielded a votive statuary undoubtedly in the tradition of the so-called Mesilim style.

Finally at Tell Mardikh the excavations by the Rome University Expedition yielded immediate evidence of the site's importance from the middle of the third to the middle of the second millennium. But the series of monuments recovered in the first years of the dig were of the Old Syrian Period and richly supplemented the earlier discoveries from this period at Alalakh. Moreover they yielded material for the most part going back to Middle Bronze I, whereas at Alalakh this phase had been covered only by soundings. In 1969 Tell Mardikh was identified with Ebla in consequence of the discovery in the previous year of an inscribed bust of an Eblaite prince. This was a foretaste of the further discoveries from the third millennium which were to be made from 1973 onwards.

The finds of the Sixties at Tell Khuera and Tell Mardikh were in many ways revolutionary. One was revealed as what might reasonably be considered the first great centre of a culture of the third millennium, probably in large part Hurrian. The second proved an unparalleled source of material from the formative phase of the Old Syrian Period, at the beginning of the second millennium, and represented a North Syrian environment which without doubt was of predominantly Amorite population. But while the discoveries of Tell Khuera and Tell Mardikh remained largely isolated, a new era of Syrian archaeology opened with the appeal launched in 1967 by the Directorate-General of Antiquities at Damascus for the rescue of the historic sites of the Euphrates valley threatened by the artificial lake to be formed by the Thawra Dam, near the village of Tabqa, in the area of the medieval city of Meskene. The appeal for international collaboration from Damascus moved into a second phase in 1971, when UNESCO took the whole programme under its patronage. After an accurate inventory of the sites, drawn up by M. N. van Loon on the basis of a first census by A. Rihaoui, there was an unprecedented concentration of expeditions over a relatively small area of the Euphrates valley. This had always been neglected, but has now been shown to have had extraordinary importance during at least three phases of the Prehellenistic archaeology of Syria, Late Bronze II, Early Bronze III-IV, and the Protohistoric Period.

	1964	1966	1968	1970	1972	1974	1976
Tell Hadidi						Dornemann (1974)	
Tell Mumbaqat						Orthmann (1973)	
Tell Habuba Kabira				Heinrich (1969)		Strommenger (1973)	
Tell Kannas		Finet (1967)					
Jebel Aruda					Franken/Van der Leeuwe (1972)		
Tell Halawa							Orthmann (1975)
Tell Selenkahiyya	van Loon (1965)						
Meskene					Margueron (1972)		
Tell Fray						Bounni/Matthiae (1973)	

Figure 5 Chronology of Archaeological Exploration in the Lake Assad Region

For the fourteenth and thirteenth centuries B.C. the greatest centres explored were the tell of Meskene on the right bank of the Euphrates, and Tell Mumbaqat and Tell Fray on the left bank. The Prehellenistic settlement of Meskene was intensively excavated by a French expedition under J. C. Margueron. Following the discovery of several hundred cuneiform texts of the Middle Syrian Period it was identified with the ancient Emar and thus with the greatest centre of the region during the time of Hittite rule. Emar had been rebuilt perhaps at the beginning of the fourteenth century B.C. on the site of the modern excavations, by means of impressive earth-moving and terracing operations on the bluffs of the Euphrates. The new city was perhaps a little way off the Early and Middle Bronze Age Emar, of which no trace has been found, and has yielded in quantity remarkable evidence of sacred and profane architecture, temples with long cella and axial entry, houses with three rooms, of regular construction on stepped terraces. Striking parallels with Emar are offered by Tell Mumbaqat, excavated by an expedition of the Deutsche Orient-Gesellschaft headed by E. Heinrich and his successor W. Orthmann and Tell Fray, excavated by a

joint expedition of the University of Rome and the Archaeological
Excavation Service of the Damascus Directorate-General of Antiquities headed by A. Bounni and the writer. At Tell Mumbaqat, where the
excavations can continue because the tell is situated at the very edge of
the lake, one large temple is of the same type as those of Emar and one
of the city gates is in an excellent state of preservation. But the greatest
interest of this important centre is undoubtedly in the possibility it
offers, already to some extent realised, of following the development of
the settlement throughout the whole of the Late Bronze Age or longer.
The position of Tell Fray, relatively very near to the Thawra Dam,
where work was already almost finished, did not allow an exploration in
depth but only one extensive exploration in 1973. The important level
Fray IV, which was destroyed during the reign of the Hittite great king
Hattusilis III (or perhaps a little later, and anyhow around 1250 B.C.)
during the wars between Hittites and Assyrians for the control of this
frontier region on the Euphrates, revealed among other things a temple

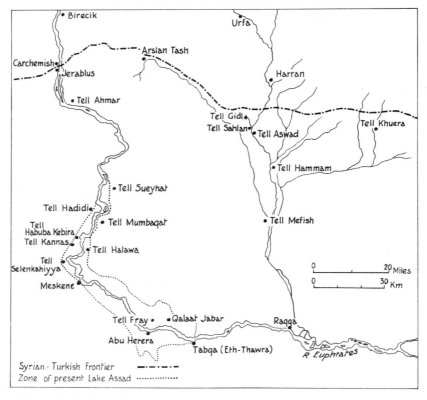

Figure 6   Archaeological Sites of the Euphrates Valley and the Balikh Basin

similar to those of Emar and Tell Mumbaqat and a second larger sanctuary, in the North Mesopotamian tradition.

For the final phases of the Early Bronze Age, covering the last centuries of the third millennium, particular importance attaches to the huge settlement of Tell Selenkahiyya, on the right bank of the Euphrates, which was excavated by expeditions first of the Oriental Institute of Chicago and then of Amsterdam University, both led by M. N. van Loon. Other discoveries relating to the same period were the most important level at Tell el-Abd, excavated by a Syrian expedition under A. Bounni, the remarkable necropolis of Tell Halawa, explored by a German expedition led by W. Orthmann, and an important phase at Tell Sweyhat, where the excavations were directed by T. A. Holland. Other centres of this region, such as Tell Hadidi, where an American expedition led by R. Dornemann was at work, are remarkable for the succession of cultures attested by their stratigraphic sequence.

But the most sensational results of the exploration of the Tabqa region were undoubtedly the unexpected yields from sites which flourished at the end of the fourth millennium in the Protohistoric Period. Its most important city was without question the great continuous single centre which corresponded to the two present tells of Kannas and Habuba Kabira. The first of these was explored by a Belgian expedition led by A. Finet, the second excavated extensively by a German expedition under E. Strommenger. It is probable that the little hill of Tell Kannas was the religious and perhaps also political centre of the great city settlement of Habuba Kebira, the enceinte of which has been brought to light over a good part of its length and is characterised by a rectilinear mud brick curtain wall with salient quadrangular towers. The architecture, glyptic, and pottery of Kannas and Habuba for this period fully correspond to a very advanced phase of the Uruk period and perhaps to the Jemdet Nasr period in Southern Mesopotamia. The temple buildings on the two sites are of unusual interest and closely recall the wonderful tripartite architectural structures of Uruk IV, consisting typically of a nave cut by a transept. The same architectural elements and an identical material culture were discovered in the same region by the Dutch excavations directed by H. J. Franken and S. E. Van der Leeuwe, at Jebel Aruda on the right bank of the Euphrates.

With the conclusion of the works on the Thawra Dam in 1974 and the formation of the great Assad basin, the greater part of the sites explored in the most recent years have disappeared beneath the waters of the lake, dominated by the ruins of the picturesque medieval fortress of Qalaat Jabar.

While the expeditions continue their work on those sites which have remained intact on the borders of the lake, normal archaeological activity is being resumed after the extraordinary concentration in the Euphrates valley, with due regard to the historical data which have emerged from the most recent years' excavations. In chronological order these data may be thus listed:

1. The Tell Habuba Kebira, Tell Kannas, and Jebel Aruda excavations have reopened the whole problem of how the city culture of the upper valley of the Euphrates and Northern Syria was formed.

2. An advanced city culture, probably Hurrian, of the third millennium has been identified in the area of the Khabur, of which one important centre was certainly Tell Khuera.

3. The great Eblaite civilisation of which Tell Mardikh, or Ebla, was certainly the cultural and political capital, has been brought to light. It was certainly North-West Semitic and of the third millennium.

4. Evidence has also been provided by Tell Mardikh of one of the greatest cities of the Archaic Old Syrian Period, the age when the Old Syrian culture was formed, to become fully developed when Yamhad dominated Northern Syria and was one of the principal Amorite kingdoms of Western Asia.

The most recent, and very promising, developments of Syrian archaeology have been to some extent at least determined by these new points of view. The important Tell Brak site was reopened in 1976 by a British expedition under D. Oates and we may hope that it will enable us to answer many questions of chronology concerned with the phase previous to the Palace of Naram-Sin, and cultural questions too perhaps, regarding the differences between the culture of Upper Mesopotamia and the contemporary culture of Northern Syria revealed by Ebla. A contribution of equal moment may be the excavations begun only in 1976 by an American expedition from the University of Los Angeles under G. Buccellati at Tell Ashara, the ancient Terqa, on the middle course of the Euphrates. For the Protosyrian Period both Mature and Late, and for the Archaic Old Syrian Period at least until the age of Hammurabi, Terqa should provide some decisive indications on the relations between the North Syrian and Mesopotamian cultures.

The extraordinary concentration of archaeological research in the Syrian area in recent years and the general adoption of the most up-to-date techniques of investigation by the expeditions working in Syria are laying the groundwork for a new historical understanding of the significance of Syria in the individual periods concerned. To realise that Syrian archaeology has become a fully mature structure based on work in the field we need consider only two points. First, the establishment of a line of archaeological research no longer has to follow a slender thread of occasional finds but takes its place in an exact framework of historical enquiry, with investigations in parallel. Secondly, the whole development of archaeological research has changed. It is no longer a matter of isolated cultural episodes emerging from the obscurity of an almost total lack of evidence, but of whole environments brought to light and defined by historical situations which can be identified in space and time.

2
The Tell Mardikh Excavations and the Rebirth of Ebla

In 1964 the University of Rome decided to undertake some excavation work in Syria. The question was where. In answering it there was a certain convergence of interest between the Italian philological tradition on the one hand, as exemplified in the work of G. Levi della Vida on the Prehellenistic cultures of Western Asia, and on the other the habitual alertness of Italian archaeologists to historical questions of what in the western and central Mediterranean is called the 'orientalising period'. This undoubtedly pointed to the Phoenician cities of the coast, or perhaps to the Aramaean centres of the northern interior. But this tradition, however illustrious, was typically philological rather than archaeological. The requirements of progress in the then state of scholarly research imposed other considerations, and it seemed in the end more logical, though perhaps rather bold, to be guided in the choice of a site by recent archaeological discovery and the historical problems thereby raised.

So it was that in the spring of 1964, following a brief surface survey with these general principles in mind, the University of Rome pre-sented to the Directorate-General of Antiquities in Damascus an official request for permission to excavate two archaeological sites in the Aleppo region. They were Tell Mardikh, a large tell situated about fifty-five kilometres south-south-west of Aleppo, and Tell Afis, a smaller one about ten kilometres north of Tell Mardikh. The authorisation was immediately granted for both sites with wholehearted generosity by S. Abd-ul-Hak, then Director General, in that spirit of open-handed collaboration which has always characterised the cultural politics of the Syrian Arab Republic.

Of the two sites Tell Mardikh in the immediately preceding years had been the centre of attention with officials of the Directorate of Antiquities in Northern Syria because it had been scoured by clandestine excavators. Although it was of unusually large size it did not at that time lend itself to a plausible identification with any known ancient centre. Tell Afis, on the other hand, where in 1901 the Aramaean stele of King Zakir of Hamat and Hazrek had been found by chance, could in all probability be precisely identified with the Hazrek of Bible texts and the Khatarikka of Assyrian sources. Though decisive proof is still lacking, Tell Afis does seem to be the very citadel of Hazrek where Zakir about 800 B.C. was besieged by a powerful coalition of princes of Syria and Anatolia led by the King of Damascus, whom he managed to defeat. To commemorate his victory he then erected, perhaps in one of the city's sanctuaries, the commemorative stele, in which he gave thanks to Baal Shamin for the averted danger.

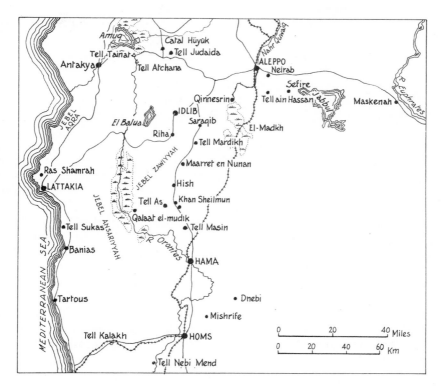

Figure 7   The Tell Mardikh Region

Thus Tell Afis was essentially an Iron Age I and Ii site, a point which had not escaped W. F. Albright when he visited the tell in 1927. It was certainly an important Aramaean centre, while Tell Mardikh appeared from surface exploration to be a much more ancient city, with special potentiality for throwing light on a definite historical problem.

1. Fundamentals and prospects of the excavations

At a preliminary glance, before any excavation had been begun, Tell Mardikh appeared objectively a site of undoubted general interest. There were evident external features which, even without an attempt at relating it to any particular context, put it among the most important of the Syrian area. Above all, there was its impressive size. With its fifty-six hectares of surface area and highly suggestive structure it must certainly have been a single great city centre for some part at least of its history. In the second place, the pottery fragments distributed over its

surface gave some general indication of approximate dates of occupation. In particular they suggested an hypothesis about extensions of
the area of occupation at the different periods represented by the
pottery. Finally, the discovery on the surface of the tell, a few years
before the Italian excavations began, of a ritual basin with two compartments and three of its faces carved with reliefs was sure evidence
that the ancient city buried under Tell Mardikh had been the site of a
highly developed urban culture.

Taken in detail these general points, already significant enough on
their own, showed Tell Mardikh to be a site urgently in need of
exploration. It seemed certain to produce a wealth of information and
throw up problems for archaeological research in terms of some definite
historical perspective.

The lay-out of the tell is very characteristic. A central hillock, almost
circular, about 170 metres in diameter, the so-called 'Acropolis', is
surrounded by a huge, almost flat depression, the 'Lower City'. This
last is only slightly modified by gentle undulations of the ground. It is
ring-shaped in form and enclosed all round by a raised ridge which
stands out from the flat surrounding countryside with rather precipitous
slopes. On the line of the raised perimeter of the tell, forming an
irregular trapeze, four noticeable depressions can easily be discerned.
They seem to interrupt the circuit, in which it is easy to recognise the
traces of the ancient defensive fortifications of the city. This typical
tripartite division of the Tell Mardikh settlement plan into Acropolis,
Lower City, and Walls made it plausible that the tell in its entirety was
to be considered as a topographical unit, concealing a single urban
occupation area belonging to a historical period still to be defined. If the
Lower City and the Walls appeared clearly connected in a single unit
over an entire period of time, there was room for doubt about the
Acropolis. It might take its structure from the presence of strikingly
monumental buildings giving the hillock a look of massive solidity. But
it might equally well be the site of an original settlement, perhaps of
limited extent but repeatedly rebuilt, or else too of successive equally
spaced occupations from the period or periods when the city enjoyed its
greatest prosperity.

The Acropolis is higher towards the north, where it reaches 431
metres above sea level, and lower towards the south-west. Its brows are
slightly raised so that its central region is insensibly hollowed out from
north to south. The hill slopes form a kind of irregular terracing, more
in evidence on the south-west side but quite visible, though in smaller
areas, on the east and south. On the west a terrace of much greater area
than on any of the other slopes extends towards the Lower City,
forming a well-defined platform. Only on the north is the slope of the
Acropolis rather steep with hardly a trace of terracing.

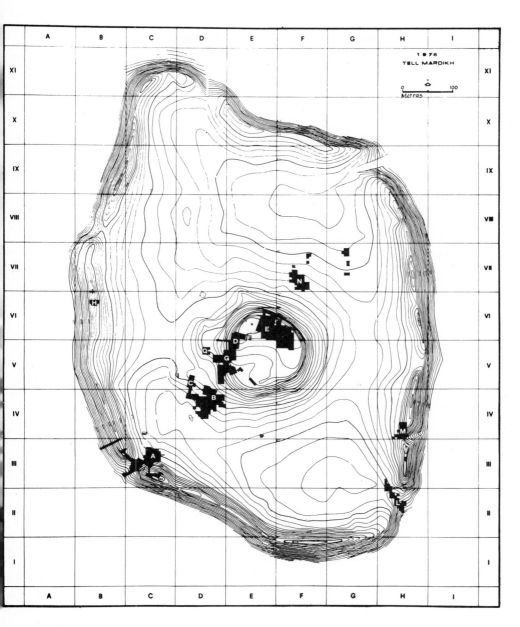

Figure 8   Relief map of Tell Mardikh with the state of the excavations in 1976
            (Letters denote various sectors of the city)

The Lower City is shaped like an irregular ring bulging out to the north and north-west on one side and to the south and south-east on the other. So since there is a shorter distance between the Acropolis and the City Wall to the east and west than to the north and south, two slight saddles raise the ground level of the Lower City in these sectors. Here, at 415–411.50 metres, it reaches its greatest altitude, while the lowest parts of the Lower City are situated not far from the depressions in the north-east and south-east lines of the Walls, at heights around 407.80 metres. The Wall in its present condition consists of a raised ridge, reaching its greatest heights of 429.15 metres in the western and 423 metres in the eastern sector, with a thickness at the base varying between fifty and a hundred metres. On the line of the Walls, besides the four major depressions to the south-west, north-west, north-east, and south-east, there are some minor breaks which seem accidental and probably derive from breaches made in the ancient fortifications. The four major depressions, if only for the remarkable regularity of their position, must mark the sites of the ancient city gates.

These elements of the topography of Tell Mardikh set alongside the details of surface pottery, gave a near enough picture of the periods concerned to serve as a plausible working hypothesis of the story of the ancient settlements composing Tell Mardikh. The preliminary exploration of the tell, before excavations were begun, in fact revealed that the surface pottery, owing to the large area of the tell, was not uniformly distributed in all sectors of the site but in distinct patterns. In general the pottery types most in evidence were attributable to Early Bronze Age IV (c.2400–2000 B.C.) and Middle Bronze Age I-II (c.2000–1600 B.C.). Fragments attributable to the Persian (c.535–325 B.C.) and Hellenistic (c.325–60 B.C.) periods were much rarer. Late Roman sherds were of altogether casual occurrence. More precisely the Early Bronze IV pottery seemed completely absent from the Acropolis, moderately in evidence in the Lower City, but abundant on the slopes, especially the internal slopes of the Walls. The pottery of Middle Bronze Age I-II could be gathered in small percentages on the Acropolis, was dominant in the Lower City, and found in concentration in limited areas of the slopes of the perimeter ridge. The pottery of the later periods, especially the Persian-Hellenistic, but also Iron Age II (c.900–725 B.C.) and Iron Age III (c.725–535 B.C.) was found exclusively on the Acropolis and the terracing towards the Lower City, being completely absent on the Walls.

Such a well-marked distribution of pottery fragments on the tell's surface called for a general reconstruction of the history of the Tell Mardikh occupations. It was of remarkable interest. The occupation of Early Bronze Age IV must have been very extensive. Though in different percentages, the sherds in question were distributed over the Lower

City or the Walls. The absence of sherds of this period on the Acropolis was evidently to be put down to the superimposition of other levels later, and they too no doubt were structurally continuous. The occupation of Middle Bronze I-II appeared without doubt to have been the most considerable and must also certainly have involved the whole surface of the tell, extending from the Acropolis to the Walls. In the following periods Walls and Lower City seemed to have been abandoned, while during Iron Age II and the Persian and Hellenistic periods there is evidence only of sporadic occupations on the Acropolis, as was perhaps the case also in the late Roman period.

From these data there followed two fundamental elements in the interpretation of the history of the Tell Mardikh occupations. On the one hand the flowering period of the great city could be placed broadly between the limits 2500 and 1500 B.C., when probably the whole territory covered by the tell was inhabited. On the other hand, after 1500 B.C., with probable breaks in continuity, of the ancient city area on the ruins of the Acropolis alone, sparse village-type occupations can be identified as forerunners of the occupation of the site in more recent periods.

What significance was to be attributed to the discovery of the carved basin in the Lower City of Tell Mardikh in the framework of this reconstruction? It must be said that in 1964 the Tell Mardikh basin with two compartments, discovered by chance in a fairly good state of preservation, then reduced to fragments by the countryfolk, but fortunately recovered by the officials of Aleppo Museum, seemed a very singular object. The 'twin-basin' type was then completely unknown. Its relief decoration on three sides was unusual. Its style, elaborate but rough, was puzzling. The decorative conception was well thought out and suggestive. Powerful half-figures of roaring lions emerge from the base. On the front face is a ritual scene in bas-relief, in which the king is seen pouring a libation before an offertory table loaded with unleavened loaves, and on the two sides figures of soldiers advancing towards the focal point of this sacral ceremony. The habit of assuming that any monumental sculpture carved in basalt and found in Northern Syria must be concentrated in the 'Neo-Hittite' period had at first prompted a proposed dating of the beginning of the first millennium for the Tell Mardikh basin. It appeared, however, beyond doubt that the actual date of this unusual fitting must be quite different. A lengthy examination of the antiquarian elements discernible in the modelling of the figures revealed clear parallels with the cylinder seals of Kültepe II, and this imposed a dating around 1850 B.C. The subjects of the carvings, but even more their style, though still far from those typical of Mature Old Syrian seal work of the years around 1750 B.C., confirmed this dating. The attribution to the nineteenth century B.C. of

this carved basalt basin found before 1964 was thus in complete agree-
ment with the surface pottery of Tell Mardikh. The basin belonged to
Middle Bronze Age I (c.2000–1800 B.C.), the central phase in the fullest
occupation of the tell and the city's time of greatest prosperity.

From this complex of data Tell Mardikh assumed an altogether
exceptional significance. It appeared as a site peculiarly suited to
provide, under systematic and intensive archaeological exploration,
information about certain aspects of cultural development in Syria
which had not until then been gleaned from any other archaeological
site. The extent and shape of the tell guaranteed that Tell Mardikh must
have been an urban centre of undoubted political importance. In the
North Syrian interior, between the Euphrates and the mountain chains
which run parallel to the Mediterranean coast, only the tell of Mishrife,
the ancient Qatna, not far from Homs, is larger than Tell Mardikh. The
surface pottery made it certain that no lesser occupation of the
Hellenistic and Roman Period would greatly impede the excavation of
the older levels, except perhaps on the Acropolis, which was of course
a worry because the Acropolis was just the place where the more
representative buildings were likely to be.

The site was completely free from any modern or even recent
presence. Over the whole surface there was not a single village dwelling
nor even, as often happens on the tells of the Near East, a local
cemetery.

But two considerations above all made Tell Mardikh appear an
archaeological site of extraordinary interest in respect of a well-defined
historical problem. The first was the question of the origins and development of the great Syrian urban culture of the Middle Bronze Age
II (c.1800–1600 B.C.) known until then almost exclusively from the
architecture and glyptics of Alalakh. Tell Mardikh in fact was the first
great centre of Northern Syria which, on the basis of concrete material
evidence from surface pottery, could have been a city of important size
continuously from the middle of the third to the middle of the second
millennium. The second consideration was that Tell Mardikh was the
first North Syrian site to have yielded, in the carved double basin, an
object of complex structural type and composition, important artistic
evidence of the period around 1850 B.C., which immediately preceded
the high point of the Mature Old Syrian glyptics of Alalakh VII. So Tell
Mardikh was without possibility of doubt a great urban centre, and
must certainly have played a leading part in the formation of the
Archaic Old Syrian culture of Middle Bronze Age I (c.2000–1800 B.C.).
Beyond that it seemed to have been an important city in the last
centuries of the third millennium, a period for which in 1964 our
material evidence was confined to the stratigraphic sequences,
important but all alone, of Amuq J-I and Hama J.

Therefore it did not seem too bold to expect that the archaeological exploration of Tell Mardikh might hold the key to the exact formulation, if not to the solution, of a historical problem of the first importance — the historical roots of the Mature Old Syrian culture. It must be admitted that by 1964 it was already clear that material evidence perhaps not unlike that which might be obtained from Tell Mardikh could also have been offered by certain other centres of similar history and equal importance, like Carchemish and Qatna. But even if difficulties of excavation due to external circumstances could have been disregarded, which they certainly could not in the case of Carchemish, sites such as these did not, like Tell Mardikh, guarantee much in the way of historical continuity until about the middle of the third millennium. In this sense Tell Mardikh in 1964 offered itself as a centre exceptionally qualified to throw light on problems of the origins and make-up of the Old Syrian culture. It seemed likely to yield information not only of the immediate antecedents of the Archaic phase of the period of the Amorite dynasties, Middle Bronze I, but also of the more remote and obscure origins of city culture in Syria, in the last stages of the Early Bronze Age, of which nothing was known till then.

2. The archaeological investigation of the site

Before 1964 the name Tell Mardikh was virtually unknown. Although not explicitly named it was certainly Tell Mardikh to which the inhabitants of the region of Saraqeb, a little town on the Damascus-Aleppo road a few kilometres north of the tell, must have been referring when in 1927 they informed W. F. Albright, travelling from Jerusalem to Baghdad, that there were three great tells in the area. The great American archaeologist was able to visit only one, Tell Afis. Of the second, Tell Tuqan, he learnt only the name. Of the third, certainly Tell Mardikh, by far the biggest of the three, whose imposing outline stands clear across the horizon for anyone on the summit of Tell Afis, he had nothing at all to say. By a remarkable coincidence, on the very same journey Albright visited, on the periphery of Raqqa, on the old course of the Euphrates, another tell of most striking size which much impressed him, Tell Biya, now identified with certainty as the ancient Tuttul, and suggested that it should be identified with Ebla. A few years later, between 1932 and 1939, during a campaign of the Carlsberg Foundation Expedition to Hama which he headed, H. Ingholt was able to visit Tell Mardikh and observe the abundance on it of pottery typical of the Hama J phase, that is Early Bronze IV. But he never managed to give news of his find to the world of international scholarship. In the years immediately preceding the beginnings of the Italian operations, Tell Mardikh was mentioned by W. J. Van Liere in the course of a series of surface surveys in which he attempted to establish the ecological conditions of vast regions of Syria in ancient times compared with the present. Finally, Tell Mardikh appeared in an archaeological sketch map of Syria compiled by B. Hrouda in the course of research work by the M. von Oppenheim Foundation Expedition to Tell Khuera under A. Moortgat.

The archaeological exploration of Tell Mardikh, begun in 1964, was carried on in regular annual excavation seasons, each lasting in the early years about six weeks and later two or three months. During the first short season a detailed analysis of the surface pottery was carried out and some very limited soundings were made on the internal slopes of the Walls, in one sector to the south-west of the Lower City, and on the west slope of the Acropolis. The expedition verified that the Middle Bronze II levels in the Lower City were close to the surface, and at least in the area west of the Acropolis not covered with any continuous later layer.

Beginning with the second season, in 1965, it was decided to proceed with the systematic exploration of the great city of the Mature Old Syrian Period which was beginning to emerge, in parallel and con- temporaneously, in all three distinct sectors of the tell — the Acropolis, the Lower City and the Walls. From 1965 on the objectives were quite clear. On the Acropolis, the Great Temple D in the western area having been identified, the aim was to continue the test trench of the first season along the summit of the hill and so locate the palace, on the assumption that this would be found, as at Alalakh, on the northern edge of the hill. In the Lower City the programme was to extend our excavations in the south-west area at the foot of the Acropolis, where the inhabitants of Mardikh village had indicated the find-spot of the carved basalt basin taken to the Aleppo Museum. On the line of the Walls it was decided to check whether the marked depressions in the perimeter ridge did in fact conceal city gates, beginning with the south-west passage, which was undoubtedly the most obvious of the four. In 1966 it became clear that our objectives were about to be realised. In the northern area of the Acropolis the Middle Bronze Age II building which began to appear was identified as Royal Palace E. In the Lower City, at the spot indicated by the local people, Temple B1 was coming to light, and on its access platform had been found a large corner piece of the carved basin previously recovered. The south- western breach in the walls was revealing itself as Monumental Gateway A.

The programme of excavations continued in the following years with the primary object of deepening our knowledge of the great city of

Middle Bronze Age I-II. For this the operations were to be extended to the private housing areas in Sector B of the Lower City and in Sector A immediately inside Monumental Gateway A, and work was to be intensified on the excavation of Royal Palace E. The situation of Palace E, unfortunately in a very bad state of preservation in its northern sector, was complex. The ashlars of the walls had been in large part removed for re-use after the destruction of the building at the end of Middle Bronze Age II. For this reason the levels which overlay Royal Palace E in the northern area of the Acropolis needed thorough investigation, with special attention to a large rustic building of the Persian and Hellenistic Age. It was also found necessary to complete some further soundings on the Acropolis in its south-west area — Sector G — in order to verify the stratigraphic situation by comparison with what had been observed in the northern area — Sector E — and possibly also to locate the ancient gateway of the Acropolis, on the not improbable assumption that this must be situated in the obvious depression in the south-west quarter of the mound.

At the end of the first five years of excavation, in 1968, a particularly important find induced us to modify our general strategy. Outside its original context, in a late Persian level, we found the mutilated bust of a royal statue in basalt, with a cuneiform votive inscription in the Akkadian language mentioning a king of Ebla. This made it seem very probable that Tell Mardikh *was* Ebla. Up until 1968 the principal aim of the Tell Mardikh excavations had been to get to know, as widely and deeply as possible, the city of Middle Bronze Age I-II. After 1968 we still had this prospect in view, and could even hope to widen the now traditional limits for such a study. But now we had a second aim — to prepare for future years the exploration of the Early Bronze Age IV city. The assurance that Tell Mardikh was the Ebla defeated by Sargon and conquered by Naram-Sin of Akkad was decisive in renewing our determination to realise that aim.

Of the two aims the second was extraordinarily attractive and stimulating. But it could not be given an objective preference. We had to know in what areas of the tell the necessary and sufficient conditions for a systematic excavation of the Early Bronze Age IV levels would be realised, and we had to wait patiently for a sounding to tell us. The conditions were two. First, the area must be free from important structures of Middle Bronze I-II, which apparently covered the entire surface of the tell, and secondly, the levels of Early Bronze IV must be present in good states of preservation. Convinced that these conditions were more likely to be realised in the Lower City and along the slopes of the Walls, where the buildings of the Middle Bronze Age ought to be less imposing than on the Acropolis, between 1969 and 1972 we started up new workings: Sector H on the inner slope of the Walls to the west,

Sector L at the presumed location of the city gate to the south-east, Sector M on the inner slope of the Walls to the east, and Sector N in the Lower City to the north. The Middle Bronze I-II levels were almost everywhere in a good state of preservation, though sometimes of no great depth. None the less we took limited soundings, especially in Sector A and Sector N, and these verified the presence of levels of Early Bronze IVA (c.2400–2250 b.c.) and IVB (c.2250–2000). These levels were very poor everywhere and, what is more, damaged by the foundations of Middle Bronze I. In certain areas of the Lower City, in Sector B for instance, every trace of the Early Bronze IV occupations had disappeared in consequence of elaborate works carried out during the Old Syrian Period I and II. The new diggings started from 1969 onward led, as we had calculated, to a considerable increase in our knowledge of the city of Middle Bronze I-II. The monuments excavated in the first five years and partly brought to light after 1969 were now joined by the Temple N in the Lower City to the north, Fortress M on the line of fortifications to the east, and City Gate L. On the other hand, the widening of the excavations in Sector B of the Lower City to the south-west led to the discovery of the large Sanctuary B2.

The problem of how to explore Early Bronze Age IV levels to a significant though perhaps limited extent remained central to the Tell Mardikh excavations. It was established that Tell Mardikh was Ebla, and clear also from the surface pottery that it had really been a centre of great importance during Early Bronze IV. It was therefore disappointing to find it so difficult, without damaging well-preserved levels of the Middle Bronze Age, to reach the city destroyed by Naram-Sin of Akkad. In the Lower City the attempts to do this had proved unsuccessful almost everywhere. On the Acropolis any hope of this kind seemed for other obvious reasons very unlikely to be realised. Very limited soundings in the cella of the Great Temple D and in a corner of Royal Palace E had immediately led to the identification of an Early Bronze IVB level. But any further progress in these sectors would have involved damage too serious to be contemplated to two important monuments of Middle Bronze I-II.

The solution of the problem, in part at least unexpected, turned up at the end of the tenth year of excavation, in 1973. In that year we decided to carry out some trial diggings on the slopes west and south-west of the Acropolis, since it had already been established in the preceding years that immediately under the Great Temple D, standing on the western brow of the elevation, the slopes during Middle Bronze I appeared to have been laid out in terraces, with intentions apparently more aesthetic than functional. The shaping of the slopes of the Acropolis into terraces continued with a certain regularity to the south-west, that is, at a considerable distance from Great Temple D, where the idea would not have made sense. So it seemed worthwhile to look for other reasons which might have persuaded or compelled the architects of Middle Bronze I to model the western slope of the Acropolis in terraces below what had probably been the city's biggest temple.

This idea, vague though it was, proved correct. The reason for the terraces in the south-western area of the Acropolis was the presence there of earlier structures, previous to the Middle Bronze Age. But what could never have been foreseen was their massive size and their function. The soundings of 1973 very quickly located walls 2.80 metres thick, of large-sized mud bricks. The pottery horizon was quite clear, and consisted of an Archaic phase of Early Bronze IV, which we called Early Bronze IVA. The structures located in 1973 belonged to a stairway of four flights enclosed in a strong square tower, and were thought to be part of a line of fortifications of the citadel or else part of a monumental building. The discovery in 1974 of two long rooms adjacent to the tower on the north and of the first cuneiform tablets led us to suggest, with caution, that the remains were those of a possibly royal building and to give up the idea of a fortification. In 1975, for the first time in the whole Tell Mardikh exploration, we concentrated excavations solely on the site of the Early Bronze IVA Building G, the outstanding importance of which was now evident. The result was the discovery of the State Archives and the definite identification of Royal Palace G.

Thus it can be said that the first ten years of exploration of Tell Mardikh were devoted essentially to the city of Middle Bronze I-II. The second decade, beginning in 1974, owing to the very fortunate assumptions made in 1973, was largely given over to the excavation of the Royal Palace of Early Bronze IVA. This task, on which the expedition is at present engaged, will be long and not easy. But the monument may be considered from now on as an extraordinary example of Mature Protosyrian architecture, with an originality of conception which must be a fundamental element of evaluation in any comprehensive historical account of the achievements of Western Asia in the third millennium B.C.

3. History of the settlements

The excavation of Tell Mardikh was governed by the prospect of giving a total, unified account of its successive settlements. Among them, the great cities of Early Bronze IV and Middle Bronze I-II were of dominant interest. Owing to the peculiar width and structure of the site we did not carry out vertical soundings there in the hope of obtaining a stratigraphic sequence of general validity. Vertical soundings no doubt have their place but they are a frequent source of partial and fallacious information on the chronology of a big tell. Moreover,

Mardikh I	c. 3500–2900		Protohistoric Period
Mardikh IIA	c. 2900–2400	Early Bronze I-III	Early Protosyrian Period
Mardikh IIB1	c. 2400–2250	Early Bronze IVA	Mature Protosyrian Period
Mardikh IIB2	c. 2250–2000	Early Bronze IVB	Late Protosyrian Period
Mardikh IIIA	c. 2000–1800	Middle Bronze I	Archaic Old Syrian Period
Mardikh IIIB	c. 1800–1600	Middle Bronze II	Mature Old Syrian Period
Mardikh IVA	c. 1600–1400	Late Bronze I	Early Middle Syrian Period
Mardikh IVB	c. 1400–1200	Late Bronze II	Recent Middle Syrian Period
Mardikh VA	c. 1200–900	Iron I	Neo-Syrian Period
Mardikh VB	c. 900–720	Iron II	or
Mardikh VC	c. 720–535	Iron III	Aramaean and 'Neo-Hittite' Age
Mardikh VIA	c. 535–325		Persian Age
Mardikh VIB	c. 325–60		Hellenistic Age
Mardikh VII	III-VIIth centuries		Late Roman and Byzantine Age

Figure 9   Archaeological and Historical Phases of Tell Mardikh

the remarkable size of Tell Mardikh would probably have frustrated any such hope, even if carried out on the Acropolis, and certainly on its slopes. Any sequence so obtained would have been ambiguous about the real succession of occupations, representative only of one small locality in the huge city area, and with apparent gaps that are actually reflected in the archaeological investigation.

With such complex changes of occupation in the course of its history, there must have been many breaks and interruptions of use in the various areas of Tell Mardikh. Even so bedrock was reached by the excavators at various points of the Lower City, both in Sector N to the north and in Sectors B and C to the south. West of the Acropolis, the rock was simply laid bare by erosion in some places, carrying off at least some remains of the Middle Bronze II city. On the Acropolis itself, however, virgin soil has not been reached at any point, although there are numerous indications that the present central mound of Tell Mardikh must cover an original rocky knoll, barely emerging above the level of the surrounding countryside.

The earliest ancient traces of a human presence so far detected were in the Lower City, in the B Sector, where fragments of 'Chaff-Faced Simple Ware' have been found immediately over the rock. This pottery is characteristic of the Amuq F horizon and dated in absolute terms between 3500 and 3300 B.C. It is the only trace of the village of Mardikh I (c. 3500–2900), which probably had its centre on the Acropolis mound.

Almost nothing is yet known of the occupations of the first half of the third millennium. A short sounding, however, in the most northerly area of Sector G on the slope down from the Acropolis has brought to light a very limited stretch of a courtyard or street, flanked by parts of rather well-preserved structures of mud brick, which were subsequently covered over by the impressive masonry of the Great Temple D. This remnant of occupation, which immediately precedes the Royal Palace G, must be attributed to a final phase of Early Bronze III (*c.*2750–2400 B.C.) corresponding to the latter part of Mardikh IIA (*c.*2900–2400 B.C.). This is how we have labelled the Ebla occupation parallel to the Early Dynastic Period in Mesopotamia and to the phases of Early Bronze I-III in the Syrian area. The internal divisions of this period as they actually appear at Tell Mardikh require further study. It must be said, however, that this final phase of Mardikh IIA is characterised by the presence, though rare, of the typical 'Red-Black Burnished Ware', as the Khirbet Kerak pottery is called, in very characteristic reddish examples. So far, however, the usual moulded decorations have not been observed. Very probably it was during this period that the expansion of the Ebla occupation in the Lower City took place. It is not yet possible however to draw its boundaries.

It was in correspondence with what it seems appropriate to define as Early Bronze IVA that Ebla emerged as a big city. It was of considerable extent from this time on, and probably approximated to the city area of the Middle Bronze Age as defined by the ramparts. Of this great centre of Mardikh IIB1 (*c.*2400–2250 B.C.), which is the city of the Royal Palace G and the State Archives, no other monuments are known. It can however be stated with certainty that the occupation extended, on the south-west, to near the later Monumental Gateway A, and on the north and north-east, as far as the area of Sector N. It is thus possible that the line of extensive fortifications of Middle Bronze I conceals the structures, technically no doubt altogether different, of the perimeter walls of Mardikh IIB1, which may have followed a very similar line.

In general the ceramic horizon of Mardikh IIB1 is near enough to that of Amuq I and in part to the older phases of Hama J, with the important exception of the 'Red-Black Burnished Ware', which is largely present in the Amuq but completely absent in Mardikh IIB1. This occupation is further characterised by more sophisticated and better quality pottery. In terms of absolute dating the divergencies from Amuq ware, if not be to be understood in a purely geographical sense, must be taken as placing Mardikh IIB1 slightly later than Amuq I. The important art work of the Royal Palace G indicates a cultural environment very close, figuratively and ideologically speaking, to that of the Akkad dynasty. The end of Mardikh IIB1, which is marked by serious devastation, was therefore very probably the work of Naram-Sin of Akkad, around 2250 B.C. It cannot be completely ruled out, although it seems very much less likely, that the burning of the city is to be attributed to Sargon of Akkad, around 2300 B.C. It is, however, the later date which from various indications it has seemed advisable to adopt.

The succeeding great city, Mardikh IIB2 (c.2250–2000 B.C.) would be parallel in date with the end of the dynasty of Akkad beginning with the last years of Naram-Sin, with the Gutian domination, with the second dynasty of Lagash, and finally with the third dynasty of Ur. In the traditional archaeological terminology this phase should be called Early Bronze IVB, corresponding in its entirety to the ceramic horizon of Amuq J and to the middle and late phases of Hama J, characterised by its abundance of 'Painted Simple Ware' and the presence of 'Smeared-Wash Ware' as Mardikh IIB2. The remarkable Mardikh IIB2 culture developed directly out of Mardikh IIB1. There is no break in evolution between the two phases but merely an interruption due to external causes which must have brought about a temporary political collapse at Ebla but certainly did not put an end to the culture represented so vigorously by Mardikh IIB1. Very little is yet known of the city of Mardikh IIB2, but its range must certainly have been similar to that of Mardikh IIB1, as shown by soundings in the Lower City. The catastrophe which overwhelmed the older city must have imposed drastic changes on the civic installations of Mardikh IIB2. This too ended in destruction, around 2000 B.C., though the date is largely conventional. Its traces are conspicuous wherever the material of Mardikh IIB2 is found.

The rebirth of Ebla with Mardikh IIIA (c.2000–1800 B.C.) took place in Middle Bronze I during the period of domination of the Isin and Larsa dynasties in Mesopotamia. The ceramic horizon of Mardikh IIIA, typical of the Middle Bronze Age culture of the Syrian and Palestinian area, corresponds completely with that of Hama H. Its appearance constitutes a clean break with the Early Bronze IVA-B cultures, though there are certain elements in which some signs of continuity can be traced. The quality of the pottery, much less varied in type and technically less skilful, and the carinated shapes, which characterise many types of this phase, are the most general and the most constant distinctive indicators of the new culture. It corresponds in date with the period of emergence of the Amorite dynasties, not only in Mesopotamia but also in Syria. Tell Mardikh at the beginning of the period once more becomes a great city. Its extent is clearly marked by the line of the Walls, consisting of a tremendous embankment of beaten earth surrounding the whole urban area already inhabited, and perhaps also spaces for future occupation. Mardikh IIIA seems to have been a period of great prosperity. The greatest of the city's monuments were for the most part founded then, especially some of the major sanctuaries, on the sites of more ancient buildings of Early Bronze IVA-B which had been destroyed. Architectural techniques took on a characteristic aspect. There was a flowering of artistic production displayed in the custom of dedicating votive statues in the temples and the great carved ritual basins, expressions seemingly of an independent and solidly acknowledged political power.

The following phase, Mardikh IIIB (c.1800–1600 B.C.), corresponding in broad terms to what it seems useful to define as Middle Bronze II of the Syrian Area, is a natural development out of Mardikh IIIA. There are no substantial changes in what appear to be the fundamental culture of Mardikh III. In the final phase of the Mardikh IIIB occupation there are evolved pottery types which appear to be on the same line as certain new forms characteristic of Middle Bronze IIB-C in Palestine, though with more archaic and conservative features. During Mardikh IIIB there was a considerable decline in monumental artistic production, though perhaps not a total disappearance. Probably therefore there was a loss of the political power and prestige which must originally have characterised the great city of Mardikh IIIB. Not much seal work from this period has been found at Tell Mardikh, though the Mature Old Syrian Period was that of the grand manner of Syrian seal cutting. The reason perhaps is simply that the remains brought to light so far by our excavations in Royal Palace E have been noteworthy for their extent on the ground rather than for their state of preservation. All the same, the few cylinder seal impressions recovered are among the finest examples of this refined art. At least one of the sealings, made by a cylinder of the type known as 'Mitannian with Old Syrian elements', must be dated to about 1650 B.C.

The date of the destruction of Mardikh IIIB is very difficult to determine. Like the cylinder seal just mentioned, the evolved forms of the pottery, rare as they are, show that the end of the occupation must be placed between 1700 and 1600 B.C. That it was a destruction rather than an abandonment of the settlement is clearly proved by the thick layers of ash which seal the levels of Mardikh IIIB where their state of preservation is good. The problem of a precise dating, although internal evidence of an absolutely reliable kind has not been found, must be considered in relation to the political history of North Syria in the century beginning in 1700 B.C. In this framework two major possibilities can be assessed. Either Mardikh IIIB may have been destroyed in consequence of internal upheavals in the kingdom of Yamhad — in which case no precise dates can be suggested. Or as a vassal of Aleppo it may have fallen to the assault of the Hittite Great King Hattusilis I, who took Urshu in the last decades of the seventeenth century B.C., or of his successor Mursilis I, responsible for the conquest and annihilation of Aleppo itself in about 1600 B.C. This second guess does seem highly probable. With the destruction of Mardikh IIIB there was a decisive collapse of city life at Tell Mardikh, and a crisis of this magnitude seems more likely to have been connected with the murderous invasions of the two Old Hittite Great Kings, the second of whom put an end to the First Dynasty of Babylon with the capture of Hammurabi's city. It is very difficult to say then whether it was Hattusilis, I, the conqueror of Urshu, who brought about the fall of Ebla around 1650 B.C., when he was perhaps encircling Aleppo by depriving it of its most powerful vassals and thus making things much easier for his successor; or Mursilis I, the destroyer of Aleppo and Babylonia, who after seizing the capital of Yamhad would undoubtedly have had the vassal cities at his mercy. Both possibilities are likely and we have no means at present of deciding between them. In any case this final destruction of Mardikh IIIB must have occurred between 1650 and 1600 B.C. in the time of one of the last two kings of Yamhad, Yarim-Lim III or Hammurabi II.

The destruction of Mardikh IIIB marks the irrevocable end of the great urban settlement of Tell Mardikh, which with two destructions, in 2250 and 2000 B.C., flourished for eight hundred years, from about 2400 to about 1600 B.C. With brief interruptions it maintained a position of political and cultural primacy which must have had its highest point at the time of Mardikh IIB2, during the Mature Protosyrian Period. During the Old Syrian Period there were two phases. The first, Mardikh IIIA, must again have been one of cultural and political hegemony, certainly under Amorite dynasties, and perhaps with a more restricted range. The second phase, Mardikh IIIB, was the age of domination by Yamhad, whose fortunes Ebla followed until the final act.

After 1600 B.C. the Walls and Lower City of Tell Mardikh were finally abandoned. On the Acropolis modest and limited rebuildings can be traced among the remains of Palace E during the Late Bronze Age. But in the present state of our knowledge we cannot even properly speak of settlements corresponding to Mardikh IVA-B. Almost all the remnants of this phase, always in the Acropolis area, in fact consist of fragments of dwellings put together haphazardly from construction materials of the monumental buildings of Mardikh IIIA-B.

During the Iron Age (c.1200–535 B.C.), while nothing is known of Iron Age I (c.1200–900 B.C.), sporadic structures of Mardikh VB (c.900–720 B.C.) reveal that the Acropolis of Tell Mardikh was used for the building of what were probably special installations for a particular purpose, dictated no doubt by its exceptional strategic position. This perhaps is how we must explain the remains of a massive structure with small casemates on the western brow of the Acropolis and the levels of the same period in Sector E, in the northern area of the central summit of the tell. Both on the Acropolis and in some parts of the Lower City rubbish pits provide evidence of the burnished red slip ware typical of this phase.

So it is probable that the Acropolis of Tell Mardikh was used as an internal look-out point of the Aramaean state of Hama and Lagash, and it is even probable that these modest installations were destroyed in 720 B.C. when Sargon II (721–705 B.C.) conquered Hama and annexed the whole territory. None the less, in the third phase of the Iron Age, during the time of the Assyrian and Babylonian domination, a modest village must have continued to exist during the Mardikh VC phase (c.720–535 B.C.).

At a moment which cannot be exactly fixed but cannot have been too early in the Persian epoch a big country house was built in the northern and north-eastern sectors of the Acropolis. This was during Mardikh VIA (c.535–325 B.C.). It was built largely of stone re-used from the ruins of the great city, which at that time were mostly still above ground. There were several phases in the life of this building. Its remains even today rise to a considerable height, and it was still in use in the Hellenistic Period — Mardikh VIB (325–60 B.C.). But it is difficult to say exactly when the building in its final version was abandoned for good. The last evidence of any occupation at all on the Acropolis is some remains of houses of which only the foundations are preserved, emerging on the surface of the northern and eastern areas of the Acropolis (Mardikh VIB Final).

But before becoming a desolate tell Tell Mardikh experienced one more occupation particularly suited to its character of a dead city. On the western terrace which prolongs the foot of the Acropolis towards the Lower City, at a moment which cannot yet be exactly dated, but in the late Roman or possibly Byzantine period, a tiny community of Stylite monks must have installed themselves. It was only in 1976 that indubitable traces of their occupation were found.

From then on Tell Mardikh fell into a long abandonment which was to continue until our own times, but for one very short interval when it was used as a fortified camp. Perhaps it was merely for one military campaigning season. No indication of this use has survived in any form of settlement but the breach in the walls, still clearly visible today, marking Monumental Gateway A of the Mardikh IIIB city, had been blocked with great ashlars re-used from an Islamic building. The stones bear still visible Kufic inscriptions with simple benediction formulae which have been in part placed upside down and must therefore have been ignored, either because they could not be read or from wilful disregard. If we remember that the armies of the First Crusade did actually pass through the Tell Mardikh region on their way down from Antioch, and that in A.D. 1098 they vigorously invested the important medieval city of Maarret en-Numan, it is not improbable that Tell

Mardikh, with its extraordinary ring of ramparts, may have given hospitality, even if only for a few weeks, to detachments of the Frankish army, before returning to its long oblivion.

4. The identification of Ebla

The picture that could be drawn, as early as 1968, of the occupation history of Tell Mardikh, was in view of the then backward state of Syrian archaeology fairly exact. The ancient city there buried, it was clear, must be one of those Syrian centres which flourished from the second half of the third millennium to the middle of the second and of which ancient sources supplied some examples. In particular the western cities mentioned by Sargon or Naram-Sin of Akkad — Ebla, Yarmuti, Ulisum — all or almost all seemed to have met with a catastrophe either in the third millennium itself or about the middle of the second, when, at the latest, their role as great cities must have ended. This was even the case with Tuttul and also Arman, if this was not an ancient name of Aleppo. There seemed no doubt however that Tell Mardikh was indeed a city of Northern Syria with a history similar in general lines to that of the cities with which the kings of Akkad came in contact.

Until 1968 there were only some general pointers to the identification of the ancient name of Tell Mardikh. But the discovery already mentioned, of a big torso fragment of a basalt statue with a votive inscription in Akkadian, gave definite grounds for a solution of the problem.

The torso was not in its original context, having been re-used in the Persian-Hellenistic period in the south-west region of the Acropolis, and is very difficult to date owing to its lack of any particularly significant characteristics. Probably it is to be assigned to the beginning of Middle Bronze I, since it has some stylistic features which would place it in an initial phase of the Archaic Old Syrian Period a little before 1900 B.C. A cuneiform inscription preserved on the bust begins in the right-hand section of the back and, passing on over the right shoulder, extends over the whole torso, according to a custom well attested in votive statuary in Mesopotamia, where however the space reserved for the inscription is frequently more limited or at any rate the inscription is more tidily arranged. On palaeographic grounds a quite general dating, to around 2000 B.C., is indicated. The language of the text is an Akkadian dialect close in some aspects to Old Assyrian.

Though the inscription has some expressions uncertain and difficult to interpret, the general structure is quite comprehensible:

To the goddess [Ishtar] a basin (?) Ibbit-Lim, the son of Igrish-Khep, the king of the Eblaite 'League' (?), introduced (into the temple). In the eighth year of Ishtar, from when she 'shone forth' in Ebla, a statue the same Ibbit-Lim for his life and the life of his sons (caused to be made and) Ishtar was very pleased with him. That statue before Ishtar, his lady, he erected . . .

The fundamental datum contained in the inscription is of course the mention of Ebla in two different but very significant contexts. The name of the city appears both in the title of the royal personage who dedicated the statue and in the dating formula which defines the year of the votive act. While the central term of the title is very imperfectly understood, there is no doubt that the dedicator of the statue, Ibbit-Lim, was the son of a king of Ebla and that the statue was put up in a temple in a year that took its name from the goddess Ishtar of Ebla. It will be clear that these points on their own were not enough to clinch the identification of Tell Mardikh with the ancient Ebla. In the first place, it could have happened that a prince of Ebla would have dedicated a statue of himself in a temple of another city. That said, it will also be clear that the finding of the statue must cause us to give our closest attention to the possibility of an identification.

Obviously, the only way to settle the problem was to compare the history of the occupations of Tell Mardikh as reconstructed by archaeology with the history of Ebla as gleaned from written sources. Only if there were a substantial correspondence between the two kinds of evidence could the identification be put forward.

In 1968 in fact, although the excavations in the Palace G area had not yet been begun, the succession of occupations of the tell was already clear enough to permit the comparison and make it informative. At once a positive finding emerged. The period of the first great urban settlement at Tell Mardikh, Mardikh IIB, between 2400 and 2000 B.C. approximately, corresponds to the period of the most frequent and most significant allusions to Ebla in the Mesopotamian texts. In copies of the Old Babylonian Period inscriptions have come down to us, the originals of which must have been engraved on monuments of the time of Sargon of Akkad (c.2340–2284 B.C.):

Sargon, the king of Kish, won thirty-four battles. He destroyed the fortifications as far as the shores of the sea. He caused to be tied up to the pier of Akkad the ships of Meluhha, the ships of Magan, and the ships of Tilmun. Sargon [the king] prostrated himself in prayer at Tuttul to the god Dagan. [Dagan] gave him the upper country: Mari, Yarmuti, Ebla as far as the Cedar Forest and the Silver Mountains . . .

Some years later, on certain votive objects, Naram-Sin of Akkad (c.2260–2223 B.C.) puts his name followed by the titles 'the strong, the king of the four regions, the conqueror of Armanum and of Ebla' and describes his successes against the two western cities as undertakings never yet achieved by anyone 'since the creation of humankind'. A century after Naram-Sin, Gudea of Lagash (c2143–2124 B.C.) records in the inscription on one of his statues that several kinds of timber considered necessary for the sacred buildings of his city came from the 'plateau of Ebla, from the city of Urshu'. Economic documents of the same period from Lagash record the arrival of linen from Ebla.

During the Third Dynasty of Ur (c.2112–2004 B.C.) the references to Ebla accumulate, although only Shu-Sin refers to the city in a royal inscription and groups the city with Mari and Tuttul. The other frequent references, always in economic documents, mostly from Umma and Puzrish-Dagan, but also from Lagash and Nippur, concern single personages of Ebla, especially messengers and merchants, revealing not only an active presence of the people of Ebla in south-central Mesopotamia but also specific and intensive economic and commercial contacts of the land of Ebla with the land of Sumer in the Neo-Sumerian Age.

The second point in favour of the identification of Tell Mardikh and Ebla to emerge from the comparison of the archaeological and epigraphical evidence concerns the Mardikh III period (2000–1600 B.C.). In this second great phase of prosperity in the city's fortunes the references to Ebla in the Mesopotamian area become rarer. The reasons may be not only that Ebla itself was less important but also that the political relations between the major Mesopotamian centres and the West were looser and that the number of economic documents preserved from this period is smaller. It is none the less significant that peoples of Ebla and Mari are mentioned in a text of Ishbi-Erra of Isin (c.2017–1985 B.C.) right at the beginning of the Isin period in the first years of the twentieth century B.C. Ebla appears again in an Old Babylonian place-list, and in the myth of the journey of the god Nanna to Nippur it is said that the timber comes from the 'forest of Ebla'. A very doubtful reference, on the other hand, is in a dating formula of Sumulael of Babylon (c.1880–1845 B.C.). But in this same period individuals of Ebla are present at Kanesh in Cappadocia, the famous Old Assyrian trading colony. Above all, in the texts of Alalakh VII, the Syrian city of the kingdom of Yamhad situated not far from the mouth of the Orontes, Ebla reappears on several occasions. A dating formula of King Ammitakum of Alalakh, between 1700 and 1650 B.C., takes its name from the marriage between a son of the king of Alalakh and a daughter of the king of Ebla. A text of the same archive records the visit of a king of Alalakh to Ebla.

A negative point of some difficulty may be seen in the failure of the economic texts and diplomatic documents of the Archives of Mari to mention Ebla in the decades immediately preceding Hammurabi of Babylon (1792–1750 B.C.) and the first thirty years of his reign. Such a gap may seem all the more serious because, as is well known, the Mari letters often refer to the states of Syria and not infrequently come directly from kings of Syrian states. Moreover, there are grounds for believing that in the time of Zimri-Lim of Mari, the king who was defeated by Hammurabi, the states of Yamhad (the kingdom of Aleppo) on the north and of Qatna on the south had a common frontier. Since Tell Mardikh is situated between these two great cities, about fifty kilometres south of the former and 130 kilometres north of the latter, it seems clear that the Archives of Mari in the time of Hammurabi do fail to record the presence of Ebla in that region, in striking contrast to those of Kanesh a little earlier, and Alalakh a little later. Mari itself, however, provides the key to the puzzle. A letter there from the Babylonian chancellery itself contains the following celebrated passage:

There is no king whose power proceeds from himself alone. Ten to fifteen kings are in the retinue of Hammurabi of Babylon, as many more in the retinue of Rim-Sin of Larsa, as many more in the retinue of Ibalpiel of Eshnunna, as many more in the retinue of Amutpiel of Qatna, but there are twenty kings in the retinue of Yarim-Lim of Yamhad.

It was in Hammurabi's reign that Yamhad probably reached the peak of its political power and this is the exact situation and system of political control so succinctly described by the letter. Yamhad's hegemony and the intense fragmentation of the period of the Amorite dynasties both in Mesopotamia and in Syria are clearly demonstrated by the text. It suggests that Ebla was probably one of the petty kingdoms subject to Aleppo in the time of Yarim-Lim of Yamhad. It must still have been a great city but probably no longer enjoyed political independence. For that reason it escapes mention in the internationally oriented Mari archives.

There is thus a complete general correspondence between the history of Ebla as derived from the written sources and the history of Tell Mardikh emerging from archaeological exploration. Certain pieces of evidence specifically emphasise the similarity between the two chains of evidence. First, in the period in which we now know that Ebla was the centre of a political and economic power of great prestige — Early Bronze IVA — Naram-Sin of Akkad boasts of the conquest of the city as an extraordinary feat, evidently very conscious of the international weight of the defeated rival. This quotation, which contains the only clear allusion to the political power of Ebla in sources outside the city itself has now met with an extraordinary confirmation in Royal Palace G and in the Mardikh IIB1 State Archives. Secondly, after its destruction by Naram-Sin of Akkad, about 2250 B.C. or a little later, a first mention of Ebla records that its commercial relations were now with the city of Urshu in the region of the Ebla plateau. Here Ebla seems to have been introduced simply in order to explain the whereabouts of Urshu to the citizens of Lagash. Perhaps Urshu's political power was only recent, and evidently the name of the more ancient capital was still vividly remembered by educated people in South Central Mesopotamia. This was a time for which the Mardikh IIB2 settlement is abundantly attested by pottery of Early Bronze IVB on the tell itself. But with the removal of the Residency elsewhere after the destruction and abandonment of Royal Palace G, there had evidently been a great political upheaval. Thirdly, and lastly, when after the emergence of Yamhad Ebla became perhaps one of the greatest vassal states of Aleppo, the city enjoyed a period of what was probably only economic prosperity, without the vigour of high artistic achievement which had characterised Mardikh IIIA. This final period, Mardikh IIIB, was ended by the same disaster which put an end to the kingdom of Yamhad.

While the Lower City was abandoned after the final destruction of Mardikh IIIB in around 1600 B.C., there are, as already noted, on the Acropolis evident traces of rebuilding on the ruins, especially those of Royal Palace G, during the Late Bronze Age, but these are no more than the remains of a village, not to be compared with the splendours of the great city of the Mature Old Syrian Period.

Parallel with this last poor evidence of a sort of continuity of life on the Acropolis are the latest citations of the name of Ebla in written sources. A Text of Alalakh IV, about 1450 B.C., mentions a man of Ebla. In a fragment of a Hurrian ritual from Boghazköy, in an otherwise obscure context, the cities of Aleppo and Ebla appear side by side. In a great Middle Assyrian god list from Assur the 'goddess of Ebla' is included. Finally, about 1250 B.C., a text from Emar, the present Meskene, recently brought to light, mentions a man of Ebla.

In contrast with the previous centuries, after 1600 B.C. the references in non-religious texts to Ebla are connected with single isolated individuals, and there are no further allusions to kings or governors of the city. More strikingly still, the texts have been found in Syrian centres, Alalakh or Emar. Ebla has disappeared also from the economic documents of Mesopotamia and does not appear in the Hittite texts of Hattusas. It is evident that from then on these were simple allusions to a modest village without political importance, to be passed over entirely but for its great past, of which there must have been still conspicuous evidence in the immense ruins long used as quarries of stone. The sense of the ritual fragment from Hattusas and the list from Assur is different. These are traditional texts and Ebla appears in them not for what it was in the Late Bronze Age but for what it had been in the past. Nor is it surprising that the Ishtar of Ebla should be worshipped in Assyria if we remember the close relations between Ebla and Assur, now documented for about 2350 B.C. by the Archives and on the statue of Ibbit-Lim dedicated to Ishtar.

Perhaps the most significant of the references to Ebla in the period following its destruction at the end of Middle Bronze II is in the great geographical list which Tuthmosis III (c.1490–1436 B.C.) had engraved at Karnak in memorial to his Asiatic campaigns. There Ebla appears at a short distance from Aleppo. This piece of evidence, for long overlooked by scholars even in the most recent years, bringing Ebla and Aleppo together as in the Boghazköy ritual fragment, could have saved them many mistaken identifications of Ebla with places far from Aleppo, north-east of Carchemish. Tuthmosis III's citation is not surprising. Even today the tell of Mardikh stands out imposingly in the gentle undulations of the North Syrian plateau and certainly when the Egyptian army crossed the kingdom of Mukhashshe, as that part of Syria was then called, the ruins of Ebla must have made a tremendous impression, all the more so in an area where the city settlements at the beginning of the Late Bronze Age were passing through a period of upheaval.

It is almost certain that with the beginnings of the Iron Age the name Ebla with its ancient and glorious associations disappeared. There is some trace of it still in Neo-Assyrian texts, but they no longer have any connection with the powerful Syrian city, only with a female deity still accorded traditional worship in the East, though the memory of the original place of her cult had very probably been lost. It is possible that the limited settlements of Iron Age II and the Persian and Hellenistic periods had acquired new names under the influence of the Aramaean-isation of the region. Nothing however can be said for certain about this. The modern name Mardikh, which is certainly puzzling and owes nothing to Arab tradition, may be derived from a late Syriac place-name.

The identification of Tell Mardikh with Ebla, proposed immediately after the discovery of the Ibbit-Lim torso, was greeted with ill-founded scepticism in certain quarters. Yet it was based in 1969 on the correspondence between two categories of evidence, archaeological and epigraphical, concerning Tell Mardikh on the one hand and Ebla on the other. First suggested by a crucial find of an Eblaite prince's inscription, the identification was based essentially on historical considerations and from them drew its strength. When in 1974 the first royal texts of Mardikh IIB1 were discovered and in 1975 the collection of the documents of the Archives of Royal Palace G emerged, the growing weight of evidence became too much even for a few irreconcilable sceptics.

3
Ebla in the Mature and Late Protosyrian Periods (c.2400-2000 B.C.)

It is still impossible to say anything much about the origins and growth of Ebla into the great city it became in the later phases of Mardikh IIA. What is certain is that the development occurred during the historical phase which it is convenient to call the Early Protosyrian Period (*c*.2900–2400 B.C.) and which was largely contemporary with the Early Dynastic Period (*c*.2900–2340 B.C.) in Mesopotamia.

In the Mesopotamian area, as is well known, the great urban developments came about in the preceding Period, the Protohistoric (Early Historic) (*c*.3500–2900 B.C.) and particularly in the so-called Uruk Period (*c*.3500–3100 B.C.). In the Early Dynastic Period, on the other hand, while city life spread rapidly, social structures and institutions began to appear, and their formation, at least in some major centres, was already complete in the Early Dynastic II Period (*c*.2750–2550 B.C.). It is quite possible that in the Syrian area the urbanisation process was more gradual and less generalised, so as to appear retarded in absolute date compared with Mesopotamia. In any case it seems certain that the settlements of Mardikh IIA did not extend very far into the Lower City, while it is possible that the occupation of Ebla was only gradually extended during the final phases of this period. This process must, however, have been complete by the beginning of Mardikh IIB1, which is to be put around 2400 B.C.

1. Mardikh IIB1 (c.2400-2250 B.C.)

Mardikh IIB1 was the period of the first great urban centre of Ebla, which as I have indicated was of considerable extent. There are levels of this phase next to City Gate A beside the south-western section of the Walls of the Middle Bronze I-II cities and north of the Acropolis in Sector N. Though much ruined, they show that the Mardikh IIB1 settlement probably had a similar extent to that of Mardikh IIIA.

This supposition is based on the excavation itself, and seems confirmed by the written evidence of the contemporary archives. There are in fact allusions in the texts to the four city gates of the time, each unmistakably named with a divine name. The Mardikh IIIA-B city has four gates arranged almost symmetrically about a fairly regular ring of walls, and it seems quite probable that they were put up in the same places as the earlier gates of Mardikh IIB1. These original gates were no doubt the first to be so located, just as Mardikh IIB1 was the first Ebla

Date	Northern Mesopotamia			Northern Syria				
3500								
3400	Early Uruk Middle Uruk	Nineveh III	Gawra XIIA-XI		Amuq F			
3300							Late Chalcidic Tarsus	Proto-historic
3200	Late Uruk		Gawra XA-IX			Mardikh I		
3100		Nineveh IV			Amuq G			
3000	Jamdet Nasr		Gawra VIIIC-A	Early Bronze I			Tarsus EBI	Proto-urban
2900								
2800	Proto-dynastic I			Early Bronze II				Proto-syrian IA
2700	Proto-dynastic II	Nineveh V		Early Bronze III	Amuq H	Mardikh IIA	Tarsus EBII	Proto-syrian IB
2600	Proto-dynastic IIIA		Gawra VII					
2500								Proto-syrian IC
2400	Proto-dynastic IIIB			Early Bronze IVA	Amuq I	Mardikh IIB1	Tarsus EBIIIA	Proto-syrian IIA
2300								
2200	Akkad	Assur G						
	Late Akkad Lagash II	Assur F	Gawra VI	Early Bronze IVB	Amuq J	Mardikh IIB2	Tarsus EBIIIB	Proto-syrian IIB
2100	Ur III	Assur E	Gawra V					
2000								

Figure 10   Northern Mesopotamia and Northern Syria in the Protohistoric and Protosyrian Periods

occupation to extend so far. So while the choice of location for the later gates would merely have been following tradition, the first set would have been laid down arbitrarily according to some abstract geometrical plan. The position and number of the four city gates, which in the Archive texts are placed to correspond with what were evidently the four quarters of the Lower City, suggest that when it was decided to surround the Ebla settlement with walls, the city plan was chosen to be approximately circular. At the centre of the circle was the Acropolis, with the main administrative buildings.

Of the actual appearance of the Mardikh IIB1 city, except for the only building in course of excavation, that is Royal Palace G, little can be said. It is however probable that the perimeter wall consisted of a massive curtain of unsquared stone with salient towers, probably quadrangular, at intervals, as seems to have been the tradition in other cities of the time in that region. The Lower City must have been densely packed with very modest private houses, built of mud brick and almost certainly without stone foundations. But in the Lower City area, perhaps at the foot of the Acropolis, there must have been some temples. Only one of these has been located with certainty in the north of the Lower City, on the site of Temple N of Middle Bronze II. A sounding taken over a very short section, in the ground near the west wall of the building, which has its entry on the east, has revealed that the foundations of Temple N reach bedrock at a depth of 1.70 metres in levels of Mardikh IIB1 and Mardikh IIB2. Another short sounding taken against the outer face of the perimeter wall south of the temple has revealed that the rock had a marked rise towards the Acropolis and that Temple N of Mardikh IIB1 was founded on it, well above the level of the Lower City. The Acropolis at the beginning of the Mardikh IIB1 phase was a mound certainly of smaller area and height than at present and composed of the ancient tell with its limited settlements, which must have developed around a natural limestone outcrop. As demonstrated by the soundings on its western slope, the Acropolis must certainly have had its highest zone, as it still does today, in the north-western area sloping down towards the south. Where it fell short in Mardikh IIB1 of its later extent was particularly in the south-west and perhaps also in the south, since the present terraces are actually formed by the outer limits of Royal Palace G. So far as concerns the external appearance of the Acropolis the hill slopes, at least in the excavated area, were not visible during Early Bronze IVA, in contrast with what we have been able to discover of the Middle Bronze Age citadel. They were hidden by the high walls of the façade of Royal Palace G which faced the Lower City and must have been high enough to screen from view most of the upper sectors of the Acropolis with the palatial buildings on its slopes and summit.

a. Architecture

Royal Palace G, in the present state of the excavations, has been uncovered only to a very small extent, in comparison at least with the size of its original structure. We do not know even incompletely the lay-out or function of its different parts. Although it has been explored in one fairly wide area, Palace G remains still a fragment of what must have been an extraordinary monument of its period.

What has so far been excavated extends over the slopes of the south-western area to the foot of the Acropolis. Quite a big section of one of its façades has been brought to light, in an excellent state of preservation. This is certainly the principal façade and looks out on a huge open space, a kind of large square, in part at least colonnaded. Projecting northwards from this façade, and cut by erosion on the slope of the mound, is part of a structure that extended towards the Lower City west of the Acropolis. We have also begun excavation of the wings of the Palace behind the façade, and have been able to say what purpose they served. We have uncovered a large area of the square opposite the façade, a well-preserved surface on to which the massive walls of the main elevation of the Palace had collapsed outward under the pressure of the superimposed masonry of the Acropolis.

The elements of Royal Palace G so far uncovered are: the north and east sides of the so-called 'Court of Audience'; the North-West Wing of the northern façade of the Court; the Tower with the Ceremonial Stairway at the intersection of the two façades of the Court; the Monumental Gateway opening out of the east side of the Court; a small part of the Guard House, north of the Gateway; a short section of the Administrative Quarters, south of the Gateway.

The area named 'Court of Audience', rather incorrectly, because at the beginning it was thought to be an actual inner court of the building, is in reality a city square (L.2715 and L.2752 on the ground Plan of Figure 11), colonnaded on at least two of its sides, the north and the west, and measuring more than 50 metres on its north-south axis and more than 27 metres from east to west. The two façades (M.2614 on the north and M.2751 on the east) are massive mud brick structures on low ashlar foundations 2.80 metres thick throughout. The north portico is about 5.50 metres deep, the east portico rather less, about 5 metres. The superstructures of the two porticoes were supported by wooden columns about 0.70 metres in diameter, each fixed to the ground in a regular hole, the bottom of which was formed by a stone slab. The cross beams were about 3.75 metres long on the north side and on the east varied from 2.80 metres opposite the Monumental Gateway to 3.60 metres further south.

Several doorways opened on to the Court area. On the north side was a small doorway of which only the eastern jamb is preserved and which opened on to some narrow store chambers behind the north façade. At the eastern end of the north portico a high narrow door in an excellent state of preservation opened on the Ceremonial Stairway inside the square tower. On the east side the Monumental Gateway, spanning a broad flight of steps which ascended towards the Acropolis, offered access to the Palace proper. Again on the east side but further south a fourth door gave admittance to the inner part of the Administrative Quarters.

Under the north portico, a dais of mud brick rendered with a whitish gypsum plaster 4.50 metres by 3 metres and about 0.55 metres high was built against the north façade, near the jamb of the door leading to the store rooms. A very short main flight of three steps ascended the front of the dais and a second identical flight ascended the side adjacent to the store-room door. Slight depressions, not perfectly regular, in the central area of the upper surface of this structure, indicate that a throne and probably also a canopy were regularly placed there. This must have been the royal seat of audience. It is significant, in relation to the royal throne, that the door to the Ceremonial Stairway at the eastern end of the north portico opened towards the dais and that the other doorway in the north façade which admitted to the store rooms was beside the dais. No doubt the Ceremonial Stairway was the route followed by the king to reach the dais from his personal apartments, which were perhaps on a first floor of the building, while the small chamber and narrow corridor behind the north façade of the Court must have been the accommodation reserved for a first provisional storage of at least some of the goods which would have been brought into the Court and probably laid down in front of the royal dais.

Two buttresses of which certainly the principal function was to support the tower of the Ceremonial Stairway did duty also as screens for the two colonnades (Figure 13). While the pier of the north portico hid from view the entrance to the Ceremonial Stairway, preceded by a narrow vestibule, the pier on the line of the east portico (M.2750) formed a small chamber (L.2712) with access from the south, which was also used as a Court store room. South of the Monumental Gateway, separated by partition walls only one brick thick along the line of the colonnade, were rooms of particular importance annexed to the Administrative Quarters.

In the Court was a complex of wells and cisterns. Since only part of the square has yet been excavated, the system connected with the north portico is the only one we are quite clear about. In front of its colonnade was a well mouth served by a small underground channel, the course of which can be made out from irregularities in the pavement. This channel conducted to the well part of the rain water collected by a

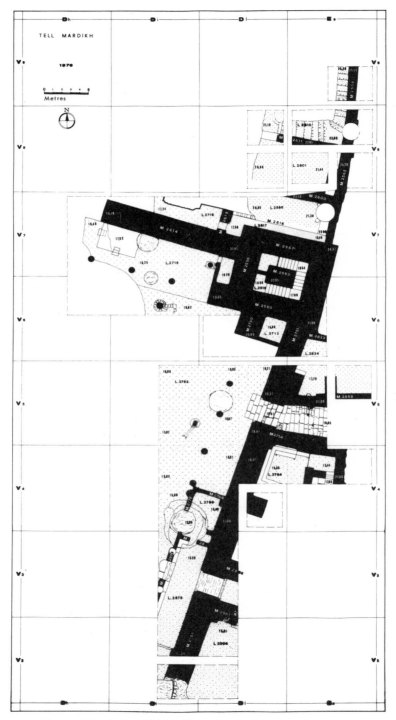

Figure 11 Ground Plan of Royal Palace G of Mardikh IIB1

cistern placed just in front of the tiny vestibule of the Ceremonial Stairway and covered by the north portico. There was a second cistern in front of the east portico. In this case the mouth of the well was closed by a stone slab of very regular circular outline, with a rectangular opening rebated along all four sides into which a dressed stone lid must originally have fitted.

The original extent of the Court cannot be exactly determined. In the northern area the paving is interrupted a little to the west of the dais, the upper part of which has in fact been damaged by this break. It may have been caused by erosion but even more probably by later cleaning up operations in the ruins of Royal Palace G. Even during the Mardikh IIB2 phase this seems to have been thought necessary, perhaps because of the danger of the collapse of walls still standing. Whatever the reason, the break in the pavement makes it impossible to say anything definite about the width of the east-west side of the Court. It can only be said that if the royal dais was situated in an approximately central position on the north façade of the Court, the width of the Court would have been about 40 metres. If we then take this probable central position of the dais as a basis of calculation and treat the façade as an architectural elevation, with the dais installed halfway between the western structure of the tower (M.2556) and the west side of the Court itself, then the east-west width of the square must be round about 32 metres.

It is still more difficult to make any guesses at the length of the Court on a south-north axis. The east façade does not offer any feature which could reasonably be supposed to have been placed in a position of calculated symmetry. This problem may never be finally solved, since nothing has been turned up by our excavations which gives any hope even in the future of getting reliable evidence. The great façade M.2751, which is well preserved at its northern end and progressively more and more ruined to the south, is broken off, perhaps for good, in square DiV2ii. Therefore, considering also the positioning and height of the terraces in this sector of the tell at the foot of the Acropolis, it seems impossible that the south-east corner of the Court can have been preserved — the corner, that is, where the southern extremity of the great eastern façade of the square should meet the southern limits of the built-up area. Yet there is one point which may give useful evidence. In square DiV2i, in correspondence with a pilaster strip slightly projecting from the face of M.2751, the pavement of the Court shows a gentle rise in the ground level, a sort of low step which seems analogous to that which marks the limit of the colonnade on the north façade. On this analogy it might be argued that we here have the beginning of the front of a probable south portico of the Court. In that case the Court would have measured a little less than 52 metres on the south-north axis, that is about 100 cubits, and a little less than 32 metres on the east-west axis, that is 60 cubits.

For the colonnades, there is sure evidence on the northern and eastern sides of the Court, but nothing can really be said about the western and southern sides, which have not yet been excavated and are very probably lost for ever. There is no reliable basis for reconstructing the roof heights of the colonnade columns, even hypothetically. The holes by which the columns, certainly of wood, were fixed to the ground are cylindrical, about 0.80 metres deep more or less with a diameter as I have already said of about 0.70 metres. On the walls of the two main façades, M.2614 and M.2751, no traces have been preserved of slots or bearings for horizontal joists, such as must certainly have formed part of the roofing of the colonnades, up to the maximum surviving height of 5.15 metres in the corner of the north façade, near the doorway to the Ceremonial Stairway. The only feature which could possibly be considered with this in mind is a thin continuous fracture line in the whitish gypsum plaster that covered the two surviving façades of the Court, at a height varying from 1.80 metres to 2 metres. Immediately below this line, which averages about 3 centimetres in thickness, at fairly regular intervals holes are visible in the two mud brick structures which must evidently have served the purpose of supporting horizontal joists.

To explain the fracture line in the plaster two suggestions may be offered. First it may be supposed that the colonnades were very high, reaching about 5.50 metres or a little less. In that case the absence of visible traces of horizontal supports for the roofs would be explained by the fact that the upright structures had survived only up to a lesser height. The thin fracture line in the rendering would then be explained as having been due to the presence in the Court walls originally of a frieze, of wood perhaps and corbelled outward in a kind of shelf, which would have had the function essentially of providing a mount for a series of large limestone eyes which have in fact been found, scattered about the pavement of the Court, especially along the eastern façade. The second possible suggestion is that the roofing of the portico was very light and might thus have been at the height of the fracture line. In that case the height of the porticoes, which could then be more properly described as low galleries, would only have been about 2 metres. For where the fracture line in the plaster today appears at only 1.80 metres in height it may be because the heavy mud brick structure has been compressed. If this second suggestion is correct the frieze of eyes could have served to decorate the front of the roofing of the galleries along the edge of the colonnades.

These two hypotheses, which seem the only plausible ones, are not at all convincing, either of them, for several reasons. Very high colonnades seem aesthetically more plausible but not very functional and, from an engineering point of view, columns only 0.70 metres in diameter at the base do not seem very secure. For very low colonnades with light roofing it is hard to see the necessity for supporting columns of such massive structure. This second case presents many aesthetic difficulties, and it is also very hard to explain apertures of such a height as that of the Monumental Gateway or of the door to the Ceremonial Stairway, the view of which would have been in great part cut off by the galleries.

At the intersection of the two façades of the Court is the tower, 10 metres by 11 metres, with the Ceremonial Stairway inside it (L.2515), in four flights built around a central rectangular pillar. In the tower, the outer walls of which are 2.80 metres thick like those of the Court façades, the steps themselves are only 1.10 metres wide. A small door opening to the left immediately after the entry to the tower gave on to a small room in the space under the third flight of steps, fitted out as a toilet. The steps of the main stairway, which are remarkably well preserved, had their treads covered with wooden boards, probably of open-work or at any rate carved, in which mosaics were mounted, probably of shell, in geometrical shapes. These tesserae, predominantly square or triangular, were arranged in such a way as to form geometrical flower designs interwoven in repeating patterns. The wooden panels have of course vanished completely, and the same applies to the mosaics, which is hard to understand if their material was shell or other less perishable material. The decorative designs can be reliably restored, however, from the impressions left in the clay by the burnt panels after the conflagration. Of the four flights of steps the first three were built solid while the fourth, the west flight, must have been open string. It is possible that a fifth flight, also open, of which incidentally no trace remains in the walls, was installed above the first. In any case whether the door of egress from the Ceremonial Stairway opened out of the fourth flight or out of a possible fifth, the Stairway must have connected the north colonnade with what must either have been a first floor of the Palace, of which all direct evidence has been lost though it would justify the great thickness of the façade walls on the east side of the Court, or else with those quarters of the Palace which were naturally higher, being built on the upper slopes or at the top of the Acropolis, east of the first row of rooms behind the east façade of the Court.

The North-West Wing of Palace G consists of a section of building emerging to the west of the northward extension of the line of the east façade of the Court. It includes two long rooms with an east-west orientation (L.2586 and L.2601), bounded on the east by a terrace wall (M.2565) which approximately follows the line of the east façade of the Court; north of that a winding stairway which starts alongside the room

L.2601 and mounts towards the summit of the Acropolis in the area of Temple D; a corridor, a small square room (L.2716), and a passage (L.2617), rather long and very narrow, which served as store rooms, immediately north of the north façade of the Court. The floors of the two long rooms of the North-West Wing were about 3.40 metres higher than the ground level of the store rooms along the back of the Court, and certainly the floor of L.2586 covered the passage L.2617, which was actually a cellar, because in the masonry of M.2557 we have found big cavities at regular distances which must have accommodated the supporting joists of the southern part of the floor of the southern long room. Since the erosion of the slope of the Acropolis has carried away the western part of the two long rooms, only the eastern half of which has survived, it is not possible to say how access was gained to them. Certainly a door connected the northern room with the winding stairway L.2610. It cannot however be ruled out that the access to both rooms or to one of them was on the lost west side and that other rooms were built to the west of the surviving area at a lower level. If this was so then the North-West Wing, as was certainly the case with all the southern part of the Palace behind the east façade of the Court, would have been raised on terraces. It would not have been a great part of the North-West Wing that would have been carried off by the erosion but only a small terminal part, consisting of rooms built on intermediate terracing between the great upper terrace to the east, that is Room M.2565 with other possible lower rooms situated to the west, on the same level as the Court.

In the east façade of the Court, the Monumental Gateway was certainly the principal access to the Royal Palace G, but perhaps also the main entrance to the Acropolis as a whole. The Gateway, in fact, is approached by three steps of big limestone slabs and encloses a flight of steps of partially stuccoed basalt, ascending to the interior of the Acropolis.

This stairway starts square to the great east façade (M.2751) with its north-north-east to south-south-west orientation and thus at first moves from west-north-west to east-south-east. Once past the gate the walls on either side are no longer parallel but diverge slightly so that the stairway fans out and corrects its direction of ascent. It thus acquires a true west-to-east direction, in keeping with the north-south alignment of the internal terraced walls of the Palace, which are still very incompletely excavated.

A door in the north side-wall of the stairway gave access to the Guard House, containing at least two rooms, still only partially excavated. On the line of the Guard House door was a great jar fixed in the ground and occupying part of the threshold. The wooden door itself, which was found torn off and thrown on the pavement, had been cut out at the bottom in the shape of the jar, which thus stood part inside and part outside the door when it was closed. This singular arrangement indicates that it was thought necessary to ensure the water supply to these rooms with the door closed, evidently in view of the sort of things normally kept in this part of the Guard House. That is, the water was poured into the jar from outside with the door locked and could be got from inside without opening it. Thus if it was found necessary to keep this small corner of the Palace normally shut off, it was no doubt because something important was kept there. It seems reasonable to guess that this something was the arms issue for the Palace garrison, or perhaps only for the guard on the Gate. This could also be inferred from what was probably a wooden loft, which has left visible traces of burning on the walls of L.2834 above a certain height. At the same time there must certainly have been soldiers of the garrison living in the Guard House because in Room L.2834, besides the jar for liquids in the threshold of the door, we found also jars of corn set in a fitted brick bench, while built into one short wall was another bench, also of mud brick, for sitting on.

The most homogeneous sector of the Palace is undoubtedly the Administrative Quarters, south of the Monumental Gateway but apparently quite cut off from it. It consisted of some smaller rooms outside the Palace proper, under the east portico, and some larger rooms inside it. In the area so far excavated, under the east portico, two such rooms are the vestibule, L.2875, with an entrance through the line of the colonnade directly facing the main door to the Administrative Quarters through the line of the great façade M.2751; and the archive room, L.2769, entered through a side door from the vestibule. The length of the vestibule cannot be determined, because a broad trench, dug in Middle Bronze I-II, partly through the doorway of the Administrative Quarters, has entirely removed the southern portion of the vestibule, destroying every trace of its southern limits, and making it impossible to tell whether there was another room south of the vestibule, symmetrical with the archive room on the north.

In the area of the Administrative Quarters extending to the east of the great façade M.2751, that is inside the Palace proper, a corridor and three large rooms have so far been identified, one after another in line. Only two of these have been partially excavated. That remaining to be explored is the central room of the three, approached by the corridor from the entrance doorway. Of the two side rooms that to the north, L.2764, had rather high multiple benches of mud brick built along part of three walls. One of the benches was encased with carved wood panels. Against the fourth wall were some fittings, so far only partially uncovered and not yet certainly identified, but seemingly brick stairs which perhaps led up to a loft. The open space to the south, L.2866, must have been very large, at least 10 metres long. It is impossible, however, to guess its function owing to the complete absence of furniture and fittings inside it.

Considering as a whole the sections of the so-called Royal Palace G so far brought to light, it will be noted how the individual sections are unified and brought together by the so-called 'Court of Audience', an urban open space of exceptional coordinating power. Although it is impossible to offer a plausible reconstruction of the Court, it is possible, as we have seen, that it measured 52 metres by 32 metres on its north-south and east-west axis respectively. The two elevations east and north must certainly have had a monumental appearance. The east elevation was probably between 13 metres and 15 metres high, as calculated from the mud-brick masses fallen into the Court and easily identified in the east-west walls of the excavation squares. The southern and western sides, on the other hand, must have been very different even in appearance. It is almost certain that every trace of them disappeared beneath the rebuilding of the great city of Mardikh IIIA. But even before that and quite soon after the destruction of Royal Palace G (at the end of Mardikh IIB1), a wall of Mardikh IIB2 was put up immediately to the west of the royal dais to contain the ruins of the Palace. This goes to show that while the remains of the north and east façades were still imposing, the remains of the west and south sides must already have almost completely disappeared. Evidently on these two sides, towards the Lower City, the elevations of the Court were formed by actual private houses. It is therefore doubtful whether the colonnades extended all round the Court.

Thus the Court of Audience was an urban open space coordinating the complex of royal buildings which made up Palace G. These emerged partly from the flanks of the Acropolis, arranged in terraces — the North-West Wing — and were partly contained by a great monumental façade, M.2751, at the back of which the Palace apartments began, again disposed on terraces up the slopes of the hill. The Court is a piece of city planning of varied function, conceived with the aim of giving monumental dignity to the administrative and residential complex on the Acropolis. The imposing east façade was intended to offer a truly monumental prospect, an elevation rising to unify from below the various sectors of the Palace set along the south-west slopes of the Acropolis. It was designed to enhance the grandeur of the main Gateway by creating a kind of scenery around it. At the very level of the Court and communicating immediately with it we find the Administrative Quarters, which had an indisputable relation with the business transacted in the Court. A similar and even more evident intention was that of the north façade, which was really a pure elevation without any architectural function. It was merely a boundary mark delimiting the

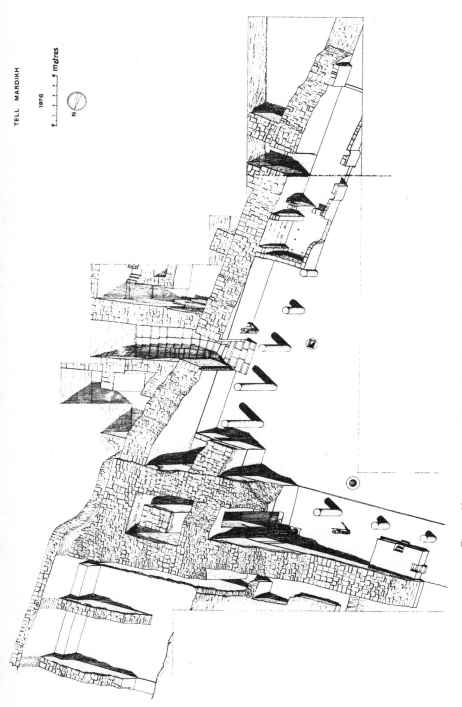

Figure 12 Axonometric View of the Ruins of Royal Palace G from the West

area of the Court, a mark designed to exalt and literally give height to the symbolic requirements of the royal dais.

As one very particular open space the 'Court of Audience' formed a threshold between the dense and intricate network of private dwellings in the Lower City and the palace apartments on the Acropolis and without a break brought the two city areas together. It thus appears as the pivot of social life in the city, a meeting place between the administrators of power and the productive forces of the community. The Court, it has been said, is on the threshold between the two areas, not inside the administrative area. And some of its most characteristic architectural achievements are nothing but devices to emphasise this position. Thus the tower of the Ceremonial Stairway can only be explained if it is the only way, or at any rate a privileged one, between the dais and the royal apartments, while the Monumental Gateway must lead primarily to the administrative sectors of the Palace.

The Court communicated with the store rooms behind the north façade through the door near the dais, with the royal apartments through the Ceremonial Stairway, with any more distant Palace apartments through the Monumental Gateway, and finally with the Administrative Quarters, which opened directly on to it, through the east façade.

The relation of the Court with the Administrative Quarters appears the most important element. In fact, those sectors of Palace G which have a clear technical homogeneity easily seen in the ground plan are the two surviving façades of the Court, the tower of the Ceremonial Staircase, and the Administrative Quarters. But since there is a noticeable shift of orientation between the Court itself and the Palace buildings inside the east elevation (M.2751) on the slopes of the Acropolis, we must suppose that something we do not yet know has caused this change of axis, and is also the reason for the curious fan shape of the stairway through the Monumental Gateway. If the orientation of the Court was not dictated by that of the Palace quarters behind the east façade, we are forced to suppose that it was determined by pre-existing structures too important to be ignored or changed, probably because of their function. In fact, soundings taken to the west of the Court along the line of the north façade have brought to light impressive remains of a building, perhaps sacred, of Mardikh IIIA-B, the structures of which are identically oriented with the Court of Mardikh IIB1. It must be inferred that very probably, at the beginning of Mardikh IIB1, there was already a sacred area to the west of the North-West Wing, and that this must have been the deciding factor in the orientation of the Court. Thus the sacred area in question would have been formally connected with the Court. The change of axis moreover provided a convenient trapezoidal area to the south for the

Administrative Quarters, which would then have been planned in close connection with the Court and at the same time.

It is possible that the site of the Court of Audience alone was originally intended to serve similar purposes to those ultimately served by the whole Palace area in Mardikh IIB1. But at a given moment, probably about 2400 B.C. or a few decades earlier, the period to which the earliest documents of the State Archives of Royal Palace G can be dated, it was decided that considerations of prestige and efficiency demanded the creation of a city square which would do duty both as a square and a court, and serve as an element of coordination of the different city buildings and provide a monumental background for the giving of audience by the powerful lords of Ebla. In our present state of knowledge it is possible that the man responsible for this original urban project was Igrish-Khalam, the first king so far vouched for by the Archive texts.

b. Small sculpture

The remains of sculpture from Royal Palace G have reached us in very fragmentary form. This is almost certainly due to the materials used and the way they were put together in the works of this Mature Protosyrian Period. The statuary of Mardikh IIB1 found in the Palace was characterised by its small size and combination of different materials. All that has actually been recovered are some miniature female headpieces in the form of wigs, sometimes intact, which must have been attached to bodies of a different material. They are usually themselves made of a blackish-grey or greenish-grey stone very like steatite, or else of lapis-lazuli. There is nothing to suggest what the bodies were made of, all traces having vanished. So they must thus have been of very perishable material.

The problem of how this small Eblaite statuary was made up can be tackled with good hopes of solution by reference to the only figurine which it has been possible to restore almost entirely, a small human-headed bull, couched. The several parts of this statuette were found scattered on the pavement of L.2764, including the human face, the animal hindquarters, the two separate forelegs, the horns, and one of the ears, all in gold leaf. Besides these, also scattered, were the front and back plaquettes of blackish-grey stone with the thick curls of the flowing beard and animal mane. The plaquettes, very thin, were concave on the reverse so that they could be mounted on the core of the figurine, which is completely lost. It is therefore clear that the core and the supporting substance of the statuette must have been in perishable material, almost certainly wood, while the exposed non-hairy parts were of gold foil and the curls of the mane and beard were in hard stone.

It may be added that the eyes must certainly have been inlaid, with shell for the whites and lapis-lazuli or blackish stone for the pupils.

It is impossible to guess the function of this miniature statuary. The statue of the bull-man could certainly be an independent artefact but it is also very probable that it was an ornament on some other object, no doubt precious and perhaps ceremonial. Of this, however, there is no evidence. As a mythical image, the bull-man couched in the standard posture of the statuette, with one foreleg folded under the body and the other partly raised and pointing to the ground is, in the contemporary mythological and iconographic tradition of Mesopotamia, one of the composite beings in the train of the Sumerian sun god Utu and the corresponding Semitic god Shamash. The function of this composite figure is to throw open the gates of heaven at dawn when the sun appears on the line of the horizon. It is a guardian of the heavenly gates. Then, when the gates are open, the sun god rises into heaven on the backs of two bull-men couched exactly in the position of the composite statuette of Mardikh IIB1.

In other cases, where the remains consist of miniature female wigs we must suppose that they probably belonged to figurines of women in which again the exposed parts of the body were of wood covered with worked gold foil, the head pieces of hard blackish or bluish stone, the clothes of different materials, and that these are lost, so that they also were presumably precious. However, for the clothing there is actual evidence, because at least one front part of a gown with flounces of wool tufts, the traditional ancient Mesopotamian dress, has been found in Palace G, and its material is ivory. So it is probable that, as in the case of the hairy parts of the bull-man, in the statuettes of human figures the gowns and cloaks were made of two pieces of ivory or bone concave on the reverse so that they could be applied to a wooden form which would support the whole. Obviously in the present state of the excavations, that is while the exploration of Royal Palace G is still in its initial stages, it is impossible to say what was the function of the figurines, though it is already possible to form a precise idea of the extremely precious nature of these images of gold, ivory, and hard stone. It should be added that the wigs and gowns are of remarkable fineness of workmanship and in no way inferior to the wonderful, meticulous lightness of the inlaid woodwork of the Palace.

As for the function of the figurines it remains very probable that all these images formed part of some precious fittings the nature of which cannot be determined. In fact in the two inner rooms of the Administrative Quarters, where the greater part of the fragments of this small sculpture have been found, we also found a number of remnants of gold foil in various shapes, hammered into decorative geometrical designs. These were certainly overlays for wooden furniture, even for pieces of

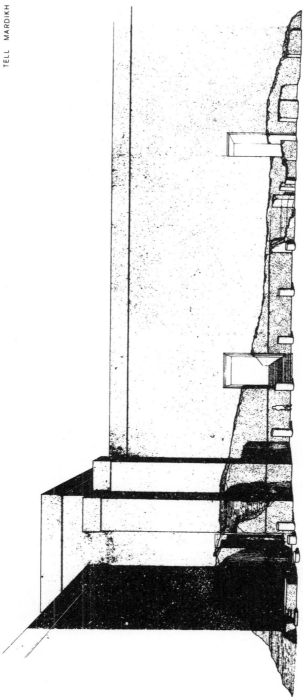

Figure 13 Elevation of the Façade of Royal Palace G

quite large size, and probably the ornaments in the round, like the figurines, were connected with these. Thus, considering the extraordinary affinity of workmanship, even from the technical point of view, between the surviving fragments in hard stone or ivory of carved statuettes from the Administrative Quarters and the wooden figures discovered in one of the rooms of the North-West Wing, we may suppose them to be manufactures of a similar type. But in the second case they will have belonged to furniture extremely fine, but almost wholly of wood, while the first were composite objects made of several precious materials and of extraordinarily skilful workmanship. Obviously the very value of the materials would have caused the objects to be looted during the destruction of the Palace. The remnants have been scattered with the consequence that any possibility of restoring the original furniture has been lost for ever.

The technique of combining various materials must have been used not only on miniature figurines in the round, for insertion in luxurious furniture, but also on larger statuettes, perhaps for votive use, on life-size images, probably of a cult nature, and commemorative bas-reliefs. One find which certainly formed part of a composite statuette is the fine turban complete in every detail, in limestone, decorated on top with spear-shaped elements which were probably inspired by the woollen flounces of a type well known from contemporary costumes, and finished at the base by a sort of regular swelling as if produced by a thick cord, the end of which hangs down on one side. Typical of this turban is a slight elevation of the central part in front. It is an item of costume which must be considered typical of Mardikh IIB1 and a head-dress, probably royal, of ceremonial character in the Ebla of that time. In fact the same turban is worn by a bearded figure who holds an axe against his chest and is clothed in a cloak with woollen flounces, a figure found among the wooden fragments of furniture ornaments in one of the rooms of the North-West Wing. The clothing, the attitude, and the head-dress undoubtedly identify him as a regal personage. Furthermore one of the figures in the train of the great goddess in a Protosyrian palace sealing of Mardikh IIB1 wears the same sort of turban, which may therefore have some undetermined connection with royalty and fertility. The turban of course has the lower part concave so that it can be applied to the head of the statuette. It was of limestone because in work of this kind a rather friable chalky limestone was used for woollen garments, while, as we have seen, the rest of the figure must have been gold for the exposed parts of the body, perhaps lapis-lazuli for the hair which partly emerged from the turban, limestone again for the cloak, and shell inlay for certain details such as the eyes. The size alone of this figure suggests that it had a votive function. It is too large to have been a furniture ornament and too small to have been a cult image. This cannot however be definitely proved unless further excavation identifies a cult room inside the limits, yet to be defined, of the Administrative Quarters.

One piece must almost certainly have formed part of a cult image. Of exceptionally fine workmanship, it must be considered a fragment, unfortunately not very substantial, of a composite female head. It could really be called a segment of a head, in greyish-green stone, of very fine grain and high polish, trapezoidal in section, with the three inner faces smooth and the fourth, outer, face accurately carved with waving locks of hair overlapping one another and ending below in six plaits carved in the round and unfortunately broken off at the base. The presence on the smaller, inner face of a large rectangular cavity like a mortice and on each of the two side faces a circular perforation shows that this surviving segment must have been combined with three others, probably lost, to form the rear part of a female head. It undoubtedly had a central stock with tenons arranged radially to hold the segments together at the back, and the face of the figure, worked in a plaque, in front. Nothing can be said about the face except that in the usual way of this kind of sculpture it could have been a piece of wood carved in high relief and covered with gold leaf. On the other hand it is certain that the head-dress must have been of different material, because the top of the head is not decorated and the locks end in an arc where it is certain that originally the base of an emblem or a separate tiara fitted, not fastened to the head but simply put on it. The exceptional fineness of workmanship and the technical complexity of structure challenge comparison between this image and the frequent Mesopotamian descriptions of divine images used in cult, characterised, as they always are, by a multiplicity of precious materials, leaving no doubt that this sadly solitary fragment must have belonged to a splendid whole, almost certainly a cult image.

Votive perhaps, but more probably commemorative in character are one or possibly several composite panels which have been very tentatively put together from scattered fragments. These were found on the ground of Room L.2866 of the Administrative Quarters and consisted of several limestone plaquettes decorated on one side with wool tufts, and some parts of headpieces in lapis-lazuli. The plaquettes are polished and flat on the back, where there are always one or two cylindrical recesses, evidently to accommodate short tubular dowels. The plaquettes are cut to shape so that their edges coincide with the borders of the skirts carved on them. The wool-tuft flounces are reproduced according to the usual regular pattern with leaf-like elements and only the bottom flounce sometimes has the single tufts carved in openwork. The headpieces have the hair in 'low helmet' style worked in very fine bas-relief with a series of big curls all round the head. But what does appear rather strange is that these headpieces, although worked in the round and not in relief, are not complete in one piece but always cut with one polished plane, so that threequarters of them are preserved. From these elements alone, the limestone gowns and lapis-lazuli headpieces, it seems possible to infer what the original composite plaques were like. They seem to have shown in profile, perhaps on a wooden panel, the figures of people passing, probably with their heads in high-relief, to judge from the headpieces preserved. Once again the bare parts of the bodies, faces, torsos, arms, and legs, were probably of wood covered with gold leaf. Although no gold-leaf fragments in naturalistic shapes have been found in the room where the rest of the plaques were found, in one of the long rooms of the North-West Wing we found the end of a lion's paw with the claw spread to seize the prey, executed in a manner which may very well have been an overlay for a rather sophisticated bas-relief. Even the size of the lion to which such a claw might belong would be in keeping with that conjectured for the original figures, would have been about 30 centimetres in height.

It is difficult to be sure about the nature and function of these plaques. The most plausible guess is that they were not unlike the votive plaques of Early Dynastic Mesopotamia, which are, however, all of limestone or alabaster without the addition of other materials. It is also certain that in the invention of this singular genre Ebla must have had some inspiration from the tradition of inlaid friezes. In some cases these too must have been used as wall pictures. From their discovery in the palace area of Mardikh IIB1 it may also be supposed that at Ebla these precious composite plaques in rather high relief had a commemorative value for the royal family and the deeds of some of its members, even though perhaps most of the themes were of a cult nature.

There is no doubt that the exploration, which has really only just begun, of Royal Palace G at Ebla is revealing an extraordinary efflorescence of this composite style of sculpture. The discovery of an alabaster fragment of a skirt, belonging most likely to a votive statue, re-used in a level of the Lower City of Middle Bronze II and datable to a final phase of Mardikh IIA, indicates a tradition that was probably maturing at Ebla during the whole Early Protosyrian Period and in its latest manifestations gave rise to the figurative achievements of Mardikh IIB1.

c. Glyptics

Evidence of seals and sealings in Mardikh IIB1 consists of over a hundred clay bullae and fragments of bullae found scattered about the floors of rooms of Royal Palace G. These often bear cylinder seal impressions, of which several are of high quality. The greater number of bullae were collected behind the north façade of the 'Court of

Audience' in the store room L.2716 and in smaller quantity near the entrance to the passage L.2617. In the Administrative Quarters too some bullae have been found, partly in the Archive Room L.2769 and partly in the inner room L.2764.

The bullae are quite varied in form but three very distinctive types prevail. First, there is one used for sealing jars, which occurs rarely but with an evident function. It is a kind of cap. A sort of fairly thick 'foil' of clay would have been stretched over the mouth of the jar, which had perhaps already been closed by another bulla in the form of a stopper stuck right into the mouth. The big cap completely covered the mouth of the jar and its circular rim fitted over on to the neck. Sealings of this type, evidently for special administrative controls and guarantees, could be double, as is proved by the finding of at least one such cap with the normal seal impressions on the upper surface and legible traces of negative impressions of cylinder seals on the lower surface, traces left by the adherence of the 'foil', evidently of still fresh clay, to a cap already sealed.

A second type of bulla, used probably for sealing caskets or small boxes almost certainly of wood, is fairly frequent in the store rooms dug out behind the north façade of the Court. It has a triangular section, with two faces relatively flat and at a right angle to one another, marked with slight furrows drawn in lines as if they had been pressed flat to a wooden surface. Between these two faces there is another, on which the cylinder was rolled to make the sealing. In this case it seems evident from the form of the bulla that the lump of clay was applied between the closed lid, no doubt projecting horizontally, and the vertical wall of a strong-box, all the more so as on one of the two smooth surfaces we often find the imprint of something which must have stuck out from the wood and can be identified with a catch or a bolt.

A third type of bulla, not very well known before, served more commonly to seal the usual closures of jars. Normally jars were closed by putting a piece of cloth across the mouth and tying it to the base of the neck with string. A big lump of clay was then generally applied to the shoulder of the jar and stuck across cloth and binding as a guarantee of the integrity of the jar. In this type of tag the lower surface is slightly concave from following the curvature of the shoulder of the jar, which was usually of large size, while the cylinder seal impressions are found in disorderly fashion all over the rest of the upper surface.

Besides these more frequent main types other kinds of bulla have been noted. They must have served various purposes. An example is the clay stopper, which preserves in negative the neck and rim outline of a flask, generally of small size with room at the top for only one or at most very few, cylinder seal impressions. Another form of very simple bulla is a thin ribbon of clay which must have been simply stuck on, to seal lighter and less cumbersome goods held together by thin cords. It is of course on the upper face of these 'ribbons' that we find cylinder sealings, usually only a single impression on each.

What makes. the bullae of Royal Palace G of Mardikh IIB1 so interesting is the high quality of the cylinders and the official character of the seals. Production for Palace use must have been of an exceptional standard and the seals were those of high officials of the Palace in its last years. This dating of the cylinders to the last generation of the Eblaite dynasty of the Mature Protosyrian Period is guaranteed by the fact that some of them have inscriptions. These are shown to have been the property of Rein-Ada and Iptura, two dignitaries of the court of Ibbi-Sipish, who are mentioned several times in the economic texts of the Archives on dated documents.

Despite the remarkable number of bullae recovered, the cylinders from which the impressions are derived are relatively few. It has been possible to restore almost completely the figurative parts of about fifteen seals, while of some others only limited sections of the decorations are known. The fundamental theme of this Mature Proto-syrian Eblaite engraving is the frieze of standing figures, usually defined as a chain of heroes and mythical beings fighting for the preservation of the flocks. The tradition to which they belong is wholly Mesopotamian and Early Dynastic, but there are many elements of a distinctive and not merely secondary kind in the Protosyrian tradition which do distinguish it from the Mesopotamian and give it a character of its own.

Though it does not appear in all the seals, the central figure in the Mardikh IIB1 work is a female deity always shown full face and probably characterised by a headpiece of two horns spreading hori-zontally from the base and a possible vertical threefold element emerging from the top of her head, and by a skirt with a series of big flounces overlapping and turned upwards and outwards. This goddess rules over wild animals and protects the flocks, as is evident from the way she is pictured in the act of holding by the neck two lions standing on their hindlegs. The lions may symbolise the forces of evil in wild nature. In another representation she is holding up a bull by one of its forelegs, and this certainly is a positive representation of the fertility of benign nature. In another she holds a lion head downwards by one of its hindlegs. Other figures play a part in the performance, in which the leading animals are almost always the lion and the bull, but very rarely also the stag. First among the others is the bull-man, in the standard representation with the lower part of the body bull-like, the bust human, the face human with bull's horns and ears. Then we have a male figure, front face, who is generally trying to tame the lion, or a female figure, also front face and similarly clothed (but with long hair falling to her shoulder in upcurling tresses) who apparently protects the bull. Finally there is a naked hero, always front face, characterised by two locks of hair spread horizontally over a low forehead. He rarely takes part in the action of the friezes but is often represented kneeling in the attitude of an Atlas with his arms raised above him and holding over his head a vaguely circular symbol, in four quadrants, composed of two lion's 'masks' opposed head to head and two others, possibly human, opposed chin to chin. Much rarer are other personages, like the female figure with face in profile or the naked hero with lion's head. There are also some characteristic decorative elements. One is the linear herring-bone border above and below the field of figures, another the curious frieze of heads of the same figures, human or mythical or animal, that play leading parts in the scenes of the principal field. These occur as decorative borders above and below on some cylinders of special refinement. Or again there is the large bull-man's head used as a secondary filler element in the lower part of the main fields of figures.

As compositions these Eblaite cylinder seal friezes from Royal Palace G are remarkable for the number of characters represented, varying in general from four to seven and reaching nine in special cases. Sometimes there are chains of figures engaged on the same action, up to a maximum of five. But for the most part the chief characters in each mythical action, varying from two to four in number, are grouped scene by scene without disturbing the apparent unity of the whole design. One constant aspect of these compositions is the emphasis of the vertical in the figures. There is a preferred avoidance of characters interlacing or assuming oblique positions. The rhythmical spacing of the figures is strictly maintained by placing the cuneiform signs of an occasional inscription either above one of the rare secondary themes or in a limited vacant space above one of the figures.

The style of the Mature Protosyrian cylinder seals is characterised by strong sculptural feeling. This shows itself especially in the lion figures with their sinuous bodies, the lively modelling from plane to plane, and the crowding of flame-like elements in their thick manes. Both in the lion's skins and also in the men's kilts minute and cunning changes in the formal dispositions of detail make for variety of design, enriched by the bodily structure of the figures. Again, in the bulls' bodies, the tense and agile drawing of muscular legs shades into the full and massive bellies, and the variety of detail again sets off the happy fusion of the basic inspiration with a taste for the taut and vibrant line. It is the line above all of these miniature carvings that, with all its gaps and lapses and the noteworthy differences of tone and varied solutions arising from them, pursues its search for a consistent, deliberate naturalism.

Figure 14   Reconstruction of Cylinder Seals from Royal Palace G of Mardikh IIB1

d. Wooden carvings

One of the discoveries which at the end of 1974 revealed that Building G must have been a residence of particular importance was made in the North Room L.2601, one of the two long rooms running from east to west in the North-West Wing. Here a great number of fragments were found of openwork reliefs in carbonised wood. Though scarred by the fire they were only rarely decomposed. Their position on the floor allowed us, partially at least, to reconstruct the original appearance of this decorated furniture from the fragments which have so far come to hand. In fact, apart from scattered smaller pieces, the finds were concentrated in two well-localised areas of L.2601, near the east wall of the apartment. One group was more to the north, near the north-east corner, and the other more to the south.

The collection of fragments found to the north were so arranged in their find-spot as to leave no doubt about the furniture they originally composed. Crushed on the floor in fact were two large fragments of a table top, formed of three boards joined edge to edge. The essential details of construction have been studied at length and carefully recorded. The boards were held together by double-pronged bone studs let into the wood at regular intervals along the butt joints. The table top had its outer edges bevelled off below and decorated above with a moulding of semicircular section carved from the solid wood, making a raised border, or kerb, a little less than a centimetre high all round. At several points, always at regular intervals, this solid moulding was interrupted so as to allow the insertion of short half-cylinders of bone, each with two upright perforations for the pins which fastened them to the wood. Attached to the bottom surface of the table top, at a constant distance of 4 centimetres from its edge, was a separate strip about 2 centimetres square in section.

All these technical elements can be fairly confidently explained and reveal an extraordinary skill in woodworking. The table top must have been faced on its upper surface with a sheet of precious metal, or more probably covered with a fabric, no doubt also precious, perhaps embroidered, fixed and held taut at the edges by the bone half-cylinders. The square rail on the under face of the table top is to be explained by the presence in it at irregular distances on its under face of rectangular mortices or small circular holes. These were to receive the tenons or dowels emerging from the tops of the figures of the openwork friezes which decorated the sides of the table. The special richness of this splendid piece of furniture in fact consisted of these friezes of figures. About 15 centimetres in average height, they were fixed to a horizontal lower rail joining the legs of the table and the upper strips fixed directly to the under surface of the table top. Decorating all four sides of the table they presented a continuous chain of images, the inspiration of which certainly comes from the known repertoire of the Early Dynastic seal work of Mesopotamia in its later phases. As I have indicated, the upper strip was set back scarcely 4 centimetres from the edge of the table. Hence the table top did not hide the figures of the frieze from anyone looking down from on top.

The southern group of fragments in this room had some pieces in an excellent state of preservation, but the condition of the whole was worse. They must result from the collapse on the spot of a fairly large and well preserved piece of furniture. They consist of a kind of side panel bordered at the top with an undecorated moulding of circular section, and ornamented at the bottom with moving animals and scenes of lions attacking gazelles. We must suppose them to be the remains of a chair with arms and back in openwork decoration. A kind of large knob in the form of a pomegranate must have been the finial of one of the arms.

The measurements of the table can be reconstructed. It was approximately 40 centimetres by 90 centimetres but there is no indication of the form, size, or inclination of the legs. The same applies to the chair. But it seems probable that the table was rather low and it is possible that the feet were slightly inclined outwards. There is not enough evidence, as I have said, to be sure of how it was supported but the legs were probably of square section, because the corner blocks strengthening the points of attachment of the legs at the intersection of the mouldings on the undersurface of the table top were also square. Moreover we found some fragments of square wooden supports, fairly stout, with one face carved to take a close inlay of rhomboidal, square, or triangular shell tesserae such as we also in fact gathered in large quantity from the floor of the room. The inlaid geometrical design on these supports is identical with that on the mouldings enclosing the decorative parts of the supposed chair arm.

On the table, the friezes on the long sides were certainly of a different kind from those on the short. The decoration of one of the two short sides is known because the openwork relief which belonged to it was found, crushed but in place, parallel with the side panel of the table. It is a scene of a lion attacking a bull. The lion has flung itself outstretched upon its moving prey, of which unfortunately the head is missing. The composition of this plaque is in horizontal lines and the animal figures are rendered in their natural positions. The long sides, on the other hand, were decorated with friezes of vertical figures, the nature of which we have not fully succeeded in explaining, because they contain both mythical scenes connected with the world of wild nature, with its benign and harmful powers, and scenes of warfare certainly commemorative in intention. Though they can often be restored from fragments, the scenes of the first type must have been rather varied and generally depend on groups of no more than two or three figures. Thus there are the naked heroes seizing the lion erect on its hind legs, grasping it with one arm by the spine and transfixing it with a short sword, the lions rampant attacking gazelles which also stand in human posture, the bull-men front face, probably engaged in taming lions, the standing lions rending goat-like animals, sinking their fangs into the throats, the heroes, probably naked, clasping in their joined hands globular flasks from which the springs of fertilising water must have gushed forth. In contrast with these scenes, which follow the beaten track of Early Dynastic tradition, there are other subjects more surprising in such company. Yet the find-spots give no indication that the two types were used separately in the decorative schemes of the furniture. The best-preserved group, of which, even so, only the torsos of the figures remain, consists of two warriors stabbing one another while a third grasps one of the two by the shoulders. Several other fragments belong to similar figures of warriors wearing breastplates, close-fitting as coats of mail, short battle kilts, and heavy square helmets with long ear-pieces.

Although we have not enough data for a solid theory, it seems possible that in the Eblaite outlook there was no great ideological jump between these two themes. In the one case men celebrated the victory of the benign forces of nature over the dark and devilish powers opposing the order of the civilised world, in the other they exulted in human triumphs over enemies who opposed the assertion of a just social order desired by the gods. It may thus be that in the table frieze there were only, as it were, slight interruptions to separate the themes of the figurative field, which were not felt to be all that distant from one another. These pauses in the frieze could perhaps have been marked by certain figures which do not seem to fit either the mythical or the warlike scenes. Typical of these is a figurine of a girl of which only the upper part is preserved (bust and face). Her hair is arranged in an elaborate coiffure with a 'helmet' of braids framing her face, and she wears a cloak with a fringed border visible over her breast. This girl image, which was certainly frontal and has been slightly altered from its original form by some twisting of the wood during the fire, must have been essentially ornamental and could not have been inserted in any narrative context, because at least on one side the rectangular mortice for inserting a horizontal tenon has been perfectly preserved and its purpose would have been hard to explain if the figure had been flanked by similar figures.

A very similar conception must have governed the organisation of themes in the decoration of the chair. Of its two side panels one, apart from the geometrical designs worked in shell inlay on wooden segments, showed in an upper register processions of passing animals — a bull, a lion, a goat — and in a lower register scenes of combat between animals. In what was probably the back there seem to have been inlays of front-facing figures of larger size, probably representing royal portraits. One of these stands out both for its exceptional state of preservation and for the fineness of its carving. It is a bearded male personage wearing a turban, identical with that worn by a guardian spirit in a seal frieze or another on a statuette fragment. The figure is perhaps votive, probably royal, and was found in the Administrative Quarters. The personage holds an axe pressed against his chest, no doubt to be understood as a symbol of power. His beard is stylised, made up of spear-shaped, narrowly triangular elements and rather heavily framing the face with a schematically rayed effect. The cloak, in the traditional fashion with overlapping woollen flounces, covers one shoulder leaving the other completely bare. It is probable, although we cannot be sure from the circumstances of the find, that this male frontal figure decorated the back of the chair. If so, the back ornaments would have consisted of images essentially vertical in effect, while each arm had a frieze — perhaps solely of animals, with a decorative horizontal movement and lightened by the empty frames above them made of geometrically inlaid mouldings.

Although in badly fragmented condition these wooden carvings of Room L.2601 of Royal Palace G have distinct points of interest, especially from the art historian's point of view, which is always very valuable for dating purposes. The heavy helmets of the warriors, the upper surfaces of which are scored with a thick pattern of vertical lines, are identical with those worn by the Akkadian soldiers in the various fragments of the Nasiriya stele. This was a triumphal monument, of which the pieces are now unfortunately dispersed, attributable to the end of the second generation of the dynasty of Akkad, that is to the reign of Manishtusu, or more probably to the beginning of Naram-Sin's reign. The kilt worn by the warriors of the Ebla carvings is a light cloth attached to the waist, covering the groin and leaving the greater part of the haunches bare. We immediately recognise in it the garment worn by Naram-Sin of Akkad on the famous stele discovered at Susa and now in the Louvre. This type of costume in a more severe and rigid version already appears on cylinder seals of the late Sargonid era. But in the exact modelling of these carvings of warriors there are strong similarities with the triumphal stele of Naram-Sin. The cloak with fringed border on the female figure is a typical example of feminine costume well attested in Akkadian seal work, especially in cult and ritual scenes, while the hair styles seem to follow different fashions. Even the most traditional costume recorded from the Royal Palace of Mardikh IIB1, the heavy flounced woollen cloak of the possibly royal figure with the axe, is in the probably more ancient, Akkadian tradition. It is evident both in the style of the garment, which covers one shoulder and conceals the whole body, and in the treatment of the flounces, which are not arranged with geometrical regularity but tend to emphasise the bodily substance of the portrait.

The stylistic elements present in the Mature Protosyrian carvings of Ebla show that they belong to an advanced phase of the Akkad Dynasty, subsequent to Rimush of Akkad. Their iconographic elements share the typically Akkadian preoccupation with encounters and combats in which the emphasis is on the role of single combatants, in contrast to the Old Sumerian view, where the divine will reflected in human actions was the dominant theme. The loss of the complete contexts of the friezes prevents us from gaining any exact notion of the lines of thought involved in these scenes of war or combat. There is, however, no doubt that the very emphasis on single combatants allies them with the Akkadian vision and makes them remote from the Old Sumerian. It is no longer the anonymous mass of mortals who play the chief part in warlike actions but the destinies established by the great gods and realised on earth. In the table friezes too there were, as we have seen, scenes derived from the so-called figure friezes. There the heroes alternate with lions, goats, and bulls in chain-like series of images of protection and aggression, and the whole is without a doubt deeply indebted to the great tradition of Old Sumer in the Early Dynastic Age. All the same, even in these images there are compositions unknown to us from Early Dynastic seal work in all its abundance of surviving examples. One theme, for instance, which has a typically Protosyrian look is that of the naked hero seizing the mane of a front-facing lion with one arm from behind and driving a spear into its belly. Then, certain particulars of the rendering of the attitudes of the wild beasts and livestock, which in Ebla seem fixed but are very rare in Early Dynastic and Akkadian Mesopotamia, must reflect definite mannerisms of the Eblaite workshops. The severe naturalism of Ebla, the full and sober masses plastically rendered, certainly owe a lot to the Akkad school. But the relationship is complex and cannot be assessed simplistically in the traditional terms of an influence of one environment on another. What seems beyond doubt is that the very modes of the Early Dynastic vision appear to have been surpassed at Ebla in the atmosphere of Mardikh IIB1 by means of a conception of form inspired by the same points of view as gave rise to the Palace school at Akkad.

A singular work of admirable quality is the wooden relief of which a substantial fragment was recovered from the floor of Room L.2764 in the Administrative Quarters. It is probably the only surviving remnant in good condition of a door, carved in relief, from a kind of cupboard which housed objects deposited on some benches built into a section of the north wall. It is a short fragment showing two heads, almost certainly of dignitaries facing left. The heads are modelled in profile, with rather low foreheads, the noses rather long and hooked, the chins short and the mouths fleshy. The hair, carefully modelled, is dressed in short locks curled in disorder. The eyes, carved in limestone, were mounted in the wood. The delicate modelling of the faces, with a naturalistic insistence on the curved line, seems founded in a particular interpretation of late Early Dynastic modes. This work with its precise draughtsmanship and rich play of lines in the attitudes has a sophisticated charm and bears witness to a plurality of innovating tendencies emerging from the Early Dynastic tradition at about the same date as the furniture panels of Room L.2601.

e. Fragments of inlay

A number of fragments of figurative inlay in stone have been recovered from later levels, where they were found scattered owing to the evident re-use of the earth from the destruction of the Early Bronze

Age buildings. They must have belonged to decorative friezes with narrative subjects. These fragments are in general rather poor but when not too small can be identified as dealing with warlike and commemorative themes. The scenes must have included combats between naked warriors, figures, probably of kings or dignitaries, facing heaps of human heads from decapitated enemies, and others, still difficult to identify, with passing bulls. We are still not sure whether these were animals in pastoral contexts or supernatural beings, like the bull-men in mythological representations.

The original provenance of these fragments is not known. They seem to be datable to an advanced phase of the Early Protosyrian Period, before the period of Royal Palace G. In technique they show an undoubted dependence on contemporary Mesopotamian inlays, with some points of detail typical of this Western school. The inlays of Ebla were all done in limestone or alabaster, with some details carved in lapis-lazuli. They were so worked as to bring out the figures very lightly, with only the outlines carved in the background. In Ebla they did not yet use, as so frequently in Mesopotamia, tesserae of geometrical shape inside which the figure was drawn or single figures in profile which would then be set in bitumen to form a scene on a wood or stone backing. By contrast, the Tell Mardikh inlay fragments usually grouped together several figures forming small pictorial groups in outline. And these groups of figures were certainly to be inserted in a larger picture, where the single units must have been combined in narrative perhaps in more than one register.

Among the ruins of Royal Palace G quite a few scattered fragments of inlay of this same kind have been found. The fact that they were found among the ruins of different rooms of the building, never at destruction level on the ground but always among the debris of the mud-brick structures, makes it doubtful whether the original objects formed part of the Palace furniture. The fragments could also come from the mud bricks themselves and thus be re-used material. Another possibility cannot be ruled out. The scattering of the remains may be due to the fact that the original panels had been kept on an upper storey, for example a first-floor of the east façade of the Court. This does seem plausible. At least three of the fragments belong to one and the same frieze which is of special interest because its subject was certainly mythological and all the surviving remnants of figures are passing bull-men with faces framed by big beards.

Different subjects must have been represented on other smaller friezes in the same technique, certainly belonging to the furniture of Royal Palace G, but of which there are only very scanty traces. Thus we have a figurine of a sheep-like animal, very finely carved, and a rather stylised skirt of a possibly female figure showing a maturity of style compared with the pieces previously mentioned. But it would be really difficult to guess the decorative or narrative contexts of the pictures to which these fragments belonged.

The remains of inlay recovered from the later levels of Middle Bronze I-II among the ruins of Royal Palace G and on its floors at destruction level are striking evidence of an artistic genre which must have had a remarkable development at Ebla, with a history of its own. It is probable that the exciting panels with war and victory scenes date back to the last years of Mardikh IIA or even to the very first years of Mardikh IIB. Their subject matter is similar to what we find in Mesopotamia in this same artistic genre but their spirit is very different. The scenes of combat and triumph over fallen enemies are typical subjects for Mesopotamian stelae, while the celebration of victory in Sumer is attested by the inlaid panels depicting triumphal processions. The inlays with figures of bearded bulls must almost certainly be later, from a central phase in the history of Royal Palace G, and may have formed part of ritual panels with mythical images. Finally, some fragments too scanty for their subject to be made out but certainly more mature and refined in style and technique than the earlier pieces must be dated to the last years of the Mardikh IIB1 Palace.

f. Pottery

The ceramic horizon of Mardikh IIB1, and that of Royal Palace G in particular, is very homogeneous and uniform. Our knowledge of it is largely based on observation of the levels of destruction and collapse of the structures of the great Palace building of Sector G. Here we can be sure of a clear and unambiguous context. Sherds of Mardikh IIB1 are also largely present, in disturbed contexts, among the accumulations of material heaped together in erecting the ramparts of the surrounding city wall at the beginning of Mardikh IIIA. Since it came from the rooms of the Royal Palace, it is possible that the Mardikh IIB1 pottery so far noted was of a special, highly-prized quality, or at any rate that it includes examples which are rare elsewhere. This is to emphasise that certain peculiarities of the pottery from Royal Palace G of Mature Protosyrian Ebla can best be explained if Ebla was in fact the major centre both culturally and politically of what has been defined as the 'chalice culture' of Northern Syria. Furthermore, it is quite possible that in what was the capital of the most powerful state of the day the pottery of the Royal Palace included some special types not in common use.

The pottery most usual in Mardikh IIB1 was the so-called 'Simple Ware'. These are generally thin-walled, wheel-made, in small to medium sizes of a very clear whitish, yellowish, or greenish colour, with

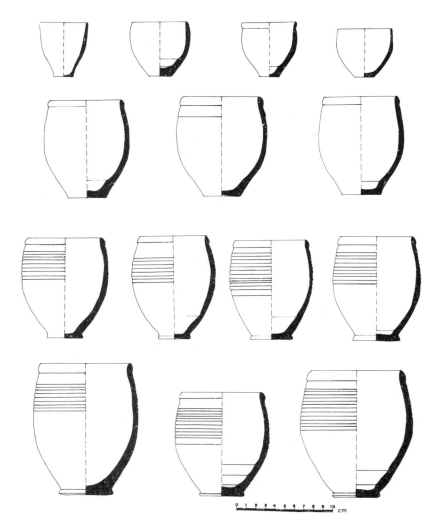

Figure 15   Pottery of Mardikh IIB1

very small grits. The vases in this type of ware are generally well fired
and sometimes have a metallic ring. Among the small-sized vases the
dominant and characteristic shape is the beaker, roughly cylindrical
above and with varying degrees of constriction towards the base. The
base is sometimes flat but often ringed, with a strong concavity between
the ring and the central disc. Very often in the smaller beakers, and
always in the medium or larger beakers, the outer surface of the vase is
characteristically 'corrugated', that is encircled with very regular wheel-
made undulations in the upper, almost cylindrical part of the body. The

rims for the most part are very slightly thickened externally. In the Mardikh IIB1 horizon the beakers are never painted, as is the rule in the following phase of Mardikh IIB2.

Quite frequent among the small-sized vases in 'Simple Ware' are the small cups with slanting walls and expanded rims, while the more usual type of cup in this phase, of which we have both medium and large examples, is slightly closed in shape with the rim strongly thickened externally. The ware of cups of this kind is often of an intense greenish colour, or deep pink or violet. They are normally better fired than the

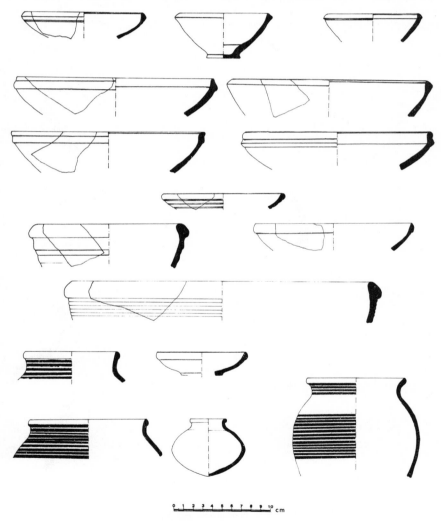

Figure 16 Pottery of Mardikh IIB1

beakers, and the metallic resonance is more marked. Still rare in this phase, on the other hand, are the cups, markedly open in form, with a rim characteristically thickened by being folded over on the outside and moulded externally rather than swollen. This style of moulding of the vertical outer face of the rim will become characteristic of the cups of Mardikh IIB2. Moreover, this same manner of working the rim will be completed by a painted decoration and used also for painted beakers.

Among the vases of middle size, less frequent but quite typical of the 'Simple Ware' of Royal Palace G, are the juglets of closed shape with

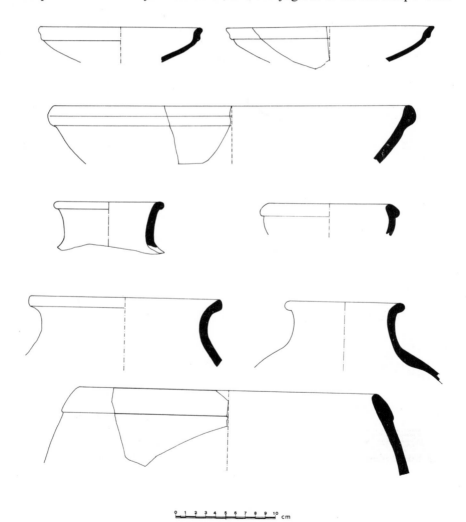

0 1 2 3 4 5 6 7 8 9 10 cm

Figure 17   Pottery of Mardikh IIB1

oval body and very short narrow neck, short everted rim and edge slightly thickened on the outside. This type of vessel was also produced in a ware with very thin walls, strongly fired, of an intense greyish-green colour, with a 'corrugation' of the surface not in rather broad undulations as is typical of the beakers, but with fine incisions closely spaced and regular. Also characteristic in this type of pottery are the juglets of globular shape with rather expanded body, the shoulder very flattened and a high neck of almost cylindrical shape with rim slightly everted, thickened on the outside, and grooved internally. A form of vase similar to this last but with the neck decidedly narrower has a tubular strainer fixed to the beginning of the shoulder. All these varieties are usually in the 'corrugated' ware with closely spaced and fine incisions.

Although of limited occurrence, a special kind of 'Painted Simple Ware' is typical of the ceramic horizon of Royal Palace G at Ebla. It is so far attested in only two forms of juglet. One is an oval vessel of very small size, not larger than a beaker, with a short, very narrow neck and everted rim. The other is a medium-sized vase, also oval, but with broader base and neck. Both these types have an application of monochrome paint in bands on the rim and shoulders, in colour brown, blackish, or very dark violet. This kind of 'Painted Simple Ware' is certainly the forerunner of the much more widely distributed and technically perfected 'Painted Simple Ware' which is characteristic of the Mardikh IIB2 horizon. In that period the painting, black or red in colour, laid in bands and usually combined with linear or waved incisions on the painted surface, was applied to almost all the current types of 'Simple Ware'.

A particular form of painted pottery is represented in Royal Palace G by small hand-made juglets of a typical yellowish-brown ware often with a light greyish-green inner wall. The shape of these juglets is very characteristic. They always have a flat, very slightly concave base, but the outline of the mouth instead of being round is oval. The body in consequence is a squashed oval. From the shoulder, which is very little emphasised, springs a short neck and a handle running along the whole length of the major axis. The mouth of this curious, asymmetric vessel is of trefoil structure with a slightly everted rim. The painted decoration of these juglets was applied over a yellowish wash of different intensity from one vessel to another, so that it varies from very pale to deep orange. Originally the colour of the painting must have been deep brown or greyish-black, but often in these jugs it has faded to a transparent grey, with an attractive, rather bright green gloss which is certainly the result of a colour change. The scheme of ornamentation of these juglets is by metopes or a chain of reticulated triangles evolving over the shoulder of the jug. From this more regular decorative band hang braids irregular in density and width, tumbling over the body of the jug to the base. The aesthetic effect of these ornaments, tastefully combining their elements in varied ways, is very successful, and the juglets of this kind may be called small masterpieces.

Among the types of medium-sized vases are examples of the 'Reserved Slip Ware' in which the exterior is decorated with ornaments of a generally linear movement arranged horizontally and applied by reserving the slip. The colour is mostly yellowish-cream or a very bright greenish. One type of decoration completely absent on the other hand in vessels of this general shape is the typical 'Smeared-Wash Ware' in which the surface of the jar has a wash of brown or reddish colour of varying depth spread in irregular 'smears' probably with some kind of brush and without following any geometrical pattern. The 'Smeared-Wash Ware', absent from Royal Palace G and probably belonging to the horizon of Mardikh IIB1, appears in some abundance in the following phase of Mardikh IIB2.

Among the medium and large-sized vases a well-represented type is the high jar with a wide flat base, made by hand with the rim applied on the wheel, having characteristically thin walls and a surface sometimes coated with a fine whitish wash. The rims of these jars, set on relatively narrow necks, are flared, with a rounded lip ending in a sharp edge below. Jars of this type were undoubtedly for liquids, probably specifically for storing oil or wine, so that various examples have been found in the Palace store rooms behind the north façade of the Court of Audience. Other jars, however, were used for storing grain. Some of these have been found in one of the rooms of the Guard House of the Palace, fixed and partly set in a bench built against one of the walls. The ware is whitish, of globular shape with a large mouth and a rather straight everted rim. Other jars, perhaps serving similar purposes, but more frequent, of very light brown ware, were also globular in shape, but with a narrower mouth and no neck as the previous ones but with a thick, rounded rim ending below in a sharp edge. One last characteristic and usual type of jar was made of greyish, lightly fired clay, with a rather porous grain, almost always with a light whitish or bright greenish slip. This type of jar, with a rather squeezed oval shape, is characterised by a flaring rim with almost vertical outer edge moulded with two or three parallel indentations, giving it a typically waved look. It is possible that jars of this type were used to carry and store water, as a jar of this type was fixed on the threshold of the Guard House door, on the north side of the stairway ascending from the Monumental Gateway of the Palace.

In the sphere of so-called kitchen ware the cooking pots of Mardikh IIB1 were globular in form, of the kind known as 'hole-mouth', with the rim thickened and sometimes expanded outward. Some large cups have also been noted in the same type of dark chestnut ware with a

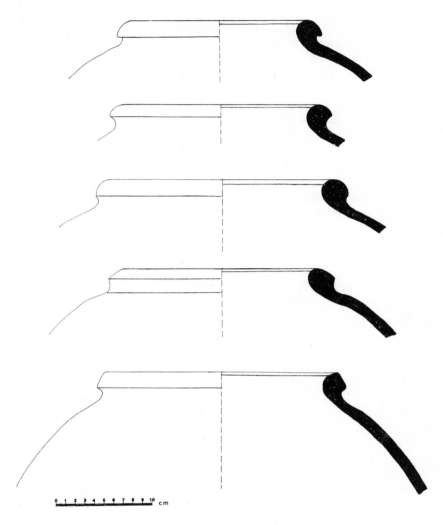

Figure 18   Pottery of Mardikh IIB1

coarse, usually striped surface and rim folded over on the outside and swollen — a form well attested among the more frequent 'Simple Ware' cups.

The ceramic horizon of Mardikh IIB1, according to the evidence we have been able to gather so far, really represents the final phase of Royal Palace G of Ebla, its materials having been in use during the last decades of the palace building. This horizon, which is very homogeneous, corresponds, with some exceptions, to the advanced phases of Amuq I, is approximately equivalent to the first three levels of Hama J, that is, Hama J8–6, and is fundamentally similar to that of Tell Selenkahiyya 3 on the Euphrates.

Like Mardikh IIB1, Amuq I is characterised by the prevalence of 'Simple Ware', frequently with 'corrugated' surface, and a steady increase in the frequency of beakers cylindrical in their upper parts, which gradually replaced the cup-beaker shape of truncated cone outline still present in the initial phases of Amuq I and altogether absent from Royal Palace G at Tell Mardikh. Even the presence of 'Reserved Slip Ware' is common to Mardikh IIB1 and Amuq I. Amuq I is distinguished from Amuq J especially by the appearance in this last period of the 'Painted Simple Ware' characterised by the painted, incised beakers absent from Amuq I and by the spread of 'Smeared-Wash Ware' of which a very few examples are beginning to be attested in Amuq I. The only substantial difference between Mardikh IIB1 and Amuq I is the total absence at Ebla of the 'Red-Black Burnished Ware' which typically is present in high percentages in Amuq I. But it must be remarked that in the Amuq sites there is a noticeable drop in the quantities of 'Red-Black Burnished Ware' as we pass from the earlier levels of Amuq I to the more recent. It is not improbable that this typical pottery of Anatolian origin, known also by the name Khirbet Kerak Ware from the Palestine site where it was largely identified, may already have completely disappeared by the end of Amuq I, as it certainly had by Amuq J. In any case the lack of evidence at Mardikh IIB1 for Khirbet Kerak Ware can only be interpreted in chronological terms as an indication that Mardikh IIB1 was rather later than Amuq I, always remembering that the ceramic horizon of Royal Palace G represents in fact the real end of Mardikh IIB1. It is probable that Khirbet Kerak Ware had not been widely diffused in the Syrian interior, though it is very well attested on the Mediterranean coast from the Amuq area to Palestine, for the very reason that it had probably followed a line of diffusion along the coast from the eastern part of the Anatolian plateau to Palestine, without penetrating, except sporadically, into the Syrian interior. All the same, rather in the same way as it has been found at Hama, Khirbet Kerak Ware has turned up at Ebla. We have recovered a very few fragments, dated to the end of Early Bronze III in a very advanced phase of Mardikh IIA, in a very limited sounding on the western slope of the Acropolis where the structures previous to Royal Palace G were brought to light.

Hama J8–6 fully corresponds to Mardikh IIB1, particularly in the wide diffusion of unpainted beakers with 'corrugated' surface and in the presence of the simpler types of the older 'Painted Simple Ware'. The sophisticated painted juglets of the Ebla Palace, however, are lacking here as in Amuq I. Among the large-sized vases again there are striking correspondences. Only the typical Mardikh IIB1 jar, perhaps a water

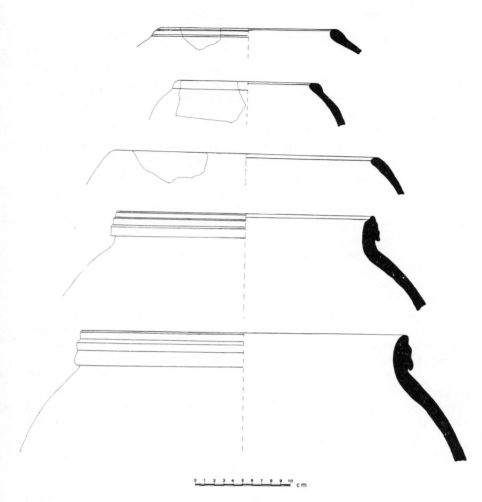

Figure 19 Pottery of Mardikh IIB1

jar, with rim moulded on the outside, is not found at Hama J except in a
rather generalised form. The developments known from Hama J4–8
are fundamentally the same as those characteristic of Mardikh IIB2,
with the widening of the 'Painted Simple Ware' style to take in nearly all
the 'Simple Ware' types and the decadence of the 'corrugated surface'
pottery.

Tell Selenkahiyya 3, though it shows the Khirbet Kerak pottery on
the wane compared with previous phases, has a ceramic horizon similar
over all to Mardikh IIB1 both in the preponderance of the characteristic
'Simple Ware' in the forms known at Ebla and especially in the refined
production of the painted juglets with a flat oval base. This Euphrates

centre was undoubtedly contemporary with Mardikh IIB1. Its ancient name will probably be among those listed by Enna-Dagan in the account of his campaign against Mari along the great river route. And here too the painted beakers are found only in Selenkahiyya 4, which like Mardikh IIB2 in absolute chronology comes out around 2000 B.C. or according to one suggestion about 1950 B.C.

On a general view, the Mardikh IIB1 pottery is homogeneous with that of inland Syrian sites like Hama and smaller localities like Khan Sheykhun rather than that of the centres nearer to the coast, like the Amuq tells, or indeed that of the Euphrates sites, from Tell Selenka-hiyya to the underground tomb of Tell Barsip and the necropolis of Tell Halawa. To mention only a few points, the 'corrugated' beaker forms of Ebla are more noticeably cylindrical than those in the northern regions, the base is in general small, and the shape thus more strikingly chalice-like. As for the cups with swollen rim, their bases are quite peculiar, of ring type with a protruding central disc — a form which seems native to the Syrian interior. These peculiarities may also explain the complete absence of Khirbet Kerak pottery at Ebla, since the stronger the local tradition, the less likely are we to find imports of external origin.

Certainly the Ebla of Royal Palace G was the political and cultural centre of greatest prestige in the Syria of Early Bronze IVA, as the State Archives show quite clearly. Undoubtedly also, as we may infer from the strong similarities of the Mardikh IIB1 pottery, the source region of this culture was the Syrian interior, over an area extending probably from the neighbourhood of Homs to north of Aleppo and from the mountains of the Jebel Ansariyya to the Euphrates. From several indications it seems highly plausible that in the fertile areas of the valley of the southern course of the Orontes — the regions of the Ghab and the Rug — and of the lower course of the Orontes — the area of the Amuq — fundamentally similar cultures evolved, though they may have been marginal to the major centres. The same must be said of the Euphrates region. The Ebla culture of Early Bronze IVA must have exerted an influence along the course of the great river approximately between Jerablus and Raqqa, that is between the ancient cities of Carchemish and Tuttul, together with the most important centres in the actual area of the present Lake Assad, round about Emar, also on the left bank of the Euphrates. On the outskirts of this area, in the Royal Palace G period of Mardikh IIB1, we can no longer speak of an Ebla culture. This applies not only to the coastal region from Ugarit southward but also to Upper Mesopotamia, and probably even to the Balikh basin. There is evidence in these regions for material contacts in Early Bronze IVA-B between their leading centres and the North Syrian culture of Ebla proper, but the respective ceramic horizons have essentially different sets of characteristics.

We still await the results of the scientific analyses now in progress on the wooden material from Mardikh IIB1, and in particular the radiocarbon tests of fragments of the Palace joists. Meanwhile the findings based on correspondences between Amuq I, Hama J8–6, and Selenkahiyya 3 tell us a good deal about the absolute chronology of Royal Palace G at Ebla. Amuq I, apart from the general picture it gives of this culture, must be placed in the period of the Akkad Dynasty, beginning perhaps in the last years of the Early Dynastic Period. This may be inferred among other things from the presence in its levels of the typical so-called 'chalice' pottery known particularly from Til Barsip. This has been associated also with certain characteristic metal implements, and their combined occurrence dated to the time of the royal cemetery of Ur or a little later. For Hama J6 and J5 the radiocarbon datings are given as 2310 and 2230 B.C. respectively with a possible error either way of about 120 years. For Hama J4–5 the determination is about 2210 B.C. Selenkahiyya 3 is unequivocally dated by a cylinder sealing of classical Akkadian style which makes impossible any higher dating of the level in which it was found.

Thus the data from all the major centres of the North Syrian culture in Early Bronze IVA converge. They clearly indicate that the absolute dating of the ceramic horizon of Mardikh IIB1 must correspond to the very last decades of the Early Dynastic Period and a great part of the period of the Akkad Dynasty. There are possible inconsistencies between this chronology and the higher one proposed for a ceramic horizon like that of Tell Khuera, but these may be only apparent. Moreover, though Tell Khuera has undoubted similarities with Mardikh IIB1 it does not correspond throughout a given range. I conclude that these doubts are insufficient to change the proposed dating, for two reasons. First, partial affinities have not the same value as wide-ranging correspondences due to cultural unity, and secondly, high chronologies for centres of remote regions need absolutely unchallengeable proof, since such centres are so likely to be backward in their cultural development.

2. Mardikh IIB2 (c.2250-2000 B.C.)

After the savage destruction which put an end to the Mardikh IIB1 settlement our excavations have not turned up any evidence of interruption in the continuity of occupation. This would indicate that Ebla was probably not abandoned even for a short time as a result of the war in which Royal Palace G was burnt down. The transition from Mardikh IIB1 to Mardikh IIB2 is marked by the destruction of the Palace but not by any real break of cultural development.

We have not yet carried out any wide-ranging excavation of levels attributable to Mardikh IIB2. But there is evidence enough that at the beginning of this new phase the Ebla settlement had about the same extent as in the preceding one, though there may well have been some gaps in the great expanse of urban development, probably due to reconstruction problems. Sure traces of a Mardikh IIB2 settlement have been identified in Sector N north of the Acropolis and in Sector A near the South-West Gate, as well as in Sectors B and C south-west of the Acropolis. Yet, though the extent of settlement was thus probably the same, there is no doubt that there must have been substantial changes particularly in the urban lay-out of the Acropolis area. In fact, the sector of Palace buildings on which the dynasty of Igrish-Khalam had lavished its greatest effort, the Court of Audience area with its panoramic elevations, was abandoned after the destruction attributed to Naram-Sin. This is easy to understand. The greater part of the imposing east façade of the Court, rising to over 13 metres, collapsed and crumbled into the square, forming a precipitous heap of fallen masonry. The very remains of the massive Palace walls could hardly be distinguished among the crumbling mounds of mud brick. It was quite natural that this ruined area should have been thought useless for further settlement and abandoned. It was probably dangerous, too, because of the continuing possibility that parts of the brickwork still standing would give way. In fact we have evidence that this was so. During the Mardikh IIB2 phase the Court of Audience area of the destroyed Palace G must probably have been walled off by a mud-brick structure, possibly not even very high, of which traces have remained in the doorway in the north elevation of the Court near the dais. Inside the main elevation of the Palace north-east of the place where the Monumental Gateway had been, in what is known to have been a ruined area of the ancient tell of Early Bronze III, where the ground is already almost level towards the brow of the Acropolis, the debris was flattened to accommodate the limestone slabs of a broad flight of steps leading to the open space in front of the Temple of Sector D.

Thus there was a radical change of function in the area south-west of the Acropolis. Royal Palace G was not rebuilt. In its place, along the whole western edge of the Acropolis, a monumental approach was laid out to the sacred building in Sector D which was the predecessor in Mardikh IIB2 of the Great Temple D of Mardikh IIIA-B. A sounding taken inside the cella L.202 has proved that this temple of Middle Bronze I-II with its massive stone foundations rests on an older sanctuary. The necessarily limited test trench has brought to light several noteworthy features of the older (Early Bronze IVB) building which we have not yet been able to interpret fully. These are: a room with exactly the same orientation as the cella of the Great Temple D,

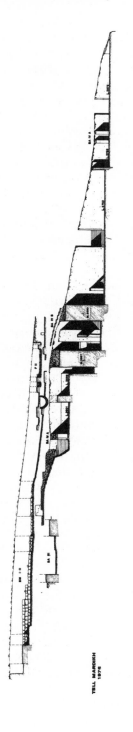

Figure 20 North-South section of the West Slope of the Acropolis, with the Great Temple D of Mardikh IIIA, the flight of steps of Mardikh IIB2, and the Palace G of Mardikh IIB1

bounded by two containing walls to the east and west, which run exactly underneath the two containing walls M.201 and M.205 of the Middle Bronze cella; a short flagged pavement of basalt and limestone, higher than the floor of the room and bounding it to the south, situated a little further north than the entrance to the Middle Bronze cella; two great monolithic column bases fixed in the floor of the room next to the containing walls and the flagstone pavement. The curious drop in level from this pavement to the room with the columns leaves us in some doubt about the orientation of the building to which these remains belonged. But the exact superposition of the walls indicates that the room with the columns was a temple in the Mardikh IIB2 phase just as it was later and almost certainly connected in some way with the Palace buildings of the Acropolis. Access to this Temple D of Mardikh IIB2, of which so little is known, must have been given by the stairway which certainly at the beginning of Mardikh IIB2 sealed off at least the ruins of the Guard House of Palace G.

The question where the Palace of Mardikh IIB2 was built after the abandonment of Sector G is not easy to answer with confidence. The most important reason is that we do not yet know the extent of the Palace buildings of Mardikh IIB1. But it seems certain that these must have been widely spread over the Acropolis, if only because of the texts which mention three 'palaces' in that area. So it is probable that in the late Protosyrian Period there was a reduction in the Palace zone. A very limited sounding in a corner of the court of Palace E of Middle Bronze I-II has revealed in that part of the Acropolis thick destruction levels densely packed with ash and characterised by pottery typical of Mardikh IIB2. Thus it is evident that while there are no Mardikh IIB2 levels in the south-western area of the Acropolis, such levels are abundantly present in the northern area under Royal Palace E of Mardikh IIIA-B. During Early Bronze IVB in consequence the Palace area is confined to the Acropolis and leaves out the whole south-western sector. Or else the Palace area has been removed from the south-western to the northern sector of the Acropolis. But nothing is yet known of the Palace buildings of Ebla in the Late Protosyrian Period.

Pottery material of Mardikh IIB2 is plentiful in the heaps of re-used soil which make up part of the core of the great ramparts constructed around the limits of the settlement boundaries at the beginning of Mardikh IIIA. The material derives from the great works completed in an early phase of Middle Bronze I, when the reconstruction of the city was put in hand in the first decades after 2000 B.C. The works involved the transport of enormous quantities of soil from the destroyed quarters of the city of Mardikh IIB2 to the outskirts of the city area for the construction of the ramparts of Mardikh IIIA. These works, perhaps

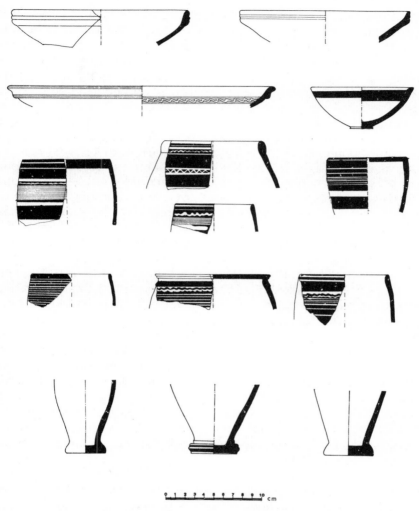

Figure 21   Pottery of Mardikh IIB2

necessitated by the rebuilding of Archaic Old Syrian Ebla, must undoubtedly have been responsible for the disturbance and cutting down,
sometimes even complete removal of levels of Mardikh IIB2 in the
Lower City and perhaps also part of the Acropolis.

The ceramic horizon of Mardikh IIB2 is fairly well known simply
because of these great quantities of material piled up in the ramparts of
the city perimeter. It fully corresponds to that of Amuq J and to that of
later levels, from J4 to J1, of Hama J, being characterised essentially by
the appearance and spread of the 'Painted Simple Ware'. The most

usual form of this type of pottery is that of the beaker in which the 'corrugated' surface prevalent during the Mardikh IIB1 phase becomes steadily rarer, and gives way to decoration painted in black or a good deal more rarely in red or brown, in very fine parallel lines or wavy lines obtained by incising the surface after it has been sprinkled with paint. Though the beaker is the most usual form of 'Painted Simple Ware' it is also true that an identical painted decoration of bands of straight horizontal lines or incised undulations does appear, much more rarely, either on small jars or on cups of a very open shape, with rim folded over and moulded on the outside. The ware in these types is almost exclusively of a light yellowish colour or, more rarely, very light pink. The very light greenish, thin, well-fired ware of Mardikh IIB1 becomes much less frequent, as do all the well-fired vase wares of which the walls have a metallic ring. However, compared with the previous phase, there is progress especially in the greater elaboration of forms. Thus typical of this phase are the rims folded over and moulded externally in the beakers, as already previously in the cups, and the beaker bases with projecting fillet. But most characteristic of Mardikh IIB2 and very frequent are the 'bell-shaped' beaker bases with their interior space reproducing in negative the strong convexity of their exterior.

Matching the spread of painted pottery there is a reduction of 'Simple Ware', the types of which are in most cases like those of the preceding phase. However, there are a few innovations, limited to the late phase of the Protosyrian Period. The most interesting is a cup of very open form with the rim vertical on the outside, incised with parallel lines to form three or four fillets. Among the types already recorded for Mardikh IIB1, the cups with rims moulded on the outside are very much more widespread than previously and the moulding is larger and more emphasised. Cups, however, with the rim expanded outwards become less frequent.

Another typical innovation of Mardikh IIB2 is the 'Smeared-Wash Ware', used for vases of medium or large size, almost exclusively of the type of high, approximately oval jars, with a broad flat base and the rim wheel-made. These jars have a decoration of apparently confused smears, in a more or less deep brown or reddish wash, spread over the upper and central surface of the vase. Among the other types of pottery with special treatment of the surface the 'Reserved Slip Ware', already recorded from Mardikh IIB1, becomes rarer in this phase.

Taken altogether, although there are no safe or easy verdicts to be given about the ceramic horizon of Mardikh IIB2, since the material mostly comes from disturbed though fairly homogeneous contexts, there is no doubt that the pottery of the late Protosyrian Period does not just follow the Mardikh IIB1 tradition but represents the peak of its development. The pottery of Mardikh IIB2 is distinguished from that of

Mardikh IIB1 both by precise innovations of type and form and by evident changes in the percentages of already recorded types. But substantially in every case we have to do with the refinement and perfecting of lines of development already present in the Mature Protosyrian Period. The ceramic horizon of Mardikh IIB2 is the most eloquent proof that the destruction of the Royal Palace G of Mardikh IIB1 was undoubtedly a grave political crisis and probably produced an economic recession, but did not interrupt or arrest the cultural development of this Protosyrian Period in its later phases. What the Tell Mardikh excavations have not yet established is whether Ebla in the Mardikh IIB2 phase, after the destruction of Royal Palace G, once more resumed the political role it had filled in the resplendent period of the State Archives.

About the end of the Mardikh IIB2 settlement the archaeological evidence leaves no doubt. The city was destroyed by a fire the traces of which are conspicuous wherever remains of Mardikh IIB2 levels have been preserved. This applies as much to material found in its original place as to material transported in successive loads for filling operations. Examples of the first have been seen in some of the soundings in Sector E on the Acropolis, of the second on the ramparts of the City Wall. The dense greyish soil of tightly compacted ash which can still be seen on the surface of the internal rampart slopes is evidence of a destruction which must have convulsed the whole city area. It is very difficult to fix the exact date of this tragic event. As I have already said, the 2000 B.C. dating is purely formal. On the other hand, comparative evidence from other contemporary centres of the Syrian area, all of which from the Amuq to Hama show the same destruction, indicates that the catastrophe which overwhelmed the Late Protosyrian culture must in any case be dated in the various Upper Syrian cities which were affected by it between 2050 and 1950 B.C. Between these upper and lower limits, some years may be found to separate the various destructions from one another. What is certain is that in the decades around 2000 B.C. the centres of the Protosyrian culture were involved in a disastrous crisis which devastated the whole area, putting an end to its development with fire.

4
Ebla in the Archaic and Mature Old Syrian Periods (c.2000-1600 B.C.)

The foundations and base structures of the Middle Bronze I buildings are laid directly on the ash-packed destruction levels of Mardikh IIB2, at least in the Lower City and on the Acropolis in the site of Royal Palace E. Sometimes the brickwork is founded directly on the rock as a result of the gigantic earth-moving operations when huge volumes of rubble from the destroyed city were shifted. On the other hand there is no consistent trace of any period of abandonment of the settlement after the sack of Mardikh IIB2. It must therefore be supposed that the devastated city was immediately rebuilt by the conquerors, who seem to have been responsible for the profound changes which altered the appearance of the civic centre.

As I have already indicated, there is a clear break between the Mardikh IIB1-2 culture and that of Mardikh IIIA-B. The ceramic horizon radically changed and innovations of architectural technique are reflected in a transformation of the physiognomy of the city. Previously, though we have as yet no direct evidence, the city almost certainly had a surrounding wall with salient turrets at intervals as we know to have been the case with some minor centres of the region, like Tell Munbatah and Tell Sabha. In the new city these were replaced with the high, wide ramparts which even today give it the strange aspect of a range of hills.

The settlement of Mardikh IIIA must very rapidly have assumed a role of great economic importance and renewed cultural prestige in a profoundly changed political situation. It is probable that this pre-eminence of Ebla was maintained throughout the whole Archaic Old Syrian Period until 1800 B.C., when it is almost certain, though again we have no direct evidence of the event, that the city came under the suzerainty of Yamhad. It is difficult to say how this might have happened. While there seem to be no traces inside the city of a destruction of the settlement of Mardikh IIIA, there is a clear filling of ash at no great depth covering the earliest pavement of City Gate A in the south-west section of the City Wall. Thus it is probable that the city was conquered on that occasion but then immediately surrendered, and thus, by almost peacefully accepting the hegemony of Aleppo, saved itself a repetition of the terrible disaster of about 2000 B.C.

Although a series of stratigraphic controls would have to be carried out in different sectors of the Lower City in order to confirm how very few superimposed levels there are of Mardikh IIIA-B even in the areas of private houses, it seems certain that the development of the Ebla culture from the Archaic to the Mature Old Syrian period went on without any interruption or general crisis of occupation. The reason for this poverty of Middle Bronze I-II levels at Ebla, if conclusively proved by our further explorations, will have to be sought. But our most recent investigations, like those in the still puzzling monumental building of Sector Q, on the western terrace at the foot of the Acropolis, excavation of which was begun in 1976, indicate that there were no important efforts of rebuilding during the Mardikh IIIA and IIIB phases. It seems that the original appearance of the Middle Bronze I city cannot have been greatly altered, beyond partial adaptations and restorations of buildings mostly put up during the Mardikh IIIA phase.

	Northern Mesopotamia			Northern Syria						
2000									Alalakh	Archaic
	Isin &	Assur D	Gawra V	Middle	Mardikh			Amuq K	XVII?–VIII	Old Syrian
1900	Larsa			Bronze I	IIIA					Period
	Period									
						Hama H				
1800										
			Gawra IV	Middle	Mardikh				Alalakh	Mature
	Old Baby-			Bronze II	IIIB			Amuq L	VII–VI	Old Syrian
1700	lonian	Assur C								Period
	Period									
1600										

Figure 22   Northern Mesopotamia and Northern Syria in the Old Syrian
Period

There is no doubt on the other hand about the end of Mardikh IIIB. Wherever the floor levels of that city have been buried intact by the collapse of structures above them, the soil consists of packed blackish ash caused by a conflagration which seems to have spared, at least in part, only a few sacred buildings. Thus, for example, the Great Temple D of the Acropolis seems not to have been touched by the fire. It is doubtful what happened to Temple B1 of the south-western area of the Lower City, while it is certain that both Temple N of the northern zone of the city area and Sanctuary B2 were sacked and destroyed by fire.

Mardikh IIIB must have succumbed to warlike operations of brutal violence and ferocity, making complete havoc of the city and all its buildings and no doubt involving its inhabitants in the same destruction since the city was abandoned after the event. The few indications we have suggest a date around 1650 or 1600 B.C. for this final calamity, which we must presume was the work of a Hittite king, either Hattusilis I or Mursilis I, in the course of their campaigns against the kingdom of Yamhad also annihilating its most powerful vassals.

1. The City plan

The general city plan of Mardikh IIIA, bounded by the irregular trapeze of imposing ramparts which girdled it, again took its character from the partition into Walls, Lower City, and Acropolis. It is practically certain that these three sectors of the city centre of Middle Bronze I were built over the corresponding sectors of Early Bronze IVA-B and served the same purpose. It is likewise certain that at the beginning of the new phase there was radical rebuilding of the city which strikingly changed its ancient appearance. Several individual monuments were newly built in the Archaic Old Syrian Period in places where buildings of like function had stood in Mature and Late Proto-syrian phases. This was the case with the four city gates, as demonstrated for the later phase by the actual topography of the ruins and for earlier times by the evidence of the Archives. The same can be said of at least two of the temples, the Great Temple D and Temple N, and probably also of Royal Palace E, which may have been rebuilt on the ruins of the palace of Mardikh IIB2. A different case, which may be significant, was that of the Great Sanctuary B2. This seems to have been put up in the Lower City in an area where the previous ruins had been deliberately rased and replaced with largely virgin soil.

Thus the city plan of Old Syrian Ebla was on the whole determined by pre-existing architecture, even though in a ruined state. The ground plan of the settlement seems to have been suggested by the almost central position of the Acropolis hill. The Acropolis, seat of political power, was the necessary point of reference, both for vision and for use. The traveller entering the city area no sooner emerged from the long passages of the monumental city gates than he was confronted by the mass of the Acropolis towering above the low roofs of the houses with the imposing outlines of its official buildings, while the streets branching away from the gates, of which only the South-Western and South-Eastern Gate have yet given definite evidence, converge radially on the Acropolis. The orientation of the city gates which more or less followed that of the streets inside the city, forced a view of the Acropolis on anyone entering it the moment the small space before the gate was reached.

The rampart walls with their rather steep external slopes descended much more gently inside. Up these inner rises the houses of the Lower City must to some extent at least have crept up to the back of the fortifications. Near the top of the ramparts, except where regular sentry walks had been constructed, there were military buildings of a defensive kind, redoubts or arsenals. On the outer rampart slopes near the top, the bases of fortified towers are still visible at more than one point. Probably they were fairly high, to judge from the type of foundations, and seem to have been isolated near the crest of the perimeter. The city gates obviously were specially well fortified. The South-West Gate for one had a regular system of massive towers to protect the access to the city, facing the open country along the whole extent of the gateway on one of its two sides.

In the Lower City, which must have been the residential zone, as has been demonstrated by excavations in Sectors N, B, and A, very little is known of the real lay-out of the city fabric, which must have been traversed by very narrow alleys. Apart from the main highways, probably as I have said radiating from the Acropolis to the city gates, there must have been very few streets joining the different quarters of the city, most of them being simply to give access to the residential units. In the Lower City in different zones, both north and south-west, at the foot of the Acropolis where the bedrock at certain points makes a sudden jump in elevation of some metres, there were spurs emerging stepwise over the level ground of the houses. In about the same region of the Lower City were situated the city temples, which in their curious typology of tower-chapels must have fringed the first spurs of the Acropolis, forming a sort of girdle of sacred buildings around the hill where the administrative and residential buildings of the court were situated.

In fact all the temples and sanctuaries of Old Syrian Ebla except the Great Temple D of the Acropolis have been identified hitherto at the foot of the citadel, to the north and south-west: the Temple N, Temple B1, the probable Temple C, and the Sanctuary B2. The Building Q, identified only in 1976 on the south slope of the wide terrace which continues the base of the Acropolis westward, almost certainly also had a sacred function, though it is difficult as yet to be quite sure what function or what type of building it was. Moreover, north-east of the Acropolis, always at a short distance from the base of the actual slopes, are surface remains of structures looking very like temple foundations. Thus altogether it seems very probable that the Acropolis was surrounded by temples, and that it was on these temples that the main access streets of the city converged, so that the Acropolis itself was probably approached only from one side.

In the Acropolis, the entrance to which may have been on the south-west although the soundings taken in that area in 1969 did not succeed in locating it, were the administrative buildings of the Palace. One edge of these has been identified at the northern extremity of the hill, and at least the major city temple, the so-called Great Temple D, was erected along the western brow of the citadel. The slopes of the Acropolis even today show a curious formation of descending terraces, much less noticeable to the north, where the slope is very much steeper than elsewhere, more regular to the east, south, and south-west, modified to the west by the wide, relatively low western terrace which extends into the Lower City. These terraces, at least in part, and certainly that of the west slope, are formed of rubble, or more rarely of regular revetment walls to contain the ruins of older levels. But it is possible that elsewhere, as in the south-west zone, there were no real clearance and levelling works on the hill slopes but only some dumping of loads of material, at least during the Mardikh IIIA phase. This material as it settled over the previous ruins would have left the slopes with an irregular terraced structure, caused by the emergence towards the Lower City of the sometimes imposing remains of Mardikh IIB1. It was in fact the massive walls of the Administrative Quarters of Royal Palace G from Early Bronze IVA, covered with the usual tippings from Middle Bronze I, which made up a rather extensive terrace at the foot of the Acropolis towards the south-west.

There are no findings yet of any importance on the planning lay-out of the Acropolis. It is only certain that the Palace buildings of Old Syrian Ebla were built on a series of brief terraces getting progressively higher from south to north and that in the two highest parts — the north area and the west area — were what must have been respectively the residential quarters of Royal Palace E and the Great Temple D. These two emergent points of the Acropolis were the poles, ideological as well as topographical, of the centre of power of the Middle Bronze I-II city. The Palace, by now, it seems, completely separate from the city pattern and isolated in the rock of the citadel, extended with at least one of its rooms over the precipitous slopes of the Acropolis, while the broad steps of the west slope of the citadel formed a panoramic platform on which stood the long building of the Palace Temple of the Acropolis, probably dedicated to the great patron deity of the city and its reigning dynasty.

We have seen that the ground plan of Mardikh IIIA reproduced in its general lines, though no doubt with some divergencies, that óf Ebla in the Mature Protosyrian Period. But it is still impossible to say whether it was conceived in the same ideological terms. In Mardikh IIB1-2, as the Archive documents have to some extent made clear, the view seems to have prevailed of the great city state as an epitome of the universe. The fact that the new city of Mardikh IIIA preserved from the older one the position and number of the city gates, the siting of the temples at the base of the Acropolis, and the displacement of the major buildings of the citadel, would indicate that the traditional key to deciphering the city's topography must have survived from one culture into the next. One thing, however, must have changed. The Old Syrian culture in its extensive break with the past at the threshold to Middle Bronze I must have brought a new taste to bear on the architectural interpretation of its city life.

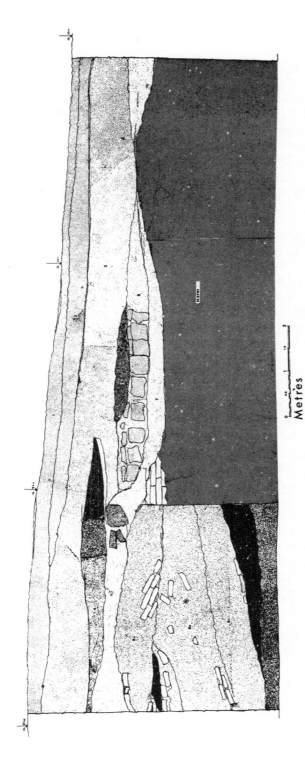

Metres

Figure 23   Stratigraphic Section from North to South at the Site of the Court of Audience of Royal Palace G

2. Architecture

Important evidence of the architectural achievements of Mardikh IIIA-B has been brought to light by our excavations. They give a broad and informative picture of Old Syrian Ebla, though some important monuments which have been identified, like Royal Palace E, are still very far from being completely understood. The extension of the areas explored has permitted us to study in detail all the more important architectural typologies thanks to the evidence of what must have been one of the most important political centres of the Archaic Old Syrian Period.

The perimeter wall of the settlement of Mardikh IIIA consists of a powerful rampart, with an elevation of nearly 20 metres above the open plain and nearly 12 metres above the level of the Lower City. The base of this enormous mass of beaten earth varies around 50 metres in thickness, though this is a rather tentative measurement owing to the very nature of the internal and external slopes. All round the rampart, the ground outline of which is vaguely oval, there may be seen at the foot of the fortifications a continual dip or trough which increases the height of the rampart in relation to the normal ground level. Evidently part of the soil piled up in building the rampart came from the land below. In the present condition of the terrain surrounding the tell we cannot speak of a regular fosse. But neither can we rule out the possibility that the trough of today was once a ditch which has been largely filled up by the soil washed into it and also partly eroded and levelled, so that its original appearance can no longer be recognised. The construction of the rampart was verified in 1970 by the digging of a not very deep trench along a section. Its core is formed of superimposed layers of reddish clay soil and whitish lime chips, alternating or in some zones replaced with heaps of ash-packed archaeological debris and ceramic material, almost exclusively of Early Bronze IVA-B, with a wide predominance of the Mardikh IIB2 phase. It is clear that the non-archaeological reddish and whitish soils came from the ditching operations at the foot of the rampart outside the city. The greyish soil with pottery and plaster fragments came from the great levelling works among the ruins of the destroyed city of Mardikh IIB2.

The rampart had at the base a facing of dressed stone. This has actually been identified only at one point west of the South-West Gate of the city, where it has survived up to a height of about 1.50 metres. But certainly this kind of stone revetment must originally have been much higher. The upper part had a rendering only of a kind of whitish gypsum plaster in some sections of the perimeter to the east and of light greyish beaten clay to the west. Stone bases for small forts or simply watch towers still visible on the ground have been identified for certain on the outer slopes of the west and south ramparts. On the east rampart are remains of foundations of works undoubtedly connected with defensive installations, but these are localised on the internal slopes. Similar fortification works left traces also in the north-west section of the ramparts, where they project into the open country, perhaps for the protection of the North-West Gate. These seem to have been fairly consistent before the excavations began but have now almost disappeared owing to the plunder of building materials.

The great rampart which protected Old Syrian Ebla up to the final destruction of the city about 1600 B.C. must have been put up at the beginning of the Mardikh IIIA phase, when the rebuilding on its Protosyrian ruins was put in hand. The evidence that this was so is provided by the pottery in the soil tippings of which the rampart itself is made. As I have said, the pottery of Mardikh IIB2 is abundant in this soil while that of Mardikh IIIA is completely absent. This evidence can only be interpreted as meaning that when the building of the ramparts was begun large areas of the Lower City still had exposed ruins of the Mardikh IIB settlement. Moreover, since the re-used soil contains no sherds of Mardikh IIIA, it is utterly improbable that the ramparts were put up later, during the Mardikh IIIB phase, without using any archaeological spoil from the previous two hundred years, that is Mardikh IIIA. In other words, the complete absence of Middle Bronze I pottery in the soil of these fortifications forces us to assume that the ramparts were put up at the beginning of Mardikh IIIA, when obviously there would not yet have been any substantial quantities of spoil from that period in the city. This dating of the ramparts of Old Syrian Ebla to Middle Bronze I agrees also with our inference that the Mardikh IIIA city was of considerable political importance, not only independent but even perhaps in a position of leadership. A later date, in the Mardikh IIIB phase, would not accord with the subordinate position which Ebla by then occupied in its relations with Aleppo.

Of the four gates in the city wall, to judge from the type of passageways still present in the wall and the massive thickening of fortifications in the zones next to them, the two biggest must have been the South-West Gate, brought to light in Sector A, and the North-West Gate. The South-East Gate, excavated in Sector L, was certainly smaller, and so perhaps was the North-East Gate. It is probable that the South-West Gate was the most important in the city. Its extraordinary monumental structure makes it quite clear that it received very special attention, both from an engineering and from an aesthetic point of view and also for its strategic function.

Over all, the South-West Gate divides into three distinct sections: a first, outer gateway, advanced into the open country, with two pairs of buttresses flanking a single entrance; a trapezoidal courtyard open to the sky, situated between the outer and inner gateways; and the second, inner gateway with three pairs of buttresses flanking two successive entrances in line. The axis of the outer gateway, with a total passage length of 10.50 metres, is not in line with that of the inner gateway but turned somewhat northward. The inner gateway, 21.50 metres in passage length, constitutes the real strongpoint of this fortified city access. Characteristic of both gateways is the ground plan *à ténaille*, with re-entrants formed by the buttresses framing the apertures in which the gates proper were mounted. The mountings of each pair of gates, one pair for the outer gateway, two for the inner, can be exactly identified by the thrust bearings, or pivot stones, in which the vertical wooden hinges rotated. Their position shows clearly that in the second, inner and larger, gateway, the pair of gates nearest the city opened away from it, into the passageway, while the outer pair opened towards the city, also into the passageway (and away from the courtyard).

The structures of the South-West Gate deserve the closest attention. Because of their remarkable state of preservation they can be closely studied and constitute important evidence of Old Syrian architecture. Many of its apparent peculiarities of structure can be explained if we consider that only one of its two sides, the east side, was strongly fortified. The west side cannot have had any special defensive appointments. So we can understand why the city rampart which kept its normal thickness up to the junction with the west side of the Gate, there expanded till it reached 60 metres on the east side. In fact, this whole east side of the Gate was a succession of fortifications erected to protect the ingress to the city.

Beginning with this advanced gateway, the two pairs of buttresses flanking its passageway have their base structures technically similar, with great ashlars supporting the high limestone orthostats of the walls. Only on the east side and set back from the buttresses was there a robust curtain wall, which must have been the side wall of an external watch and defence tower. Access to this tower was by a narrow stone stairway which we discovered almost intact at the back of the orthostats of the inner east buttress. Corresponding with the courtyard intermediate between the two gateways, the considerable pressure of soil from the ramparts, bearing down with multiplied thickness and mass, was held in check by a fine inclined retaining wall, which still survives up to about 3 metres high, of great, roughly-hewn stones, larger in size in the lower courses and decreasing in the upper.

The defensive installation worked out for the east side of the great inner gateway is particularly impressive and well preserved. Here the whole embellishment of the side walls of the entrances and of the rooms of the intermediate enclosure with its ground plan *à ténaille* consists of enormous orthostat blocks, often of remarkable thickness, of basalt on

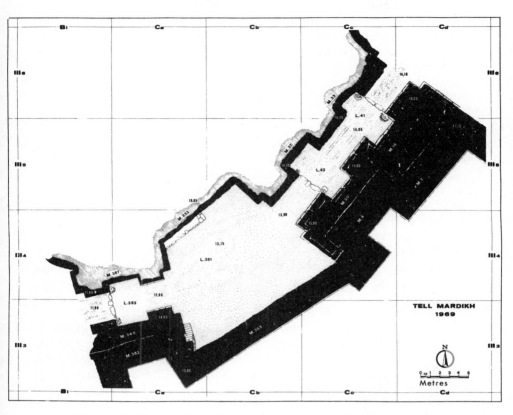

Figure 24   Ground Plan of the South-West City Gate of Mardikh IIIA

the buttress faces and limestone on the intervening recesses. These great orthostats, perfectly polished on the visible face, about 1.80 metres high and resting on a plinth of slightly projecting ashlars, have many features of interest. The basalt blocks are extremely irregular on the inside and thus, with their remarkable thickness and many roughnesses of surface, combine with the great shapeless masses of the inner core of the structure into a uniform mass. The limestone orthostats on the other hand look more like thick flagstones, are relatively well dressed on their inner faces as well, and firmly fitted between the masonry of the walls and the short lateral basalt orthostats of the buttresses. In consequence as they have had to support on a single rather long surface the enormous pressure of the mass of masonry of the bastion, they are split at several points. All the orthostats, basalt and limestone, have on their polished upper surfaces, which must have served as support bases for the upper structure of the inner gateway, a series of cylindrical holes at regular intervals. Their function was certainly to bond to the orthostats, with ties perhaps of bronze or wood, the various materials (mud brick or wood) with which the upper part of the gateway was completed. The short basalt orthostats clothing the sides of the buttresses, unlike all the others, have a slightly trapezoidal outline instead of being rectangular. This gives a slight inclination, inward over the passageways, to the tops of the ornamental faces of the buttresses.

Obviously set back from the line of the buttresses and intervening recesses but extending over the whole length of the inner gateway, the western outer face of an enormous square bastion, 21.50 metres wide, which surmounted its east side, is still well preserved. What is extraordinary is that the bastion can be completely reconstructed in its original elevation because its mass is such that, although many of the finishing and filling blocks have rolled into the gate opening, the upper part has been preserved intact, as is proved by the discovery above it of a sentry walk protected on the outside by a thick parapet. The massive walls of the bastion consist of rough-hewn blocks and must have exerted an enormous pressure on the east side of the South-West Gate, and this was no doubt the reason for the very solid and compact construction of the east base of the inner gateway, with its revetment of imposing orthostats accurately fitted to the masonry core. The totally different arrangement of the west side of the Gateway proves that the complicated construction of the east side was governed by engineering considerations. On the west not only is there no trace of an orthostat revetment to define the limits of the *ténaille* plan — which are marked by a modest socle of undressed stone — but inside these limits there are courses of irregular blocks arranged stepwise parallel to the axis of the gateway. These stone courses, seemingly irregular as masonry exposed to view, must have had the sole function of gradually taking the load of the beaten earth of the rampart, which obviously must have had much less thrust here than that of the bastion at the other end of the passageway.

The original appearance of the South-West Gate can be reconstructed in its general lines. The passageway was probably barrel-vaulted, with rings of voussoirs set radially. This may be presumed both from the position of the orthostats of the buttresses, which as I have already said were slightly inclined inward so as to close the aperture of the arch and spring the curve of the vault, and also from the Egyptian illustrations some centuries later of Syrian and Palestinian citadels, the gates of which are always roofed with arches.

As to its date, the South-West Gate must certainly have been put up in an initial or central phase of Mardikh IIIA. But it was destroyed, at least in part, perhaps at the end of Mardikh IIIA, and the damaged portions were afterwards rebuilt so as to leave the general plan unchanged. The only important renovation of which we have evidence and which must date from the last years of Mardikh IIIB was an inclined revetment wall built against the original perimeter wall of the open-air courtyard. Since this secondary structure closed the stairway which certainly led to the outer tower, it is probable that the revetment was a hasty piece of restoration to the Gateway, carried out to avoid dangerous falls of material from the bastion and the eastern rampart, at a time when the outer gate, or at any rate its defence tower, had already been abandoned.

In comparison with the monumental South-West Gate the South-East Gate was modest enough. It had a narrow passageway which seems to have taken the direct weight of the ramparts on either side and was approached by a fine flagged pavement. The badly-damaged condition of the ruins of the South-East Gate, due to the removal in relatively recent times of the great base stones of the walls, prevents our reconstructing this gateway with any confidence. It was certainly of secondary importance.

On the internal slope of the east rampart, near its summit and not far from the South-East Gate, was the so-called Fortress M, a small arsenal of compact ground plan consisting of a single rectangular block 12.50 metres by 27 metres, of masonry, the northern section of which was subdivided into six rectangular rooms arranged two by two, diminishing in size from south to north and paved with mud brick. The southern section of the Fortress was reserved for the entrance, consisting of a small vestibule leading to an angled stairway which must originally have ascended to the terrace of the building. It is characteristic of this peculiar military building that the six rooms had no doors at floor level. They were evidently reached by ladders from the terrace above, which itself was reached by the entrance staircase, leading directly of course out of the Lower City. The function of the fortress must have been dual, adapted both to storing arms under guard and readily available on the city ramparts in case of attack, and to keeping watch and ward over the eastern sector. The rooms of the Fortress, as is natural following the capture of the city at the end of Mardikh IIIB, were found practically empty and covered with thick traces of greyish and reddish soil from fire and ruin. One important clay bulla of the 'ribbon' type was found with a sealing from a fine cylinder of the Mature Old Syrian style, which must probably have served to seal a bundle of objects of unknown nature. On the floor of one of the rooms was a pear-shaped mace of polished limestone. Finally, in the space underneath the stairs, we found two wonderful bronze spear heads with the name of some personage inscribed on one face and of a type characteristic of Middle Bronze Age II.

In the ring-shaped area of the Lower City, all round the temples

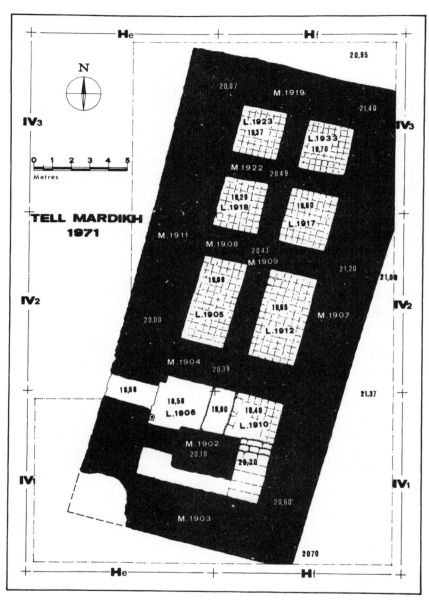

Figure 25   Ground Plan of Fortress M of Mardikh IIIA-B

standing at the foot of the Acropolis, there were private houses. The
best-preserved parts of houses so far excavated are those of Sector B
south-west of the Acropolis. Sector A inside the South-West Gate is an
area of excavation still too limited to give an adequate idea of the

ground plans of any domestic units. The private houses of Sector B, to the east and south-east of Temple B1, are built by a technique usual in all the buildings of Mardikh IIIA-B. The walls normally vary in thickness according to load, between 0.70 metres and 0.40 metres, and are regularly made up of two distinct parts, a foundation or base of undressed stone, emerging variously from the ground but for the most part between 0.40 metres and 0.90 metres in height, and a square upper structure of mud brick. The bricks are generally greenish-grey or yellowish-red in colour and about 0.31/0.32 metres square and 0.12 metres high. The basic house type of Mardikh IIIB, as found in Sector B, consists of a vestibule which sometimes takes the form of a narrow, relatively long corridor, a rather wide rectangular courtyard, and two rooms, normally approached through the wall opposite the vestibule. Sometimes the houses are arranged in a very regular manner on this scheme. This is the case with the domestic unit pivoting on the courtyard L.1518, preceded by the vestibule L.1157, and giving access to two unexcavated rooms through its north-east wall. It is probable that this house was enlarged at a later date towards the east, where there was perhaps a second small dwelling centred on the modest courtyard L.1148. Sometimes again the module of house with vestibule, courtyard, and two rooms on the same side, which must have constituted the minimum unit of habitation, must have been enlarged to the more elaborate scheme with rooms on two or even three sides of the courtyard. This is the case with the house, again in Sector B of the Lower City, which extends around courtyard L.1145, with vestibule to the south and rooms on the north, east, and perhaps south sides, while on the west is the main outer wall of the house.

The temples hitherto identified for certain in the Lower City are Temple N, north of the Acropolis, and Temple B1, south-west of the citadel. We can only guess at the possibility of a temple similar to these in the remains of great basalt blocks found in line in Sector C, near Sector B on the west, which may be part of its substructures. Temple N, the largest of the Lower City, is a very simple building, with a single chamber oriented to the east, and with surrounding walls about 3 metres thick at the sides and about 4 metres at the far end. The cella has a width of 7.50 metres and against the wall opposite the entrance had a kind of broad step or ledge, running the whole breadth of the precinct and between 3.40 metres and 2.80 metres deep. Near the south-west corner of the cella lying on the ground were two great slabs of basalt. A third great monolith, polished on the upper face and with one end cut into a sort of spout, was placed towards the centre of the cella at a slightly oblique angle to the wall.

Near the basalt slabs and behind the third, which was certainly an offering table for blood sacrifices, there was originally a splendid lime-

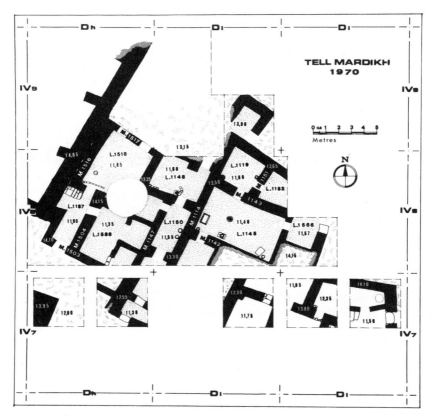

Figure 26   Ground Plan of Residential Area of Sector B of Mardikh IIIB

stone basin with two compartments, decorated in relief on all its outer
faces. Its rear part, protected by the wide ledge, was found in position
but badly cracked. The front part, evidently broken off at the time of
the destruction and sack of Mardikh IIIB, has been removed, no doubt
because of the reliefs on the principal face. Unfortunately nothing is
known for certain of the façade of Temple N. The front of the building
has been removed by the erosion of the tell without leaving a trace.

Temple B1 in the south-west part of the Lower City is of very similar
construction but smaller in size. It was oriented towards the south and is
relatively well preserved, though large sections of the outer side walls
have been plundered of their great limestone foundation blocks, laid on
the rock as in Temple N. The cella of Temple B1, 4.50 metres wide and
10.50 metres long, was approached by two flagged steps. The entrance
to the sacred building had the same width as the cella because there was
no façade wall, nothing but the edges of the side walls. Fixed in the

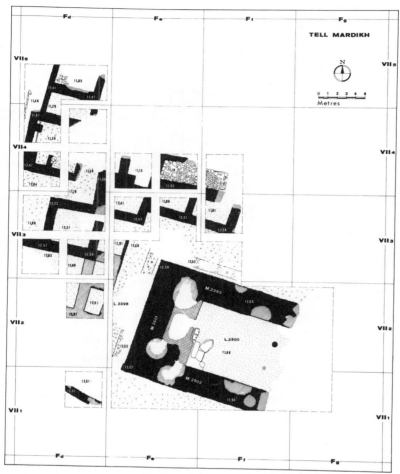

Figure 27   Ground Plan of Temple N of Mardikh IIIA-B

pavement 3.60 metres from the threshold of the building two small limestone pivot stones were found, with a slight central cavity. These certainly could not have served for the support of heavy rotating hinges but could have offered seating for wooden poles to support a fairly light crossbeam, probably used to hang a curtain. This sacred building, too, had a ledge along its rear wall, less deep than that of Temple N and formed of rather big blocks of partly dressed stone. As we know, Temple B1 was where the carved basalt twin basin found before the start of the Italian excavations must have stood, since a fragment of this same fitting was later found by us on the approach steps to this temple. As in the case of Temple N, the basin must originally have been inside the cella at the back.

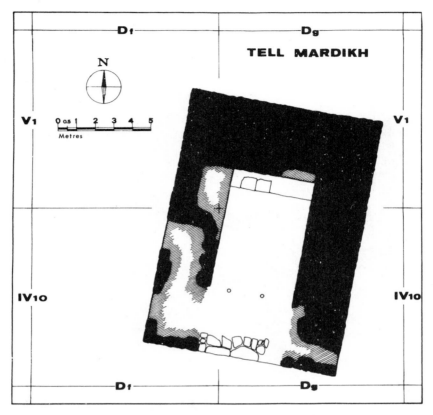

Figure 28 Ground Plan of Temple B1 of Mardikh IIIA-B

A cult building very different in type and structure from the characteristic temples with single cella of Old Syrian Ebla is Sanctuary B2, a
large building situated in the southern zone of Sector B and separated
by a small open space from Temple B1. Sanctuary B2 is a large building
of compact but irregular plan, only approximately square, with a side of
about 33 metres. We can be confident that its ground plan has been
correctly elucidated in general because the eastern section is in such a
good state of preservation. A large part of the building to the south-
west has been carried away by the erosion of the Lower City, on a slight
slope to the south in this area. The entry to Sanctuary B2 was on the
west side. Although it is difficult to attempt a satisfactory reconstruction of the building as a whole owing to its lack of elements of
symmetry, it was probably approached by a short stairway flanked by
two antae. Immediately behind the façade was a courtyard, L.2145,
which measured 11 metres by more than 13 metres. This was flanked to

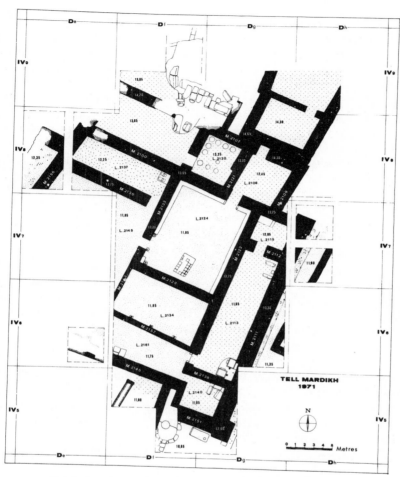

Figure 29 Ground Plan of Sanctuary B2 of Mardikh IIIB

the north by a long cella, L.2137, where in the north-east corner was a small bench of mud brick into which two big basalt mortars were built with their pestles still in position. It is also possible but in no way certain that a similar long chamber flanked the outer courtyard to the south. From the courtyard was the entrance to the great central cella, L.2124, certainly roofed, 8.90 metres by 10.65 metres, along the west, north, and east walls of which ran a low bench one brick thick. Near the south wall was a rectangular mud brick dais about 2.20 metres by 1.40 metres. Adjoining this on the south is a smaller enclosure, L.2134, which may have been a room of unknown use or possibly an internal courtyard to give light to the surrounding rooms. On its south wall there must have been three engaged pillars, it seems solely for ornament. But the small cellas of square ground plan and the big oblong cellas which alternated in a disorderly fashion around the great cella must one and all have served specific cult purposes because they have sacred fittings still in place and well preserved. Thus in the south-east corner cella there was an altar with two antae. In the long cella L.2113, 14.60 metres by 4 metres, there was again near the north-east corner an altar with two antae, lateral and standing free. In the opposite south-east corner there were two splendid basalt offering tables, dressed and polished, for blood sacrifices. In the little north-east cella L.2115 and in the long cell L.2161 to the south there were other installations of which only the bases have survived.

The Sanctuary B2 then seems to have been a complex of sacred rooms for cult, sacrifices, offerings animal or vegetable, and it must have been connected with particular rites and not a temple dedicated to a deity. Although the problem of the interpretation of the building cannot be resolved on the basis of the evidence we have, it was undoubtedly connected with a series of cavities in the adjacent rock, narrow tunnels and big holes of very uncertain use. Among these cavities some, in the near-by Sector C, were certainly used as tombs. But the free space north of Sanctuary B2, between it and Temple B1, in fact covered an area of the rock layer containing tunnels covered by great monolithic lintels. It is therefore possible that there were conceptual links between Temple B1 and Sanctuary B2, and we cannot but ask whether the whole complex cult building was not connected with shaft tombs, evidently for persons of special importance, and with functions concerning the cult of the dead. But it must be reiterated that this supposition rests on nothing more than the nearness of the building to an area which was certainly of funerary significance and the fact that it was completely different in type from the temples dedicated to deities.

The largest cult building so far discovered of Mardikh IIIA-B is the Great Temple D on the Acropolis, which, as we have seen, was erected on pre-existing structures of Mardikh IIB2 and had an over all length of about 30 metres. The foundations of the temple are massive affairs of 4 metres thick for the side walls and 4.90 metres thick for the bottom wall. Above, the two side walls are reduced to a thickness of 2 metres. The type of arrangement is longitudinal and tripartite. A short vestibule approached by two flagged steps is followed by an antecella much broader than long. The third chamber, the cella, has the same width as the two others (7.20 metres) but is much longer (12.40 metres). The cella also has a low bench along the far wall opposite the entrance and a square niche opening into this imposing rear wall. It was in this cella, in its south-west corner, that the limestone basin with carved sides was found intact.

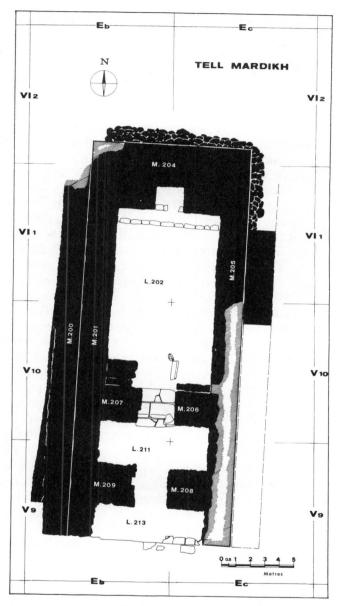

Figure 30   Ground Plan of Great Temple D of Mardikh IIIA-B

The Great Temple D must have had some noteworthy architectural decoration. Overturned on the pavement of the antecella we found a great block of worked basalt, with the hindquarters of a couched lion on two of its faces. The other two faces are finely polished. Undoubtedly the couched lion, which must have decorated the approach to the antecella, was a composite sculpture made up of three basalt blocks. The total length of this apotropaic figure must have been about 2.80 metres. The walls of Temple D were protected on the outside by heaps of rubble piled up against them, evidently to safeguard the integrity of those parts of the building most subject to damage.

The foundation of Great Temple D goes back to the beginnings of Mardikh IIIA, and the first flooring of the three chambers can be assigned to this phase. It is of very fine workmanship with layers of limestone and basalt chips laid on a clay base to form the finely cobbled preparatory mix on which the top surface of very fine white plaster was laid. The second floor, of simple beaten earth, belongs to a later phase, probably at the end of Mardikh IIIB. It was in this phase that a basalt table of offering with two small hollows for liquids was installed in the cella, in front of the bench in the back wall. During these two ancient phases, the cult image must no doubt have been lodged in the back niche, while an imposing circular basalt basin on a decorated pillar pedestal, which was found in fragments near the north-east corner of the cella, was with the carved limestone basin the most important installation of the Great Temple. After the final destruction of Mardikh IIIB the city's most holy place was still not entirely forsaken. After the walls of vestibule and antecella had collapsed, but with those of the cella still partly standing, during the phase of Mardikh IVB around 1250 B.C., the precinct was still in use, with a very different religious background from that which had given rise to the palatial Great Temple. By then the cella had become a simple little temple, and the cult image of the Old Syrian Period, resplendent as it had no doubt been, had given way to two basalt baetyls standing behind the table of sacrifice.

Royal Palace E has been identified in the northern area of the Acropolis, but it is certain that only a small part of it has yet been brought to light. The section hitherto explored must probably have been the north wing of the building, with an organic structural ground plan of its own. It is centred on a fairly wide courtyard, L.156, about 15 metres wide, which on the west was backed against a thick double containing wall, to the north and east was surrounded by a series of small fairly regular rooms, and to the south was bounded by a sort of loggia.

Careful study of the small sectors of Royal Palace E brought to light around this north wing gives an indication of the great extent of the Palace building and its detailed lay-out. In the first place, to the east of Rooms L.724 and L.759 of the north wing, both communicating with the court, at least two other rooms are to be seen, one of which, L.761, is specially large. Both must give on another courtyard situated to the

east, because they have no communication with the rooms of the north
wing. In the second place, to the south of the supposed gallery, L.1645,
there are other rooms, only just identified, the floors of which are about
2.10 metres below the paved floor of the gallery. In fact this appreciable
drop is covered by a slightly inclined retaining wall, but the two areas
are undoubtedly in communication with one another because a short
sloping corridor leads from L.748 in the southern quarters to the gallery
of the north wing. In the third place, in the south-west area of the
excavation, there were further terracing structures, though with
smaller differences in level, between Room L.745 to the south and
Room L.463 to the north. Only on the west do the great, irregular
retaining walls seem to shut off an area where the spoil heaps from the
destruction of Mardikh IIB2 are particularly high.

These findings show that Royal Palace E must have been of much
greater extent than so far detected. To the east there was no doubt
another courtyard with rooms of the same technical finish as those on
the north and east sides of the courtyard already excavated. To the
south there began series of rooms built on a lower terrace, both to
the south of the supposed gallery and to its south-west. Undoubtedly the
architectural finish varied from one part of the Palace to another. Thus
both the north wing and the section adjacent to it on the east had no
foundations to their walls but stout bases finished with orthostats, very

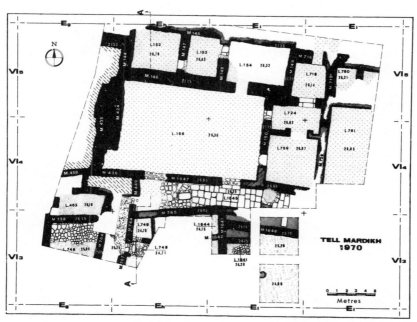

Figure 31   Ground Plan of Royal Palace E of Mardikh IIIA-B

fine floors of plaster laid on a triple base of limestone cobbles set in a layer of clay, doorways with thresholds of polished limestone slabs, usually flanked by basalt jambs. Compared with these two quarters north of the Palace all the rooms brought to light south of the terrace line have a technically more modest finish. It is very difficult to explain this difference. There are serious objections to the suggestion that the northern section might be older, since the rooms of the north wing are built directly over the destruction levels of Mardikh IIB2.

The architectural achievements of Mardikh IIIA and IIIB are the work of a culture with a remarkably uniform style of its own. These buildings of Ebla in the Old Syrian Period are closely linked with one another in technique, in type, and in their use of space. Their family likenesses cover so broad a range and betray such a deep-rooted heritage of experience and tradition that it becomes a very pressing question how this culture originated and was formed. The question is all the more interesting if the culture was in fact independent of the Protosyrian world just before it, or at any rate did not closely or directly depend on that world.

3. Sculpture

The artistic production of Old Syrian Ebla belongs almost entirely to the phase of Mardikh IIIA. It seems to come almost to a complete stop with the beginning of the Mature Old Syrian Period, when other Syrian centres, Aleppo at their head, must have been busy exploiting the ferment set up in the Archaic phase essentially at Ebla. Typologically and functionally a great part of the sculptural work of Ebla seems original in conception and peculiar to that city, even though it is possible to make out an external origin for some of its typical pieces of sculptured furniture. All the plastic art of Ebla seems to serve votive needs or the demands of cult or ritual. There is no trace of commemorative art works conceived in an ideological and less immediately religious spirit.

The votive statuary, examples of which have not hitherto been found in a temple at Ebla, is represented by fragments, sometimes even in good condition, of male statues, only in one case identified by an inscription. The statue of Ibbit-Lim, prince of Ebla, which furnished the key to the identification of the city, is a remnant of a basalt figure, probably standing, in which the descriptive elements are in great part sacrificed to an austere formal vision. In the bust of Ibbit-Lim every attempt at modelling or search for plastic form is rejected in favour of a rather abstract manipulation of volumes. The statue is very difficult to date since it was found out of archaeological context but must have been made in the early years of Mardikh IIIA. Certainly the four-square treatment, without any real interest in vividly naturalistic forms, is remote from the sensibility of the advanced phase of the Old Syrian Period, while certain stylistic elements seem to rule out any dating as high as the end of Mardikh IIB2. Thus, though the figure cannot be dated with certainty to a definite period, if only because of its poor condition, a combination of rather tenuous archaeological and epi-graphic evidence seems to point to the beginning of the Old Syrian, with its formal complexity.

A large statue, unfortunately without a head, of a king with the cup of offering is no less difficult to date. It too was found unstratified, near the South-West Gate. Though some stylistic elements in this statue, especially in the costume, seem more archaic than in the Ibbit-Lim torso, the most probable date for this piece, too, is the beginning of Mardikh IIIA. It has some points of resemblance with the reliefs of Mardikh IIIA, while we know nothing of any large statuary of Mardikh IIB2. Undoubtedly the formal vision of the two statues seems rather close. Both speak with a tongue as rough and severe as the most archaic of the Old Syrian reliefs of Tell Mardikh.

There is one case where a chronological succession of some credi-bility can be established. That is in the ritual reliefs on the carved twin basins, where we have a rather better range of evidence. Apart from some remarkable fragments, all from the sacred area of Temple B1 and Sanctuary B2, three major monuments of this type give a thorough and wide-ranging account of the Archaic Old Syrian art of Ebla. They are the twin basins of Temple B1 in basalt, of Great Temple D in limestone — an intact example — and the important remnant from Temple N, also in limestone.

Though their general dimensions vary considerably, these fittings are of more or less constant type. They are rectangular basins with two approximately square compartments side by side. No more than three of the outer faces are decorated on those from Temple B1 and Great Temple D, and this is probably the usual case, but on the shattered basin from Temple N it is certain that all four sides had reliefs. To judge from their subjects, the actual basins must have had something to do with a sort of sacred banquet, in which the principal participant was the king, sometimes together with the queen, sometimes alone. The banquet theme is indeed the principal theme of the sculptural decoration and figures on the principal face of all the basins of which enough fragments survive.

Of the three more complete basins the earliest must have been that discovered before the excavations of Temple B1 began. This basin, like another of larger size, has a fine decoration of roaring lions' heads thrust out frontally, running along the base of its three carved faces. In the upper register of the principal face is the usual banquet theme and a long bull-man figure which is also typical of these basins. On each of the two side faces is a file of armed men advancing to converge on the front face.

The limestone basin of Great Temple D must be a little later in date than this last one. Its principal face shows in the upper register the scene of the sacred banquet with the two leading participants, the king and the queen. He is followed by dignitaries and soldiers, she by servants. In the lower register is a drove of passing animals. The two sides are very interesting since they depict elements of mythical events. On one side, above, facing front and vomiting streams of fertilising water, a composite dragon-like creature confronts a naked hero, also front face, holding some fish. Below, a hunter seems about to strike a lion or bull both of which apparently confront one another peaceably. On the other side a monstrous great creature with a lion's head is seizing two passing lions by their hind legs as if to overcome them.

The basins can be dated by stylistic features, such as the stylised rendering of the dress, the type of stirrup jars carried by the servants, and the design of the table of offering on which the banquet is being served. All these elements establish the date of Temple D as around 1850 B.C., or a little later, because it has exact points of correspondence with the conventions of Cappadocian seal work from Kültepe II, with fine pottery from Byblos, and with several Old Syrian and Cappadocian cylinder seals engraved with similar figurative designs. But the repertory of themes of the limestone basin is undoubtedly derived from an Early Dynastic and Akkadian tradition. Examples are the naked hero with the radiate beard, the composite monster, perhaps also the encounter between bull and lion. Even the general organisation of the scenes represented on the principal face of the basin is a typical Early Dynastic Mesopotamian scheme. Finally, we note that the same type of twin basin, unknown elsewhere, is known in the form of a miniature object from Nippur.

The third basin has come down to us only in part from the sack of the cella of Temple N and its most important carvings have vanished. All that remains are the front-facing goddesses from the sides and the fine frieze of bearded dignitaries, facing one another in pairs, on the rear principal face. Once again it is the stylistic features which suggest a date around 1800 B.C. for this basin, on which we cannot but admire the principal decoration, the undulating and agile rhythm of the old dignitaries embracing and facing one another, perhaps to solemnise by this rite a pact or alliance.

From archaising fragments like the warrior's head in relief on a basalt plaque of Great Temple D to works like the limestone basin of Temple N we can view the progress of the workshops of Ebla towards the classical language of the Mature Old Syrian Period. But it is almost certain that unfortunate political developments prevented Ebla, after being without doubt one of the major centres of the Archaic Old Syrian culture, from continuing to play a leading part in the classical epoch.

4. Glyptics

Glyptics were the only Old Syrian artistic genre to have been fairly widely known, from the cylinder seals marketed by clandestine excavators. Yet the exploration of Tell Mardikh has so far yielded only a very few seals of Middle Bronze I and some cylinder seal impressions of Middle Bronze II. All the same, it is probable that Ebla was one of the most important creative centres of Mature Old Syrian seal work, even though we have no evidence of any early activity of this kind. That is to say, the finds in this field show that there were at Ebla cylinders of excellent workmanship in the Mature phase of the Old Syrian Period, whereas the seals gathered from the Archaic phase are stylistically homogeneous but of no great artistic value.

All the seals which can be dated with assurance to Middle Bronze I belong to a single stylistic class of nineteenth-century date. They are small seals, rather short, with a very monotonous pattern of figures consisting of a file of personages schematically rendered with deep incisions and according to graphic conventions recalling cylinders of other stylistic classes from the age of Larsa. Despite their remarkable stylisation, these cylinders have some iconographic kinship with the decoration on the carved basins of Mardikh IIIA. The seal work of Archaic Old Syrian Ebla seems to have been a modest product, highly standardised or certainly of common use. The artistically unambitious quality of these cylinders is no doubt also due to the fact that they were not works of art from palace workshops but mass-produced objects of current use. As regards their background it can be said that cylinders of the same class have been found, infrequently, both in Northern Syria and in Anatolia. So they may be a fairly commercial North Syrian product, diffused also in Anatolia in a phase of intensive contact, such as was the age of the so-called Old Assyrian colonies of Cappadocia.

The glyptics of Mardikh IIIB are known to us only from sealings which give evidence of a very particular use of cylinder seals, already typical of the Syrian area in the Protosyrian Period. The cylinders were rolled on the wet clay of the shoulders of jars before firing and thus the pottery received the impression of the seal, which was probably that of the high official who owned the jar. Obviously the cylinders were also used to seal the clay bullae intended to guarantee the integrity of covers

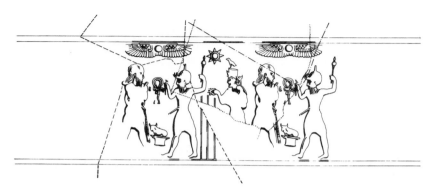

Figure 32   Reconstruction of a Mature Old Syrian Cylinder Seal of Mardikh IIIB

sent or stored. While the only bulla of Mardikh IIIB yet discovered came from Fortress M, all the fragments of jars with Mature Old Syrian seal impressions were gathered in the area of Temple B1 and Sanctuary B2 and belong to two splendid pieces of Middle Bronze II seal work. The repertoire of these cylinders is very clear and characteristic of the best Old Syrian seal work of the so-called *bello stile* phase preceding the manneristic cragginess of the later phase. The iconography is also highly characteristic. In one of the cylinders Hadad appears, the great god of the hurricane with the high spiked tiara and horns in front, his right hand grasping the mace with which he strikes the clouds, his left extended with the axe and reins with which he governs the animal symbolising his fertilising power (a bull couched on a small podium in front of him). Beside Hadad is another great deity of the Old Syrian Period, whose iconography is well known from contemporary seal work and is very probably to be identified with Anat. This goddess wears a long cloak and on her head the characteristic cylindrical tiara with horned base and on it a bird, probably a dove which in later ages was still one of the symbolic creatures associated with Atargatis. In front of the two deities is a shrouded dignitary wearing the cloak with folds characteristic of Mature Old Syrian seal work, while above them the winged sun of Egyptian iconography, meticulously worked, presides over the composition. An *ankh* sign, the Egyptian symbol of life, appears in the field between the gods and their worshipper. Another *ankh* is held in the hand of the goddess, who thus seems symbolically to be conferring life on the owner of the seal. The cylinder is exceptionally large, measuring more than 7 centimetres high, and is one of the most beautiful pieces of Old Syrian seal work which have been preserved to us. It must be dated around the last quarter of the eighteenth century B.C.

Another seal, known only from the sealings found in the sacred quarters of Sector B, is to be assigned to this date. A rather later date perhaps can be suggested for the original cylinder of the bulla sealing of Fortress M, where the composition is more complicated and unusual because of the frieze of animal figures under the principal scene with its several personages. Among these certainly is the goddess Anat once more and a probably royal figure, characterised by the high oval tiara of the Old Syrian kings of the Amorite dynasties of North Syria.

The Old Syrian seals of the Mardikh IIIB sealings are art works of an exceptionally high standard. Even among the remarkable achievements of Middle Bronze Age Syria they stand out as masterpieces of any age. It is perhaps significant that in the larger and better quality seal from Sector B no royal figure appears, though this is otherwise frequent in Old Syrian seal work. Assuredly the cylinder did not belong to a king, but unfortunately the cuneiform inscription is too incomplete in all the sealings preserved to allow any guess as to what it said. It is undoubtedly strange that such an exceptional cylinder was the property of a dignitary in the period in which the kings of Ebla, no doubt because they had lost their independence, could not even have statues or basins put up in the temples. The suggestion may be made that the seal was not the work of Ebla artists but from Aleppo, in view of the undoubted dependence of Ebla on Yamhad during those years. Nothing however can be said for certain on this score since we have yet no data for attributing specific features to individual schools of engraving in the Mature Old Syrian Period.

5. Pottery

The pottery of Mardikh IIIA makes a clear revolutionary break with that of Mardikh IIB1-2. At the beginning of the Archaic Old Syrian Period there is a sharp decline in the technical level, seen most clearly in the grain of the new ware, which now has, even in the smaller vessels, thicker walls, rather coarse ingredients, firing less hard, surfaces less finished. Almost all the vessels are now wheel-made, but there is a complete disappearance of the wares characteristic of Mardikh IIB2 with its rather sophisticated products and tradition of painted caliciform ware. The only traces of the Mardikh IIB2 culture preserved by the new ceramic horizon are in the undulations, which now decorate the large jars and are incised, whereas at the end of the Late Protosyrian Period they were used in the painting of small vessels.

The ceramic horizon of Mardikh IIIA is characteristic of Middle Bronze I, dominated by carinate shapes in all types of vessel. The range of wares is now much more limited. A very clear whitish or yellowish ware predominates, its surface quite often grained with limestone grits, and occurring in many more or less markedly pink variants. Much less frequent but equally characteristic is a chestnut-brown or greenish-brown ware of which the surface is often burnished with a stick.

In the smaller vessels of whitish ware the most ancient Mardikh IIIA forms are small rather closed cups with a classic carination at the base of the shoulder and rim slightly flared. More frequent but likewise archaic, though they do seem to persist longer, until in the course of Mardikh IIIB they probably disappear altogether, are the cups of rather closed form, with classical carination about halfway up the vase and rim almost vertical or slightly flared, always marked with a few parallel incisions on

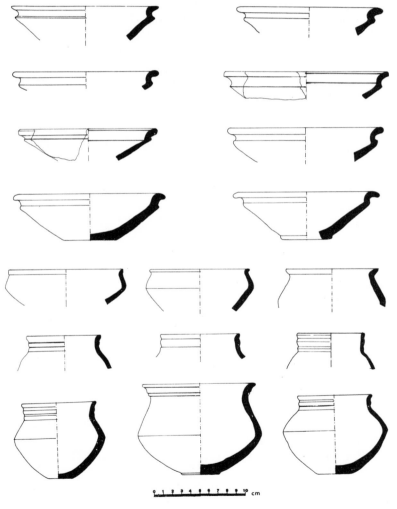

Figure 33   Pottery of Mardikh IIIA

the outer face which produce a series of typical fillets. The most frequent of the Mardikh IIIA forms, which however continues in evidence with decreasing frequency in Mardikh IIIB, is the characteristic open cup of the Syrian interior in Middle Bronze I. Distinctive elements of form are the oblique walls with flat or much more rarely disk base; the high, very sharp carination under the rim; the flared rim with the edge arched and sometimes downturned. The small cups, almost funnel-shaped with infolded rim, also belong to the Mardikh IIIA horizon, although less in evidence.

Always in the same type of pale ware, dominant in frequency among

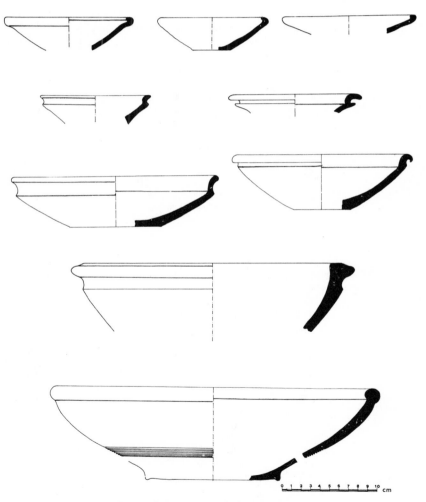

Figure 34　Pottery of Mardikh IIIA

the medium-sized forms, is a cup with rather convex walls, characterised by an almost horizontal rim expanded on its upper face and with
a ribbing a little below the rim. This type of vase is frequent also in
relatively large sizes. Among the closed forms a very common one not
only during Mardikh IIIA but also in Mardikh IIIB is the oval jar with a
short flared neck and the typical everted rim. There are many varieties
of this characteristic projecting rim but the sharp look of its lower
extremity is common to them all, the upper face being frequently
rounded. A morphologically similar juglet, which is found both in
Mardikh IIIA and IIIB, has the rim outfolded and bulging over a

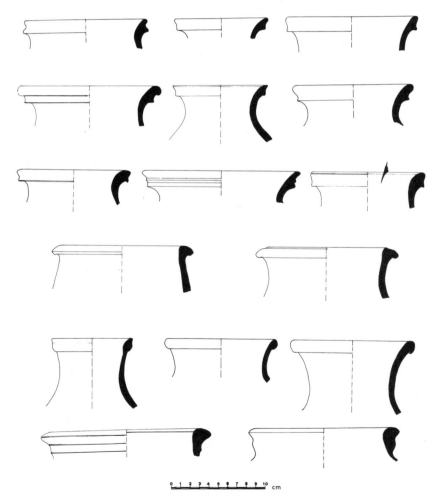

Figure 35   Pottery of Mardikh IIIA

cleanly everted neck. Finally there are also many examples of a juglet with a rather globular body, fragile because thin-walled, the low neck with a marked middle rib and terminating above in an expanded rim with the upper face often convex.

Among the medium to large vessels there are two frequent and distinctive features, apart from the carination which is often present in vessels of substantial size: the expanded rim, sometimes horizontal, sometimes convex, sometimes downturned, sometimes marked with fillets on the upper face, and the combed decoration in horizontal or waved bands. Always with these characteristics, there are large deep

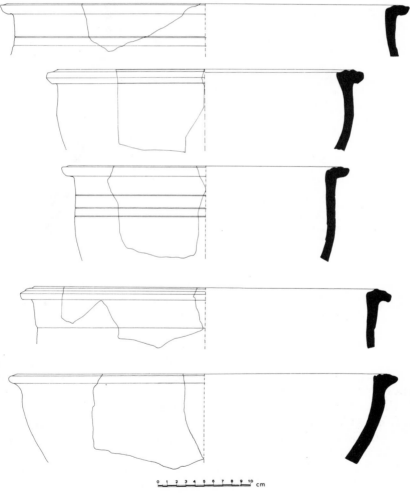

Figure 36   Pottery of Mardikh IIIA

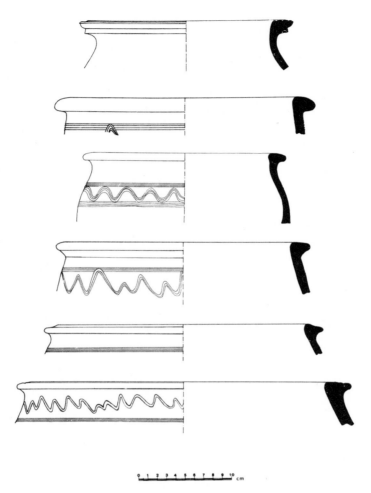

Figure 37   Pottery of Mardikh IIIA

cups in which, because of the open form, the carination eases off into the roundness of the outline; jars with mouth almost closed and oblique shoulder; and, above all, even in middle-sized vessels, carinate jars of vaguely biconical shape.

In the dark chestnut or greenish ware various types of cups and dishes occur, of which the most distinctive element is the rim infolded and slightly expanded, or else expanded inward and outward, sometimes typically set on the thinning of the cup wall. Some types, among the simplest, have the rim merely thickened and rounded, while those more highly developed have a ribbing under the rim which is set obliquely and projects inward and outward.

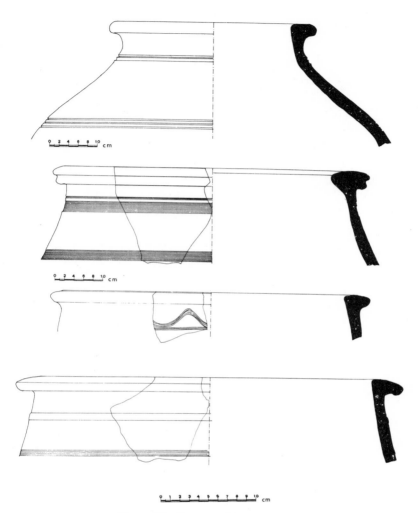

Figure 38   Pottery of Mardikh IIIA

The picture of the pottery of Archaic Old Syrian Ebla that emerges from the exploration of Mardikh IIIA levels is remarkably uniform. In its general characteristics the Mardikh IIIA horizon agrees well with the innovations typical of the initial phases of the Middle Bronze Age in the cultures of the coast and the Palestine area, so much better known than those of inland Syria. Both the pottery types, such as the characteristic dark brown or greenish, often burnished, ware, or certain specific elements of form, such as the widespread use of carination and the almost exclusive use of flat or disk bases, are distinctive aspects of the beginnings of the Middle Bronze Age in the Syro-Palestinian area. But

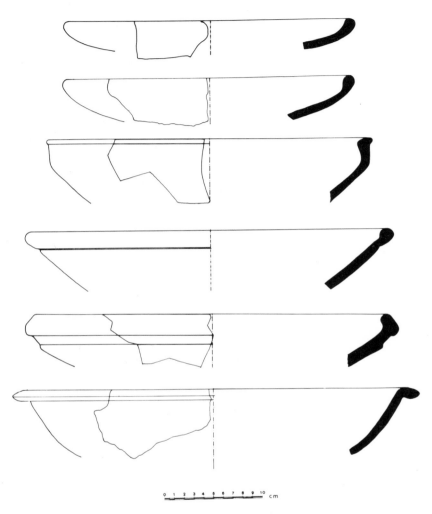

Figure 39   Pottery of Mardikh IIIA

taken as a whole the Mardikh IIIA horizon completely corresponds to that of Hama H and appears typical of the cultural situation of inland Syria, which was more isolated and conservative than the coastal area and less exposed to contacts in innovatory impulses. It is in fact with the Hama H horizon that Mardikh IIIA shows an impressive series of particular similarities, such as the cup shapes with high, sharp carination or the rather closed carinate cups with vertical rims and fillets on the outer face, or the carinate juglets with combed decoration and expanded rim.

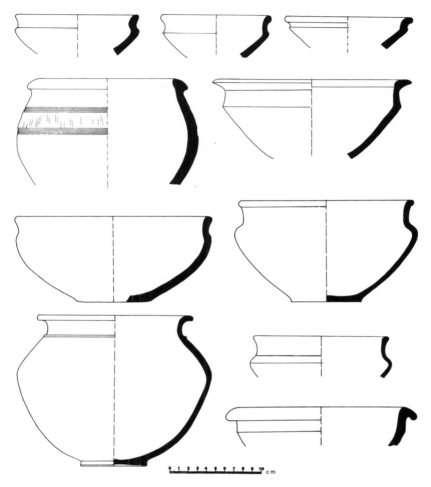

Figure 40   Pottery of Mardikh IIIB

The Mardikh IIIB phase is not characterised by extensive changes in the pottery fabrics, but more by a decline in frequency of certain types very common in the preceding phase and, above all, by the appearance beside the earlier types, of forms still rather rare but new in conception. Thus there is not only no substantial break between the Mardikh IIIA and IIIB phases but there are not even the marked innovatory tendencies characteristic of Palestine in the so-called Middle Bronze IIB and IIC phases.

In general, the Mardikh IIIB horizon is distinguished both by the spread of pottery types which were almost absent before, such as the light greenish ware which to a minor extent appears together with the

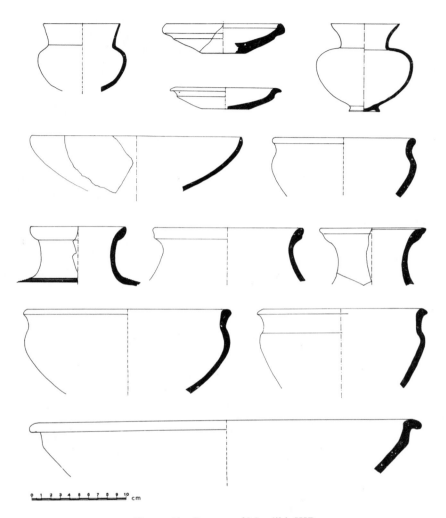

Figure 41 Pottery of Mardikh IIIB

still prevalent whitish or very pale yellowish ware, and by the tendency to rounded rather than carinate forms, and finally by the increased use of ring bases. However, some typical new forms do occur, even though very rarely. The most characteristic of these are the cups of closed shape, narrow everted rim, and body expanded above. Vases of this type, unknown in Mardikh IIIA, often have a ring base and sometimes, in the larger examples, a typical collar applied to the base of the neck.

There is no doubt that Mardikh IIIB, which has two examples of clearly imported Khabur ware, was assailed by ferments of innovation more vigorous than those present in Hama H, which was very uniform

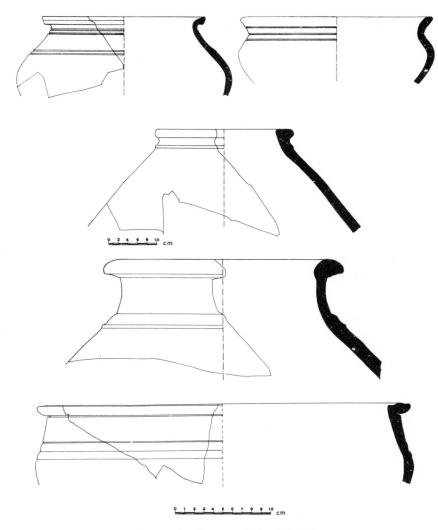

Figure 42   Pottery of Mardikh IIIB

during all its phases. One explanation of this phenomenon could be that Hama H was destroyed before Mardikh IIIB, but there is no proof of that. On the contrary it appears certain that the absence in Mardikh IIIB of quite a few of the most typical innovatory features of Palestine Middle Bronze IIC must have something to do with the premature destruction of Mardikh IIIB. This was around 1600 B.C., whereas the Middle Bronze IIB-IIC culture of Palestine is not to be dated till around 1500 B.C.

5
History and Culture of Ebla in the Period of the State Archives

Until the discovery in 1974 of the Mardikh IIB1 State Archives, the written documentation of the Syrian area in the third millennium was confined to a few dedications on archaic statues in the temples of Ishtar, Ishtarat, and Ninnizaza at Mari, a single fragment of a tablet found at Byblos, and some dozen economic texts of the Neo-Sumerian age, also from Mari. The picture the Archive tablets give of Ebla, however imperfect, is the first of its kind. It is moreover an official picture. All the tablets collected in these Archives are documents of the central administration concerning different aspects of the state organisation of the city. The greater part of the texts discovered in 1975 and 1976 are documents which the royal chancellery of Ebla wanted to preserve in its own keeping. It not only saw to the firing and hardening of a great many of the tablets but also arranged them in suitable places of custody. A considerable number of the texts date from the last years of the city of Mardikh IIB1 and must thus have been compiled a relatively short time before its destruction. Quite a quantity, however, go back to earlier times and were no less carefully preserved. They are thus not only official in subject matter but cover a fairly long period and concern probably five generations of kings. This makes them extraordinarily homogeneous, so that in several cases it is possible to follow the careers of individual personages of the court, princes and high officials.

1. The discovery of the Archives

In the excavation seasons before 1973, the year in which a section of Royal Palace G of Mardikh IIB1 was first excavated, a few very occasional fragments of clay tablets with remnants of archaic cuneiform signs in the Old Sumerian tradition had been found, especially in the excavation of Sector E of the Ebla Acropolis. These fragments, found undoubtedly out of context, must have been dislodged from their original contexts by the re-use of earlier archaeological spoil for filling or mud-brick making, or else by the ransacking of Mardikh IIB1 levels for building materials, as for instance parts of stone foundations exposed by erosion, or by the rearrangement of sectors of the Acropolis carried out during the Middle Bronze Age. It is possible that these fragments, gathered in the area north of the Acropolis, really come from the south-west slopes of the Acropolis itself, where the archive rooms of the Mature Protosyrian palace lay. It is certain that later, perhaps at the beginning of Mardikh IIIA and only on outlying fringes of the Palace area such as this, city redevelopment works were carried out including the removal of earlier debris and the building of terrace and enclosure walls.

The first finds of tablets in place in the Royal Palace G area were made in 1974 in one of the rooms of the so-called North-West Wing, L.2586. They were scattered on the floor near the bottom of a jar fixed in the ground. Undoubtedly this long chamber, one of two cut from the slope of the Acropolis, was not the original place of storage of the forty tablets. They had in all probability been taken there for consultation a little while before the capture of the Palace.

Except for a very few scattered fragments of texts gathered from the pavement of the Court of Audience, the great majority of the tablets were discovered in 1975 in two small chambers built below the east colonnade of the Court itself, one, L.2712, at its northern extremity, and the other, L.2769, immediately to the north of the 'vestibule' leading to the Administrative Quarters.

In the first of these, no doubt a small store room, about a thousand tablets and fragments of tablets were found in the mud-brick filling produced by collapses of masonry in the fire which destroyed the Palace. The tablets were found not only on the floor of the room but also above it, because they must originally have been deposited on two open shelves fixed to the north and east walls, consisting perhaps of a wooden framework plastered with clay. We know both the size of the two shelves and their height from the pavement, because on the relatively well-preserved plasterwork of the walls there are still clear traces of their outline. Evidently at the moment of destruction, when the wooden ceiling crumbled to pieces inside the room and the high, thick walls bounding the store room L.2712 on three sides also collapsed, the tablets must have fallen to the floor among the debris and often been shattered to fragments.

The second chamber, excavated over a large part of its area in 1975, L.2769, was the only real archive room hitherto brought to light in the Palace G area. This chamber has also been called, not at all correctly, a 'library', rather because of the way the tablets were stored than because of the documents preserved there. From it in 1975 some 14,000 tablets were recovered. To these must be added another 600 fragments found when its excavation was completed in the 1976 season. The great majority of the tablets of the archive room L.2769 were found in line against the east, north, and to a much smaller degree, west walls of the room. In general the texts were found up to a greater height near the walls and lower towards the centre of the room, where they were found only on the floor, scattered and separate. Against the north and east walls especially, they were piled on top of one another, and still arranged approximately on two or three fairly recognisable levels. At the moment of destruction, however, they must have slid forward from

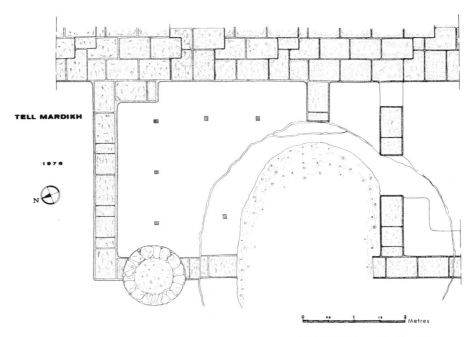

Figure 43   Detailed Plan of the Archive Room L.2769 of Royal Palace G

the walls towards the centre of the room and thus been a good deal displaced from their original positions.

While completely emptying the archive room, we obviously took care to note the find-spot of every single tablet and fragment of a tablet in relation to the walls and the level. We were thus able to make accurate observations of certain details of the floor and plasterwork of the room, from which we have been able to reconstruct with certainty the original system of storage. Along the floor were a number of holes of constant size (6 centimetres by 8 centimetres) and at a constant distance of 0.80 metres from the east, north, and west walls of Room L.2769. In the walls, especially in the north-east corner, were a number of similar regularly spaced holes (0.50 metres apart). These left us in no doubt of the type of fitted furniture in which the clay tablets were stored. The east, north, and west walls of L.2769 must have been covered with wooden shelving supported by uprights, also of wood, sunk into the floor. The actual shelves probably consisted of two boards joined edge to edge, each 0.40 metres deep and, at least along the north wall, supported by horizontal battens along the wall fixed in the corners at each end. The clearly visible holes for probably oblique brackets and the imprint left on the plasterwork itself by the pressure of the shelves against the walls are undoubted evidence that the Archive had racks of three shelves on three of its walls.

Thus the archive room L.2769 was a relatively small chamber (5.10 metres by 3.55 metres) the door of which opened into the north side of the vestibule of the Administrative Quarters, while its interior was designed specifically for the installation of the wooden shelving. In the north-east corner there had been a pilaster one-and-a-third bricks thick, projecting from the east wall. This evidently served to double the corner bearing for the horizontal battens supporting the shelves along two adjacent walls, and to reduce the span of the shelves, which, being 2.90 metres wide on the east wall and 3.10 metres wide on the north needed respectively only two and three uprights. To limit the span of the east rack near the south-east corner of the room a kind of larger pilaster had been built of the same depth, one brick and a third. It is possible that a third similar pilaster, now completely lost through the subsidence of the rock slab which has seriously damaged the whole western section of the room, was built against the west wall.

In exact correspondence with the depth of the pilasters, the shelf rack was 0.80 metres deep along all three walls and had three shelves 0.50 metres apart. In the recess formed in the south-east corner of the room by the second pilaster, resting on the floor was the bottom of a jar intentionally broken, on which lumps of raw clay had been laid, of similar shape to the tablets, not yet used but certainly put there originally ready to be inscribed.

In the excavation season of 1976, during which we further explored the area of Royal Palace G from which the written documents came and

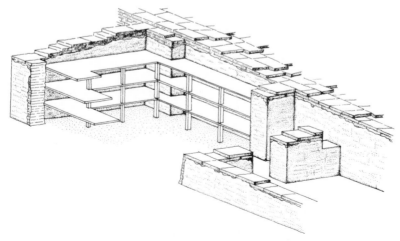

Figure 44   Axonometric View of the Archive Room L.2769 of Royal Palace G

identified the Administrative Quarters, about 450 cuneiform tablets and fragments of tablets were found in a third room built under the east colonnade of the Court of Audience, the vestibule L.2875. This room had no fitted furniture for the storage of documents, but along some surviving lengths of the north and west walls there were some low benches of plastered mud brick which may have been intended as seating. In the inner part of these benches against the west wall were some small basin-like hollows which had probably been made originally as receptacles for small objects, to prevent their sliding to the floor. In fact, though the tablets and fragments of tablets in this room were found mostly on the floor and near its north-east and north-west corners, some objects were found in the ash-packed soil above it which must be interpreted as writing implements. There were several fragments of fine bone styluses, circular in section and with relatively sharp points, and one special tool of greyish-green stone, rather more than a centimetre thick, rhomboidal in shape with two of the corners rounded and one of the two faces slightly concave as if from frequent rubbing. This peculiar implement was undoubtedly what the scribes used for erasures. On the soft clay of the tablets they could erase a line of writing by pressing with one of the two sides, or else a column of writing by rubbing with one of the faces. So it is probable that the vestibule L.2875, communicating with the archive room where the pats of clay were kept ready for inscribing, was one of the places where the scribes of the royal chancellery compiled the documents concerning business transacted in the Court of Audience.

Only one of the two rooms hitherto partially excavated in the area of the Administrative Quarters, which extended east of the great façade M.2751 of the Palace, has so far yielded cuneiform tablets. This is Room L.2764, where the few fragments already found in 1975 were increased to an inventory of almost 500 by the finds of 1976. These tablets which were found scattered on the floor, at the destruction level, and in the filling of masonry collapsed after the fire, must originally have been stored on mud-brick benches, usually one brick thick (0.40 metres), which are still to be seen along part of the north wall and along the west wall. The benches built against the west wall formed a sort of low, open shelf, while those along the north wall must have been closed by wooden doors, of which the outer faces were decorated with figures of pacing dignitaries.

In the open space of the Court of Audience, apart from a very few sporadic fragments which no doubt came originally from the archive room or from the store room of the east colonnade, about twenty cuneiform tablets were found on the floor, arranged on one or two wooden boards completely carbonised by the final conflagration. Evidently the boards were used to carry the clay documents and in all probability were precipitately abandoned on the ground of the Court at the time of the Palace's fall. The position in which they were found makes it seem likely that they came from the archive room.

The size and shape of the tablets in these state Archives is varied. The greater part of those with an administrative or economic content are rather small and round. The smallest texts in this format have two columns to a face, whereas three columns is the general rule. The diameter of the small round tablets averages around 6 centimetres with a maximum variation of some 4 centimetres to 8 centimetres. The larger round tablets have several columns to a face, for the most part four to six, and their edges rather flattened. They are up to 10 centimetres across. A second well-marked type of economic and administrative document is that of quadrangular tablets with rounded corners and blunt edges. These tablets usually have between eight and twelve columns and are about 15 centimetres in width, with height almost always a little less. A third type, also very characteristic, are square in shape and rectangular, their borders thick and flat with sharp edges. These documents, in all respects like bricks slightly thickened in the middle, accommodate fifteen or so columns, sometimes twenty, incised on faces measuring on average 26 by 24 centimetres. This type of tablet, the most frequent for economic texts of a commercial nature, seems to be limited in date to the most recent phase of the archival record. A particular variant of this rectangular form, also economic and always concerned with trade, is exceptionally large, up to 36 by 33 centimetres, with more than twenty-five and sometimes thirty columns of very close, fine writing.

Among the lexical texts all the tablet types used for economic texts occur. Thus the great word lists in Sumerian and Sumerian-Eblaite vocabularies are written on tablets with squared corners, flat faces and sharp-edged borders, as much as 23 by 21 centimetres in size, with about fifteen columns to a face and up to forty lines. A characteristic type of lexical text is found on tablets about 15 centimetres long with square corners, decidedly thick and markedly swollen in the middle of the rear face, with a few rather wide columns, between five and eight in number. Abstracts from word lists and bilingual vocabularies were also written on tablets of the round type, generally best known among economic documents.

Of literary texts two kinds have been so far identified for certain, incantations and myths. The former are known only on small, round tablets, while the very few myths identified — less than ten — when complete are written on flat-edged rectangular tablets with square corners, sometimes with about ten columns. Texts of historical character are usually written on medium-sized round tablets, or square tablets with round corners. One exception, no doubt an international treaty, is inscribed on a big square tablet, with writing actually on the flat edges as well.

In the general topography of Royal Palace G the distribution of the Archive documents is of particular importance. It helps both to identify the way in which individual sections of the building were used, and to give some idea of the criteria governing the preservation of documents. Of the rooms in which tablets were found, three certainly are significant from this point of view, the store room L.2712, the archive room L.2769, and Room L.2764 in the Administrative Quarters, while the vestibule L.2875 must have had a special function. In L.2764 the texts found were all to do with agricultural administration. In L.2712 there were only administrative and economic documents, concerning the consignment of food and drink to messengers and ambassadors sent on missions. In L.2769 most of the tablets were commercial accounts relating to the distribution of textiles, but there was also an important group of literary and lexical texts and historical documents, together with administrative and economic tablets concerning the collection of taxes or tribute in gold and silver. Finally, in the vestibule L.2875 most of the tablets found were commercial accounts of just the same kind as those in the adjacent archive room, with a substantial number of historical documents, mostly letters and decrees.

From this general picture of the provenance and distribution of document types some conclusions can be drawn. In the first place, it seems clear that the sector of the Palace we have called Administrative Quarters, although only partially excavated so far, was specifically intended for the storage of tablets, while one of the rooms, which we have called the vestibule, was probably used for writing the texts. In the second place, the location of two important deposits of tablets outside the Palace proper, under one of the colonnades of the Court of Audience, is a strong pointer to what the function of the Court was. It must have been the open space where caravans were assembled for departure and received on arrival. In the third place, it is probable that some rooms of the Palace completely isolated from the Administrative Quarters, like the room in the North-West Wing where the first group of tablets was found in 1974, were used administratively, though not exclusively so.

In the light of all this it seems clear that the part of the Palace intended for the storage of the Archive documents, and no doubt also for writing and consulting them, which is to say the Administrative Quarters, was planned in two distinct sections. On the one hand, there were the outer rooms, below the east colonnade of the Court, comprising at least the archive room and the vestibule. On the other, there were the inner rooms built to the east of the great façade of the Palace. The store room at the northern end of the east colonnade must undoubtedly be regarded as an outer annexe of the Administrative Quarters. It is important to note that the documents stored in this outer section — L.2712, L.2769, and L.2875 — all seem strictly connected with the business done in the Court itself — from the collection of taxes and tribute in gold and silver from vassals and allies to the organisation of caravans for the distribution of textiles, from the briefing of envoys about to leave for abroad to the giving of audience to foreign ambassadors and dignitaries returned from missions. The only texts we have found in the three rooms of the east colonnade which seem to conflict with this interpretation are the lexical and literary texts. But this kind of document must have issued from the Palace schools for the training of administrative officials. Some of the individual texts must be school exercises, others directories for consultation. The internal rooms of the Administrative Quarters, however, must have been for documents concerning other branches of the Administration. It seems probable that every room of this wing of the Palace was given over to a definite, specific branch. Further excavation of Room L.2764 may change this picture, and we still do not know for certain whether Room L.2764 was a place for storing documents concerned with the administration of agriculture or an office for registering agricultural transactions, though the former seems more probable. In the second case the fact that not very many documents were found in the room would have to be explained as due to there being no need to keep agricultural registration certificates for very long, unlike the registrations of government financial and commercial transactions kept in the rooms of the Court of Audience.

Taken all together, our observations on the find-spots of the tablets in Palace G throw interesting light on the archival principles employed in the Royal Chancellery of Mature Protosyrian Ebla. Apart from the one point of doubt as to what sort of archive the Room L.2764 really was, at least in part, we can say that three methods of keeping documents have been identified and shown to correspond with the different functions of Rooms L.2712, L.2764, and L.2769. In the store room L.2712, where the tablets were kept provisionally, they were deposited on two open shelves supported by wooden uprights about halfway up the wall. This little room, which was the nearest of those in the court to the royal dais, largely contained records concerning the despatch of officials on missions, most of them dating from the last ten years of Royal Palace G. In Room L.2764, inside the Administrative Quarters, where the tablets were probably stored in permanent fashion but where also administrative work was done, the texts were kept on mud brick benches projecting in various ways from the walls. This chamber was certainly an office of the part of the Palace intended for administration, with the dual function of work and storage.

Room L.2769 is an altogether special case, a real archive, where records finalised in times already ancient were preserved on wooden racks. This room had no other function but that of an archive. The very great majority of its documents had to do with business transacted in the Court of Audience. It was in fact the real archive of the Court. The tablets, mostly baked in antiquity before the fire which destroyed the Palace, were originally arranged on the shelves of the rack so as to stand up on edge, resting regularly on one of their side edges and consequently forming horizontal rows of texts, the faces of which were always arranged parallel with the walls. On every shelf there were thus a certain number of horizontal rows of square tablets on edge and edge to edge, probably separated at least in part by debris of broken tablets. Probably three walls of L.2769 were thus covered but in any case two, the north and east walls. The real archival principle according to which the documents were classified and placed on the racks will not be discovered until the study of the texts has reached a very advanced phase. After the publication of most of the economic texts concerning the distribution of textiles and collection of tribute, it will be possible to compare the data of the texts with the archaeological data relative to the position of the tablets in the archive room. For every tablet which has not been obviously displaced as a result of the fire the find-spot has been recorded, with reference to the wall of the room and the individual row, besides obviously the level.

None the less, it is already possible to glean some points of archival interest from the purely archaeological observations. Thus it may be said that the square tablets were certainly placed on the intermediate shelves, while the round ones were put on the upper shelf of the rack on the north wall or laid directly on the pavement under the rack, especially near the north wall. On the middle shelves the rectangular tablets were arranged in horizontal rows according to a rigid, precise rule. The front face of the tablet, the recto, was certainly turned towards the centre of the room, and the documents were always set up in such a way that the first column of the recto was on top and horizontal. This means that for the identification of a document the first step was to check the beginning of the writing on the recto and, given the height of the rack and the size of the tablets, it could always be easily read without getting it out. It is, however, certain that of the rooms so far brought to light in the Administrative Quarters perhaps only in the archive room L.2769 were the documents classified and kept in order according to a well-defined archival principle.

2. The language of the Archives

The writing of the Ebla State Archive texts is classical Mesopotamian cuneiform, invented in the last centuries of the fourth millennium B.C.

in Sumer to serve the administrative needs of the first centres of urban culture. Though the evidence we have is still incomplete, this culture was in particular that of Uruk, the greatest and most extraordinary urban concentration of the late prehistoric period. The tablets of the Archives must in the very great majority have been inscribed in the chancellery of Palace G itself. Only a fraction were written by Eblaite officials in surrounding centres. They show a typical stage of palaeographic evolution, corresponding to the latest phase of what is usually called the Fara Tradition, from the modern name of a Sumerian city, Shuruppak, where many pre-Sargonic texts have been found. Moreover there is no doubt that in size and shape and manner of inscription the tablets and writing of the main core of the Ebla Archives have very noticeable resemblances with the texts of the late phase of pre-Sargonic Lagash, belonging that is to the last reigns of the princes of Lagash, before Lugalzagesi of Uruk and Sargon of Akkad. They are documents above all of the time of Lugalanda and Urukagina of Lagash. It is also certain that the innovations in tablet type and in the evolution of the signs which characterise the age of Naram-Sin of Akkad in Mesopotamian documents seem altogether unknown to the Ebla Archive texts. Hence these innovations, which must be regarded as characteristic evolutions of the Mesopotamian area and probably promoted by the royal chancellery of Akkad, must either have come after the period of the Ebla Archives or else had no influence on the activities of its chancellery.

No absolute dating of the Archive documents can be inferred from these considerations. Their value is merely to indicate a broad chronological span. The palaeographic argument is insufficient on its own to define a dating. It must be said besides that in the third quarter of the third millennium, the period that the observations above would broadly indicate, Ebla in the present state of our knowledge is geographically the furthest from Sumer of any cities where written documents in the classical Sumerian cuneiform script have yet been found. Thus it is difficult to make a good guess at the possibilities of backwardness in the chancellery of Ebla compared with the great cities of Sumer and Akkad. We cannot in fact estimate, at least now, either how far Ebla was abreast with particular features of progress in Sumer or how much it was susceptible to influence from there. What can be asserted without hesitation is that the contacts between the Mesopotamian and Syrian areas were certainly intensive even in the specific fields which could be called cultural. Moreover these contacts were not only traditional relations such as might, for instance, go back a matter of decades or even centuries before the time of the Archives but actual contemporary links attested by the documents themselves. The mention in the Archives of scribes of Kish, Mari, and Emar is of the greatest interest in this connection. It is sure evidence that contact between scribal circles in Northern Syria and central Mesopotamia was continuous. More especially, these mentions are evidence of the diffusion of the script in lesser cities of Northern Syria like Emar, significantly on the Euphrates route, and show that the relations were essentially between the land of Akkad and the land of Ebla. While Mari, in fact, was the most western of the great Mesopotamian centres on the course of the Euphrates, Kish was the metropolis of the northern region of the Sumero-Akkadian area, with a predominantly Akkadian population, and the seat, according to tradition, of four pre-Sargonic dynasties.

In fact it is the evident connection between the scribal circles of Ebla and Kish which brings out a further element of uncertainty about the chronological value to be attached to the links between the North Syrian culture and that of Southern Mesopotamia. The facts in our possession relating to the palaeographic development of the Sumerian script depend almost exclusively on Nippur, the holy city of Sumer which rose and developed around the great sanctuary of the god Enlil. Almost nothing is known to us of Kish. In other words, any theories we may form from most of the Old Sumerian texts about the evolution of the script relate only to Nippur itself or to scribal schools connected with Nippur or dependent on it. Too little is known to us of documents written in the Kish area to justify any idea how far the evolutionary scheme worked out for Nippur would apply to Kish. In view then of the fact that the scribal tradition of Ebla in all probability depended on Kish, and since in the evolution of the script it is already uncertain what connection there was between the two Mesopotamian centres, southern and northern, Nippur and Kish, it must be even more uncertain what use can be made for dating purposes of the evidently indirect relation between the traditions of Nippur and Ebla.

The texts of the State Archives of Ebla are written by means of a very considerable number of Sumerian logograms, just as in contemporary Akkadian texts already known from Mesopotamia. But the language of the Ebla documents is without any doubt a very archaic Semitic language. An abundance of Sumerian logograms, the percentage of which varies according to the different types of text found in the Archives, is quite usual elsewhere. Evidently it stems from the authority of the Sumerian tradition wherever the high urban culture of Sumerian origin was diffused in Western Asia. The frequent use of such writing devices has two causes. There was the high degree of formalisation attained by Sumerian scribes, especially for writing administrative and economic documents. And then the scribes of Ebla must themselves have been steeped in Sumerian as the cultivated language of the bureaucracy and priesthood. Thus Sumerian logographic equivalents are present in very high percentages, up to eighty or ninety per cent in the economic texts, with their stereotyped formulae and technical terms. They appear less often in documents of less standard type, such as letters and decrees, where apart from introductory formulas and set phrases the formal structure is much freer. By comparison it seems that the logographic equivalents are least in evidence in literary texts.

These logographic equivalents represent in Sumerian a wide range of technical terms, not only administrative but also in the economic and commercial vocabulary. There are also many verb forms expressed in Sumerian but here it is normally a case of invariant, unconjugated forms. It is certain, however, that the language in which the texts were thought and in which they were read was a Semitic one. This is proved not only by the fairly frequent occurrence of Semitic words written phonetically, but also by the insertion of clearly Semitic conjugations of the verb in places where in other texts corresponding abbreviated Sumerian forms with a similar meaning appear. It is proved above all by the word order, which clearly betrays a Semitic syntax. A very striking feature of the script, though it is not used with special frequency at Ebla, is the so-called phonetic complement, where, appended to a noun, verb, or pronoun form written logographically, and for the most part abbreviated, in Sumerian, the final part of the word is expressed phonetically in the Semitic language of Ebla.

The language of the State Archive texts is thus Semitic, undoubtedly a local language of the Ebla region, because there is a complete correspondence between the language which is being gradually reconstructed from the documents of Royal Palace G and the language of the proper names, widely attested in the texts, of dignitaries and officials of Ebla. 'Eblaite' seems to signalise its independence of Akkadian, generally speaking, in three ways: first, rather weakly in the system of verbal aspects, since the *iqattal* form is uncertain, while there is evidence for the *qatal* and *iqtul* forms; secondly, with absolute sharpness in vocabulary, where words typical of the western regions are used instead of those characteristic of Akkadian; thirdly, in personal and place names, which here in the third millennium B.C. already conspicuously reflect traditional elements of the western, northern, and southern regions of the Semitic language domain. Characteristic of Eblaite perhaps is the prevalence of the vowel *i* in the intensive *qittil* and the causative *šiqtil* forms of the verb and certainly the presence of the prefix *š-* in the same form *šiqtil*, to be connected with the pronominal affix *-šu* of the third person. The first element would bring Eblaite closer to the North-West Semitic languages, while the second is a phenomenon typical of Akkadian but present also in North-West Semitic languages of the second millennium, like Ugaritic.

These points are already sufficient to distinguish Eblaite from

Amorite even in its most ancient phases, as attested by the proper names of Amorite type preserved in the texts of the third dynasty of Ur, from the last century of the third millennium B.C. In contrast with Eblaite, the third person singular pronominal suffix in Amorite is -*u* and -*hu* matching the prefix of the causative form of the verb which is *a*- and *ha*-. There are other highly characteristic differences between Eblaite and Amorite even in the general framework of North-West Semitic languages. For instance, the Eblaite prefix *i*- for the third person singular of the verbal aspect with prefix *yqtl*, contrasts with the Amorite prefix *ya*-; while the Eblaite forms of the *enna* type, which must be completed actions of the *ḥanna* form, contrast with the corresponding Amorite forms *anana* for *ḥanana* in the *qatal* aspect of verbs with the second consonant doubled.

The archaic character of Eblaite is demonstrated in particular by the apparent absence of nominal flexion, though this still needs to be verified systematically from texts with a more articulate syntax, such as historical documents or literature. It is also shown in the presence of certain prepositions otherwise preserved only sporadically in marginal areas of the Semitic domain, like *sin* 'towards', or, unknown to North-West Semitic, like *in* 'in'.

Eblaite is thus the most ancient North-West Semitic language to have come down to us in a written documentation of such substantial quantity and varied quality as to make it comparable only with the assemblage of Ugaritic texts and the corpus of Bible texts. It was undoubtedly the literary and administrative idiom of the chancellery of one of the greatest city centres of Northern Syria. It must be regarded as having been the educated vehicle of the settled peoples of the North-West Semitic area, just as Akkadian was the corresponding educated vehicle of the settled peoples of the East Semitic area. Amorite, which is obviously not documented by texts but only by proper names, was the language of the semi-nomads of the West Semitic area. As a documented language Eblaite seems more ancient than Akkadian from the mere fact of its being written at least two or three generations before Ibrium and hence before Sargon of Akkad. But according to the lowest and most probable chronology of the texts of the Ebla Archives, it seems that Akkadian in the East Semitic area and Eblaite in the North-West Semitic area were, in the third millennium B.C., before the reign of Igrish-Khalam of Ebla, already the two great cultivated languages of the Old Sumerian Period, when perhaps the only written language was Sumerian.

The identification, preliminary but sure enough, of Eblaite as a very archaic North-West Semitic language, distinct therefore from Akkadian and in the West Semitic orbit also from Amorite, must entail a fundamentally new approach to the history of the Syrian area. The theory has been held that before the late Akkadian and Neo-Sumerian period there were no Semites in that area, so that the most ancient language of West Semitic type there must be Amorite, as known from the proper names of that period. The written documentation of Ebla in the third quarter of the third millennium B.C. forces us to reject this theory. Similarly it has been supposed that in the far western parts of Western Asia there could have been, contemporary with the evidence of Akkadian in Mesopotamia, a sort of Western or Syrian Akkadian. This too turns out to have been mistaken. On the contrary, it has been proved that in the Syrian area, probably even before the evidence of Amorite proper names but certainly at the same time, there was a North-West Semitic language spoken and written by an advanced urban culture. This linguistic type is not far from that documented in the same Ebla texts for proper names of other cities in the Syrian area — from Armi to Urshu to Emar — and from the language that, even vaguely, may be recognised in the more ancient place names of the Syro-Palestinian area.

Thus while Eblaite, in the concrete historical reality revealed by the documents, was undoubtedly the educated and administrative language of the court and chancellery of Ebla, it may probably also be typical of the city culture of the Syrian area and perhaps of the Syro-Palestinian area as well. Moreover, studies on technical aspects of the later North-West Semitic vocabulary have revealed differences between West and East, that is, between 'Syrian' and Akkadian, in some typical uses of language connected with city civilisation. It must be supposed therefore that the population of Semitic language whose idiom the Ebla Archives have now for the first time disclosed to us played the leading part in the foundation of city culture in the Syrian area. It is a very important discovery. We now have grounds for believing that the population still exclusively dominant at Ebla in the early phase of the Mature Protosyrian Period — the age of Royal Palace G and the State Archives of Mardikh IIB1 — had completed many centuries earlier, in the Late Protohistoric Period, the transition in the Syrian area from a village culture to a city culture, and following that, in the Early Protosyrian Period, had developed in more and more original forms the high civilisation which has been discovered in an advanced phase at Ebla.

3. Elements of political history

The reading of the documents discovered in Royal Palace G has not yet got beyond the preliminary stages. Our reconstruction of the political history of Ebla in the period of the Archives must for the time being therefore be equally provisional. The picture that we can barely attempt to draw of certain events of major importance related or echoed by the texts is bound up with the very nature of the tablets hitherto recovered and the difficulties of reading and interpreting them. The information about political history that can be deduced from the economic and commercial texts, though sometimes of fundamental importance, is altogether indirect in character. That from the so-called historical texts, letters, decrees, and treaties, has a quite different scope. Thus it is actually from the economic texts that we have been able to reconstruct the succession of the kings of Ebla during the period of the Archives. In texts of this type the king is quite often mentioned not only by title but also by name. More commonly still, he is mentioned by his title alone but together with the son destined to succeed him on the throne. In the economic documents of one king, moreover, it is usual for many personalities of the administration and chancellery to be mentioned, and among these we often find the name of a dignitary referred to as king in later texts. Comparative consideration of the documents thus enables us with reasonable confidence to reconstruct the succession of the kings of Ebla, even where we are not always sure that the succession was hereditary. The documents more strictly historical in their value do contain, as I have indicated, a smaller percentage of Sumerian logographic equivalents, fewer expressions, that is, of which we already know the meaning. Thus they are often still very difficult to interpret. It will not be possible to tackle these on any scale until the systematic study of bilingual glossaries has been completed. At present it has hardly begun. The historical texts in fact record important events in the political history of Ebla. But there are several cases in which only the general tenor of a document can be understood at present.

As already noted, the historical texts hitherto identified can be classified as letters, edicts, and treaties. The letters are generally despatches sent by officials to the king of Ebla on administrative problems. But there are also messages, or more probably Archive copies of messages for the Ebla chancellery, sent by the king of Ebla to officials on missions abroad or to other kings. The edicts are royal ordinances regulating particular private matters, as for instance the distribution among members of the royal family of certain cities of the kingdom or the award to a princess on marriage of a dowry consisting of a certain number of villages. The treaties, of which very few examples are preserved, tend to be abbreviated extracts of original documents which themselves in all probability were engraved on stone and deposited in sanctuaries. But at least the most important and most complete of these texts — the treaty between Ebla and Assur — is preserved on a tablet of large size, on which are reported the introductory formulas, the clauses concerning Ebla, and the concluding imprecations against anyone breaking the treaty, while the clauses concerning Assur are abbreviated. Evidently the tablet was a copy for the use of the Ebla administration.

The basis for a reconstruction of the political history of Ebla must be the particulars of its kings. There are five individuals who appear in the texts as certainly kings of Ebla and they can be subdivided into two groups. In the first group are three kings — Igrish-Khalam, Irkab-Damu, and Ar-Ennum — whose exact relationship cannot be deduced from the texts but who were at least partly contemporary with one another. In the second group are two kings, Ibrium and Ibbi-Sipish, who were certainly father and son and who very probably both had long reigns. It is certain moreover that the first group of kings preceded the second, but equally certain that there was no gap between the first and the second, because Ibrium appears as one of the dignitaries of the reign of Ar-Ennum in documents of the latter.

Although the documents of the first three kings are proportionately few, in some of them, written in the time of Igrish-Khalam, a scribe is mentioned who appears in the only document so far identified in which Irkab-Damu is mentioned as king of Ebla. In the tablets inscribed during the reigns of Igrish-Khalam and Ar-Ennum the same personalities of the central administration appear repeatedly. However, while according to the evidence of the Archives some officials of Igrish-Khalam were still active in the time of Ar-Ennum, only officials of Ar-Ennum and not of Igrish-Khalam still appear during the reign of Ibrium. So it appears certain that Igrish-Khalam reigned before Ar-Ennum, while Irkab-Damu, whose position was wrongly assigned to the end of the dynasty at a first assessment of the textual evidence, must have reigned either immediately before or more probably immediately after Igrish-Khalam.

The last two kings are referred to by the Archives much more frequently than the first. Ibrium was certainly one of the great dignitaries of the reign of Ar-Ennum, but in no document of the latter's reign does he appear in such a special position as to allow us to suppose that he was one of the king's sons. Ibbi-Sipish, on the other hand, is on various occasions expressly designated as the son of Ibrium. Moreover, it is important to observe that in several documents of the last two kings there appear the fixed formulas: 'the king and Ibbi-Sipish' and 'the king and Dubukhu-Ada'. Since Dubukhu-Ada is frequently mentioned as son of Ibbi-Sipish, the tablets with the first formula are from the time of Ibrium, those with the second from the time of Ibbi-Sipish. And it is a fair guess that since Ibbi-Sipish must have been designated his father's successor during the reign of Ibrium, so Dubukhu-Ada must probably have succeeded his father Ibbi-Sipish.

A very important clue to the absolute chronology of Mardikh IIB1 and the dating of the destruction of Royal Palace G is provided by the fact that Dubukhu-Ada, who also was mistakenly thought to have been king on the basis of the first readings, is already mentioned in texts of his grandfather Ibrium, when he was probably no longer a boy. This not only indicates that the reign of Ibrium must have been rather long, as was probably that of his son Ibbi-Sipish, but also in particular that when the destruction of Ebla put an end to the great city of Mardikh IIB1, Ibbi-Sipish was certainly advanced in years and Dubukhu-Ada was fully mature. It is thus certain that Ibbi-Sipish was reigning when Palace G of Ebla was taken and destroyed, and this is proved also by the fact that in the vestibule L.2875 the last documents written before the fire all belong to the reign of Ibbi-Sipish. It is furthermore certain that this event took place during the second generation after Ibrium, at a time when Ibbi-Sipish was perhaps very old and Dubukhu-Ada was possibly well on in his maturity.

The succession to be inferred from these considerations is thus the following: Igrish-Khalam, Irkab-Damu, Ar-Ennum, Ibrium, Ibbi-Sipish. This reconstruction is fairly certain although some doubts remain about the exact position of Irkab-Damu, who could have preceded Igrish-Khalam. An absolute chronology of the succession of the five kings of Ebla deduced from the Archive texts, independently of any assessment of the archaeological horizon of Mardikh IIB1, ought to be based on the appearance in the same texts of personalities of Mesopotamian history known from original Sumerian or Akkadian documents and also of established date. So far, from a very preliminary examination of the tablets of Royal Palace G, three such synchronisms have been found, though not one can be considered decisive. The first is between a king of Ebla, unnamed but contemporary with Enna-Dagan, a high dignitary of the city, and Iblul-Il, mentioned in an Archive letter as 'king of Mari and Assur'. The second is between Ibrium of Ebla and a certain Shariginu. The third is between an unnamed king of Ebla and Dudiya, king of Assur.

For various reasons it is not easy to evaluate these data. In the first case, the anonymous king of Ebla was presumably Ar-Ennum, because Enna-Dagan must have been a rather important official during his reign, even though he was perhaps long-lived and had important posts under other kings as well. Iblul-Il is known as king of Mari from votive inscriptions on statues dedicated by his officials in the temples of Ishtarat and Ninnizaza at Mari. In the second case the personality whose name is written Shariginu in a commercial text could be Sargon of Akkad. The written signs certainly do not quite reproduce the Akkadian pronunciation of the name but might be an attempt to render Sargon as it sounded in Eblaite ears. If this is correct then the Ebla chancellery did not use the written version of the Akkadian royal name used at Akkad itself, but a transliteration indicating dependence on oral tradition and not on written documents. In the third case, while we cannot be sure of the precise identity of the anonymous king of Ebla who concluded the treaty with Assur, the Assyrian king named in this exceptional diplomatic text, Dudiya, is surprisingly similar to the first king, Tudiya, of the king list of Assur handed down by tradition and probably elaborated in definitive form in the Middle Assyrian Period, that is about a thousand years after the time of the Ebla Archives.

Of these synchronisms, that between Ar-Ennum of Ebla and Iblul-Il of Mari and Assur is very solidly documented, but of little value. For the dates of this Iblul-Il are disputed. Some, the Berlin archaeological school in particular, put him in the so-called Period of Transition of the Early Dynastic Age, around 2600–2550 B.C. Others, especially French scholars, put him about 2400 B.C., not far from Sargon of Akkad. It must be added that the characters used in Mari votive inscriptions by contemporaries of the kings Iblul-Il and Iku-Shamagan have archaising tendencies owing to the geographical remoteness of Mari, so that they cannot be relied on to date this statuary. It follows that the contemporaneity of Ar-Ennum and Iblul-Il is important as a fact but not decisive because we have no sure date for Iblul-Il.

The synchronism between Ibrium and Shariginu is a different, almost an opposite case. Here the problem is whether the identification of Shariginu with Sargon of Akkad is legitimate and well founded. The absolute dating of Sargon is unassailable, though it must always be subject to the uncertainties of Mesopotamian chronology previous to Hammurabi of Babylon. As I have already suggested, the equivalence of Shariginu and Sargon is plausible and probable but not certain. What would be decisive for the identification would be a mention of the city of Akkad in the Archive texts of Ebla. Now, while it seems certain that Akkad is not mentioned in the Ebla texts with its traditional Mesopotamian spelling — A-ga-de^{ki} — on the first reading of the Palace G texts it was proposed to identify with Akkad a city repeatedly mentioned in the Archives, where it is written A.EN.GA.DU^{ki}, possibly to be read A-ga-du^{ki} EN and understood as 'Akkad of the King', in the sense of 'Royal Akkad', alluding to the political power and cultural prestige of the new Mesopotamian metropolis. The city of A.EN.GA.DU^{ki} was certainly the seat of a kingdom because, though without explicit mention of their names, some kings of the city are several times recorded in the Archives. There is however one text from Room L.2769 which would be decisive if a preliminary reading is confirmed. This, which still needs to be verified by collating the original, seems to follow the mention of A.EN.GA.DU^{ki} with the specification 'in the land of Akkad'. In fact, if there is definite confirmation of the mention of Akkad in the Ebla Archive texts, it will not only follow that at least the last part of the Ebla dynasty was contemporary with that of Akkad, the city known to have been founded by Sargon, but it will be a further proof of the identification of Shariginu with Sargon because the title 'king of A.EN.GA.DU^{ki}' appears at a short distance from Shariginu in the document in which he is mentioned.

The third synchronism, between an anonymous king of Ebla and Dudiya, king of Assur, is most interesting. If Dudiya of the Archives is really the same as Tudiya of the Assyrian king list, which does seem likely, the beginning of the Assyrian tradition would emerge from legend, to which it has hitherto been relegated, into history. Yet the archaeological exploration of Assur has shown that important phases of the archaic Temple of Ishtar at Assur do date from just before the time of Sargon although the attribution of the Old Palace at Assur to the Akkadian Period is doubtful, since an Old Assyrian date cannnot be excluded. For an absolute chronology of Palace G of Ebla, however, nothing of any use emerges, since Tudiya of Assur is known only from Assyrian historical tradition and not from original documents.

Lagash	Kish	Uruk/Ur	Umma	Akkad	Mari	Ebla
Enannatum			Enakalle			
Enannatum I						
		Enshakushanna				Igrish-Khalam
Entemena	Inbi-Ishtar		Ur-Lumma		Iku-Shamagan	
		Lugalkingeneshdudu II				Irkab-Damu
Enannatum II					Iblul-Il	
						Ar-Ennum
Enentarzi	Puzur-Sin	Lugaltarsi	Ukush			
					Enna-Dagan	
Lugalanda	Ur-Zababa		Lugalzagesi			Ibrium
				Sargon		
Urukagina						
				Rimush		
					Shura-Damu	Ibbi-Sipish
				Manishtusu		
				Naram-Sin		(Dubukhu-Ada)
				Sharkalisharri		

Figure 45   Proposed Chronological Correspondences between the Major Centres of Mesopotamia and Syria during the Period of the Ebla State Archives

From all this we can consider it probable though by no means certain that Ibrium, the fourth of the five kings of Ebla, was contemporary with Sargon of Akkad. In this case the predecessor of Ibrium, Ar-Ennum, would have lived in the time of Urukagina of Lagash or rather earlier, since Lugalzagesi of Uruk may have reigned some time during the first years of Sargon. Iblul-Il of Mari must in consequence have reigned over Mari and Assur in the period between Eannatum and Urukagina of Lagash, since he may certainly be considered an older contemporary of Ar-Ennum. The correspondences between the new dynasty of Ebla and the dynasty of Akkad would then continue as follows. If Ibrium lived in the time of Sargon, Ibrium's son Ibbi-Sipish must have lived in the time of the two sons of Sargon, Rimush and Manishtusu, the second and third kings of Akkad, whose reigns were short. We have seen that the reigns of Ibrium and Ibbi-Sipish must have been rather long and that the fall of Ebla certainly occurred late in the reign of Ibbi-Sipish, when Dubukhu-Ada, his son and successor-designate, was certainly no longer a child. It seems clear then that the destruction of Mardikh IIB1 occurred in the time of Naram-Sin of Akkad, nephew of Sargon. So from the probable assumption that Ibrium was a contemporary of Sargon, it would follow that Ebla was destroyed during the second generation after Ibrium and Sargon, in the time of Dubukhu-Ada and Naram-Sin. And in his inscriptions Naram-Sin in fact boasts of having taken and destroyed Ebla.

During the whole period of the Archives, which may have lasted a century and a half, Ebla must have been an independent kingdom. But the boundaries of its territory are very difficult to determine. It does however seem certain that the area of direct rule by Ebla extended in Northern Syria at least from the Euphrates in the east to the Orontes in the west, and from the Taurus Mountains in the north as far as the Hama district in the south. It is in fact even probable that the region controlled by Ebla also extended east of the Euphrates in the region of Carchemish and crossed the Orontes valley to the west, perhaps even reaching the sea, while in the north it seems very improbable that it could have crossed the Taurus range. Of the kingdoms repeatedly mentioned in the Archives, Ebla almost certainly had a common frontier with Emar on the Euphrates to the north-east, and with Hama in the south if its identification with Ema is likely. To the north-west, however, it seems probable that distant Assur, at least for a while, had frontiers in common with Ebla, which would actually indicate a temporary extension of the territory of Ebla into Upper Mesopotamia. It is a fact, nevertheless, that the Archives contain repeated references to the kings of cities which in the present state of our work it has been impossible to identify. So the suggestion of wider frontiers remains uncertain. But there is no doubt of the more restricted territorial limits. In fact there are indications that the seats of unidentified kings were mostly in Upper Mesopotamia and perhaps also on the Mediterranean coast north of Byblos. This for instance is certainly the case with the cities of Raeak and Burman, the kings of which are mentioned quite often in the Archives. The first of these must certainly be situated on the road from Ebla to Mari, a little before Emar, the second between Emar and Mari, perhaps on the Euphrates or at a little distance from the river.

The political situation indirectly illustrated by the commercial texts of the Ebla Archives must be viewed over a lapse of time, since in the span of a hundred or a hundred and fifty years the political geography of the North Syrian and North Mesopotamian area may have changed. For example in a commercial text which is certainly archaic, for a series of cities which must have been situated east and north-east of Ebla — Tub, probably the later Tuba, Raeak, Lumnan, Emar, Burman, and Garmu — there is a personage of Assur who provides for the delivery of textile goods, and no king is mentioned of any of these cities. In later texts, starting from the end of the reign of Ibrium, but especially in the time of Ibbi-Sipish, the last king of Ebla, each of these cities has a king. Now, while it is certain that Burman and Garmu were to the east of Emar, there seems no doubt that Tub, Raeak, and perhaps Lumnan should be places west and north-west of Emar. Thus it is very probable that, in the final period of the Ebla dynasty, kingdoms, almost certainly vassal kingdoms, were established right up against the course of the Euphrates, perhaps in order to strengthen the defence of Ebla's eastern frontiers. There must have been changes also in the extent of territory directly dominated by Ebla. Evidence of these is provided by the case of Armi, undoubtedly an important city of the kingdom of Ebla, and in all probability the same as the Arman mentioned by Naram-Sin of Akkad as the other western city which he had taken and destroyed with Ebla. In one archaic Ebla document, probably from the time of Igrish-Khalam, Armi has a king, while in the last years of Ibbi-Sipish, a little before the fall of Mardikh IIB1, it is the seat of a governor, though significantly enough it seems after Ebla to be the first city in the land.

Besides the king of Armi the earliest texts mention also a king of Raeak. It thus seems plausible to regard Ebla at the beginning of the period covered by the Archive documents, the time of Igrish-Khalam, as having held a position of political hegemony in a general pattern of small states governed by kings with theoretically equal prestige and dignity. Very quickly, through events of which we at present know nothing, perhaps in the time of Igrish-Khalam himself, this hegemony must have been officially recognised by the payment of tribute, not only by the kings of the no doubt more modest neighbouring principalities but also by distant and prosperous kingdoms, in particular by Mari on the middle course of the Euphrates. In this period in fact Ebla's political horizons must have been widened remarkably. The only document we can certainly assign to the reign of Irkab-Damu, the second king of Ebla, is a letter from him to the king of Khamazi probably asking him to send picked troops. Khamazi has not been identified exactly but must have been situated east of the Tigris, and the tone of the letter, in G. Pettinato's translation, seems to imply friendly relations between Ebla and Khamazi:

Thus Ibubu, the superintendent of the king's palace, to the messenger: 'You (are my) brother and I (am your) brother; (for you) who are a brother, whatever wish you express I comply with and the wish that I express do you comply with. Send me good soldiers, I pray you: you (are my) brother and I (am your) brother. 10 pieces of furniture in wood, 2 ornaments, I, Ibubu, have given to the messenger.' Irkab-Damu, king of Ebla, (is) brother of Zizi, king of Khamazi; Zizi, king of Khamazi, (is) brother of Irkab-Damu, king of Ebla. Thus Tira-Il, the scribe, has written (and) to the messenger of Zizi (the letter) has delivered.

In this pattern of expanded international relations it seems clear that Ebla had turned to a policy of controlling the lesser, nearest kingdoms without modifying their institutions or perhaps merely intervening with the appointment in certain cities of reliable kings, who in some cases must actually have been dignitaries of Ebla itself. Thus, while it seems incorrect to speak in terms of real annexations of lesser neighbouring kingdoms, the question must have become more critical in the case of independent, more distant states. The only precise indication we have on this point is significant enough. Mari was already paying Ebla a tribute during the early years of the dynasty, probably under Igrish-Khalam, and this was certainly understood by the king of Ebla as a due acknowledgment of his political supremacy.

It was very probably in the reign of Ar-Ennum, however, that a successful military expedition against Mari was conducted by one of the highest dignitaries of Ebla, Enna-Dagan. He repeatedly appears in administrative documents where Ar-Ennum is mentioned and is the author of a long despatch to an unnamed king of Ebla who can only have been Ar-Ennum. In the report, as translated by G. Pettinato, he significantly assumes the title of king of Mari and records the phases of the military campaign:

Thus Enna-Dagan, king of Mari, to the king of Ebla. The city of Aburu and the city of Ilgi, which are in the territory of Belan, have I besieged and have defeated the king of Mari: heaps of corpses have I set up in the land of Labanan. The city of Tibalat and the city of Ilwi have I besieged and have defeated the king of Mari: heaps of corpses have I set up in the land of Angai . . . the cities of Raeak, of Irim, of Ashaltu, of Badul have I besieged and have defeated the king of Mari; heaps of corpses have I set up at the confines of Nakhal. At Emar, at Lalanium, and in the commercial colony of Ebla, Ishtup-shar, commander of Mari, have I defeated: heaps of corpses have I set up at Emar and Lalanium. Galalabi . . . and the trading colony have I liberated. Iblul-Il, king of Mari and of Assur, have I defeated in Zakhiran and have set up seven heaps of corpses.

Up to this point Enna-Dagan's letter describes essentially the itinerary followed by the general of Ebla. It is evident that he must have taken probably the most usual beaten highway of Early Bronze IVA, that is the north-east route which passed along the valley between the Jebel el-Hass and the Jebel Shbeyt to reach the region of the salt lake of Jabbul, rather than the northern one which from Ebla leads to Aleppo, and certainly became the main highway during Middle Bronze I-II. Then Enna-Dagan with his army must have skirted Lake Jabbul to the south so as to reach the Euphrates at the great bend where Emar was, the present Meskene. It is very significant that there was a trading colony of Ebla in the Emar region and that its political influence evidently reached the Euphrates and was solidly attested there. It was after Emar, when Enna-Dagan must certainly have taken the Euphrates road south-eastward, that the Eblaite general entered what must have been the sphere of influence of Mari or under its direct rule. The letter continues (again in G. Pettinato's translation):

Iblul-Il, king of Mari, and the cities of Shada, Addali, and Arisum, in the territory of Burman, together with the men of Sukurrim, have I defeated and set up heaps of corpses. Sharan and Dammium, together with Iblul-Il, king of Mari, have I defeated; I have set up two heaps. Towards Nerad and into his house at Khashuwan Iblul-Il, king of Mari, has fled, bringing to the city of Nema the tribute due to Ebla. Emar too have I defeated and set up heaps of corpses. Iblul-Il, king of Mari, and the cities of Nakhal, Nubat, and Shada in the territory of Gazur have I defeated in Ganane: I have set up seven heaps of corpses. Iblul-Il, king of Mari, and the city of Barama, for the second time, and Aburu and Tibalat in the territory of Belan, I, Enna-Dagan, king of Mari, have defeated.

In the last part, no longer intact, of this exceptional document Enna-Dagan records acts that could be defined as political in his new function of king of Mari: he 'gave back the sceptre' to several conquered cities, that is, evidently, he restored the defeated kings to their legitimate power after having received their submission and accepted 'the oath' of Iblul-Il, in token no doubt of vassalage. This would indicate that Iblul-Il, who had refused to pay the tribute due to Ebla, was pardoned probably after having recognised that his rule was now over a shrunken territory that probably did not include Mari.

So closely integrated are these Archives that another text, an administrative record also found in the Archive Room L.2769 like the letter of Enna-Dagan, registers the intake of booty from the military campaign against Mari. Its total amount is given as 2193 minas of silver and 134 minas 26 shekels of gold. This document is really of extraordinary

Figure 46   The Region of Tell Mardikh and Lake Jabbul

interest since it furnishes two ulterior motives of particular importance. It says explicitly that of the sum paid over to Ebla, 1100 minas of silver and 93 minas of gold are the property of King Iblul-Il while the rest belongs to the elders of Mari. Of the whole amount it says that fifteen per cent belongs to Enna-Dagan while eighty-five per cent is to be paid over to the king of Ebla.

Enna-Dagan's campaign against Mari was not an isolated event, nor can the control of Mari by Ebla have been only a short-lived affair. During the reign of Ibbi-Sipish of Ebla a brother or son of his, Shura-Damu, became king, or better perhaps governor, of Mari. Moreover events in Mari were closely followed at the court of Ebla. An archival dating formula records 'the defeat of Mari', which could have been that inflicted on the city by Enna-Dagan. Another year takes its name from the death of Iblul-Il, who was certainly the king of Mari and Assur. A third dating formula celebrates the accession of Shura-Damu in Mari.

These pieces of evidence, though still very scattered, are already beginning to form part of a unified historical reconstruction. Yet another administrative document from Ebla mentions a 'king of Mari' not named before, a certain Ikushar, together with personalities who seem to be contemporary with Ibrium of Ebla.

If we then try to reconstruct the general pattern of relations between Ebla and Mari, it appears probable that Mari had already begun to pay tribute to Ebla under Igrish-Khalam and Irkab-Damu, perhaps when the king of Mari was the Iku-Shamagan mentioned in the inscriptions of two pre-Sargonic temples at Mari. Iblul-Il, who was probably the successor of Iku-Shamagan at Mari, must have extended his rule eastward, obtaining direct control of Assur and assuming the title 'King of Mari and Assur'. It is possible that with the control of Assur, Iblul-Il may have felt powerful enough to rebel against Ebla, and not pay the usual tribute. This act may then have provoked the victorious expedition of Enna-Dagan. He defeated first Ishtupshar, general of Mari, and then Iblul-Il himself who fled to Khashuwan in Upper Mesopotamia. For some time Enna-Dagan, in the time of Ar-Ennum, must have reigned over Mari, evidently as a vassal of Ebla. But afterwards Ikushar became king of Mari and it seems certain that with Ikushar Mari recovered its independence, if only because the new king's name seems in the Mariot rather than the Eblaite tradition. At any rate he is not a dignitary of Ebla known from the Archives. Ikushar reigned at Mari in the time of Ibrium, though it is impossible to say whether at the beginning or end of that king's probably long reign. Finally, in the time of Ibbi-Sipish of Ebla, once more a high dignitary of the Syrian city and once again a member of its royal family became king, or governor, of Mari. Since the Eblaite dating formula that records the accession of Shura-Damu in Mari is one of the three found on the floor of one of the long halls of the North-West Wing of Palace G, it is very probable that Shura-Damu seized the power in Mari late in the reign of Ibbi-Sipish, a little before the sack and destruction of Ebla.

Another historical document of great interest from the Archives is the treaty between Ebla and Assur, which takes the form of a treaty of friendship dealing with a series of commercial questions, mainly about the trading colonies. The introduction, unfortunately incomplete, must have been of particular interest, since it listed the cities under the rule of the two kings. Though it is still premature to consider the details of this international treaty, there is one obvious fundamental fact which must be considered. Ebla in the treaty has a privileged position with respect to Assur, since in the penalty clauses of the treaty the penalty prescribed for a citizen of Ebla is always less for the same offence than that prescribed for a citizen of Assur. This then is a treaty which Ebla was able to impose on Assur at a moment of unchallenged political ascendancy. As we have seen, the name of the king of Assur is mentioned in the treaty but not that of the king of Ebla. Its date therefore can only be tentatively worked out. There seem to be only two possibilities, either in the reign of Ar-Ennum, after the victory of Enna-Dagan over Mari and Assur, or else late in the reign of Ibrium or that of Ibbi-Sipish, when there was probably an expansion of Ebla, after the overthrow of Ikushar at Mari or in the preparations for it.

It would be of the greatest interest if the name of the city of Akkad were mentioned in the Ebla texts, but this, as we have seen, is yet to be confirmed. If the curious orthography A.EN.GA.DU^{ki} really conceals Akkad it would be quite natural that this city should not be mentioned in the texts before the reign of Ibrium, since if Ibrium was perhaps a contemporary of Sargon, Akkad could not have been founded before Ibrium's reign. There is, however, one possible variant of an Eblaite spelling of Akkad, nearer to the traditional Mesopotamian orthography, which still needs verification. If it is confirmed, it seems to include Sargon's city in a list of a hundred under the suzerainty of Ebla. If this first reading is confirmed, we should have to conclude that at the end of Ibrium's reign or at the beginning of Ibbi-Sipish's Akkad for a short time was paying tribute to Ebla.

These still fragmentary and unsystematic gleanings of information from the Archive documents do seem to enable us to reconstruct the broad lines of Eblaite politics in the Mature Protosyrian Period. After a first phase of expansion of Ebla in the reigns of Igrish-Khalam and Irkab-Damu, in which it achieved ascendancy over Mari, there was a struggle between Ar-Ennum of Ebla and Iblul-Il of Mari and Assur for the control of the Euphrates and Upper Mesopotamian highways. Having won a victory over Mari and installed there a high dignitary of its own, Ebla was probably confronted with a new growing power in Southern Mesopotamia. The allusion by Lugalzagesi of Uruk to a campaign of his in the west may have originated with the Mari crisis and what from then on was the menace of Ebla. Very probably the power of Ebla remained intact or increased, especially in Upper Mesopotamia. The ambitions of Sargon of Akkad must undoubtedly have seen in Ebla, whose presence on the Middle Euphrates is now so solidly attested, a grave danger. This is the reason why Sargon advanced up the Euphrates and 'received from the God Dagan of Tuttul' the western regions, from Mari to Ebla. It is probable that Sargon broke the hold of Ebla over Mari, that in consequence of Sargon's victorious campaign in the west Ikushar established himself on the throne of Mari, and that late in the reign of Ar-Ennum or early in that of Ibrium Ebla suffered a decline in its political prestige. Sargon none the less seems not to have captured Ebla but boasted of having received its submission.

It is probable that while Ibrium was still on the throne, in the middle

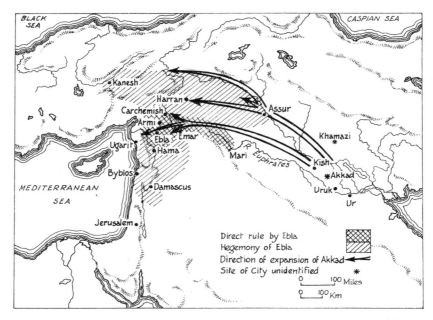

Figure 47   The Political Expansion of Ebla in the time of the State Archives

or later years of his reign, Ebla recovered a position of pre-eminence, and Sargon perhaps could no longer intervene in Upper Mesopotamia and in Syria, beset as he was by ever-increasing internal difficulties which forced him at the end of his long reign to submit to a long siege, cooped up in Akkad. Already in the reign of Ibrium, if A.EN.GA.DU^{ki} is really Akkad, relations between Ebla and Akkad improved. Akkad appears frequently as the destination of consignments of textiles to Mesopotamia, and the rare mention of other Mesopotamian cities may simply be due to the political predominance of Akkad. There is even mention of a visit of Ibbi-Sipish, perhaps when he was not yet king, to A.EN.GA.DU^{ki}. In fact the same Ibrium himself and his son Ibbi-Sipish after him must completely have re-established the power of Ebla. It was perhaps in their time that a list of cities subject to Ebla was compiled, among which appears Kanesh, the present Kültepe, a well-known city of Cappadocia in the later, Old Assyrian Period. At the same time Rimush and Manishtusu of Akkad, the two successors of Sargon, never embroiled themselves in the west but made war in the east, perhaps because Ebla could not yet be challenged. More likely still, Ebla may for some time have refrained from entanglements in the Euphrates valley and limited its own expansionist interests to the north and east. But when Ibbi-Sipish recovered the complete control of Mari and sent Shura-Damu there as governor, as had happened some decades previously in the time of Sargon, Akkad was gravely concerned by the renewal of stable control of the middle Euphrates by Ebla. General political conditions, moreover, had changed in Akkad's favour. It was no longer preoccupied with the east, which had been subdued by Rimush and Manishtusu. The cities of Sumer seem from this time on to have accepted the ascendancy of Akkad. Only the west, with Upper Mesopotamia, threatened an economic blockade of Akkad within the narrow confines of the twin rivers.

For this mixture of reasons, when Naram-Sin of Akkad decided to turn his attention back to the west, it was no longer a prestige campaign to protect some trade route but a combination of warlike operations aimed at a decisive crippling of his western and northern rivals. When Ibbi-Sipish must have been already old, Naram-Sin must have laid siege to Ebla, which capitulated, and he at once clearly realised the importance of his achievement, boasting in an inscription:

> Never since the creation of mankind has any king among kings taken Armanum and Ebla; (. . .) Nergal opened the road for Naram-Sin, the strong, and gave him Armanum and Ebla; he bestowed on him also the Amanus, the Mountain of the Cedars, and the Upper Sea. Thanks to the might of Dagan, who exalts his majesty, Naram-Sin the strong conquered Armanum and Ebla and, from the bank of the Euphrates to Ulisum, struck down the peoples whom Dagan delivered into his hands and they bore the basket of Aba, his god, and he had in his power the Amanus and the Mountain of the Cedars.

In the same inscription Naram-Sin repeatedly records having defeated and taken prisoner Rish-Adad or Rida-Adad, king of Armanum, while no mention is made of the king of Ebla. It appears very probable that Armanum of the Akkadian inscriptions was Armi of the Eblaite inscriptions, and Armi, especially in the latest documents of Ibbi-Sipish, appears clearly as the first city of the kingdom after Ebla. It is thus probable that in a period of weakness of the central power of Ebla, perhaps in actual consequence of Naram-Sin's victorious military campaigns in Upper Mesopotamia, there were disorders at Ebla to such an extent that the governor of Armi/Armanum seemed in the eyes of the Akkadian conquerors their real enemy.

Unlike Sargon, Naram-Sin left conspicuous traces of his presence in Upper Mesopotamia, from the splendid bronze head at Nineveh to the stele at Pir Hussein and especially the great palace of Tell Brak. Having defeated Ebla and assumed the supremacy of Upper Mesopotamia, Naram-Sin laid the foundations for a firm control of the conquered regions. This proves that the fundamental cause of opposition between

Ebla and Akkad was economic. Ebla by its strategic position controlled the supplies of timber from Western Syria and metals from Anatolia, the two fundamental commodities for maintaining the technological primacy of Southern Mesopotamia. In the time of Ar-Ennum first, and of Ibrium and Ibbi-Sipish later, Ebla had tried by controlling Mari to block these supplies to the land of Sumer and Akkad, at the same time developing a far-sighted policy of alliances, from Byblos to Assur, to protect its own trade in finished goods of high quality, from textiles to furniture. While Sargon could only loosen the vice of Ebla, Naram-Sin realised that the encirclement must be resolutely broken. Ebla, which had set up an effective network of diplomatic and commercial relations, no longer had the strength to organise an adequate military resistance. The conquest and destruction of the city and Royal Palace G around 2250 B.C. must have constituted a serious crisis, though not a decisive one, in the development of city civilisation in Syria. A few years later Akkad had to withdraw from its known strongholds everywhere in Upper Mesopotamia, to face the urgent menace of the Guti.

4. The economic structure in outline

The State Archive texts of Mardikh IIB1 are grouped in categories each dealing with a single section of the administration of the city. This specialisation will enable us in coming years to obtain a very accurate picture of objectively important aspects of the economy of the period. For reasons which we shall have to explore more thoroughly, these aspects were considered by the Palace chancellery as important enough to demand an orderly filing system.

So far as can be judged in the present stage of study of the Archive documents it seems that the most systematic form of registration was reserved for consignments, or what could perhaps be better called despatches, of specific finished goods — the textiles produced in the city — and the arrivals of tribute, taxation, and payments in gold and silver. It can be said that so far these statements have one general source of difficulty. They hardly ever give the reason for the operation, but the operation alone, thus combining in one document, in the first case, destinations apparently quite different, and in the second, receipts of very various origin. Thus in the textile accounts it often happens that among the consignees are listed, usually in order, the king, the queen, the princes, dignitaries of Ebla and then a number, often quite large, of cities, which may be distant, while in the records of arrivals there appear mixed up as consignors Eblaite dignitaries, cities of the kingdom of Ebla, and kings of cities almost certainly independent. The nature of the records was thus essentially bookkeeping, the aim of administration being above all to transcribe the amount of the outgoings and incomings of goods. A third section of the administration which must have been handled with special care was agriculture. These documents, as we have seen, were kept in a special room of the Administrative Quarters. Documents recording issues of rations to staff occur more rarely. One type of text in this class, however, is well represented — those concerning the delivery of rations for the specific needs of missions abroad.

There is no doubt that the special nature of the written documentation of the Archives so far recovered depends entirely on one fact. All these finds have been made in the original places of storage of the texts, and consequently belong to a homogeneous collection connected with the particular function of the Court of Audience. It was first of all a place where commercial and financial business was transacted, and hence tablets of this class predominated among those found under the east colonnade. It is interesting, moreover, that these bookkeeping records were not destroyed, but the tablets in question were carefully fired and kept for several generations. It is probable that this was done systematically, because in the Main Archive L.2769 the permanent fixtures (shelving racks) were of a kind adapted to the systematic preservation, in chronological order, of the square tablets, while the other, round, tablets were probably stored in no particular order. Thus while the commercial and financial documents were carefully preserved for five generations the texts about agricultural administration seem to concern only the last years of the life of Mardikh IIB1. Probably these tablets were not kept long but destroyed at the end of every reign or according to some other periodical rule.

The foundations of the Ebla economy must have been laid in agriculture, and the growth of the settlement was certainly due to the special ecological conditions of that region. But very soon a preponderant role was assumed by the trade in textiles. The production of these must have been developed in quantity and quality to the point where it became characteristic of the city. Moreover this trade, which is largely documented by the Mardikh IIB1 State Archives, was still flourishing in the following phase, Mardikh IIB2, to judge from Mesopotamian economic texts of the Second Lagash Dynasty, recording the arrival of textiles from Ebla. The production mechanisms are not yet known. Comparative study of the documents concerning the administration of agriculture and stock-rearing will be needed to discover where and under whose authority cloth was made. But it is probable that production was under Palace control, that is State control, and it is clear from the Archive texts that the distribution of the merchandise was totally organised by the State.

What is astounding is the size of the geographical area concerned in the distribution of cloth from Ebla. This is conspicuously brought out by the documents from the Main Archive L.2769. This very large area, besides including many centres of the Syrian region, mostly still difficult to identify, extended from the Mediterranean coast in the west to the Tigris valley in the east, and from Central Anatolia in the north to Palestine in the south. In the coastal area substantial consignments had Byblos as their destination. The importance of this city during the period of the Archives has been fully corroborated by excavations, and a further reason for its appearance in this context may well have been its central importance in the Egypt trade, of which there seems to be no direct evidence in the Ebla documents.

In the Mesopotamian area the most frequent consignments are destined for Upper Mesopotamian cities, probably in the river basins of the Balikh and Khabur. But almost none of these cities, important though they must have been, can be identified for certain. Some conclusions indeed may be drawn from the fact that often these names of cities appear in an almost fixed order with few variants, and one name which occurs quite frequently among them is Harran. Ebla obviously had close relations with the cities on the great Euphrates highway, from Carchemish, which perhaps was not yet particularly important, to Emar, which does seem already to have been of some consequence, with a king of its own, and on to Tuttul and Mari, both capitals of kingdoms. The role of Assur in this traffic seems to have been considerable, and its merchants were apparently engaged in the distribution of cloth to several destinations in Upper Mesopotamia and probably also in the Assyrian area east of the Tigris.

The South Mesopotamian region is rather scantily represented among the texts concerning the distribution of cloth. The only city which certainly appears, though not very often, is Kish. As we have seen, the mention of Akkad is doubtful. If the reading of Akkad, however, is confirmed, its very presence would explain the very rare occurrence of the cities of Sumer, which were evidently subject to the new Mesopotamian capital and deprived both of economic and of political independence. No doubt Akkad itself would have taken over the function of secondary distribution of merchandise from Ebla.

Even in the Syrian area only a few of the cities can be identified. Yet there were very many small places to which cloth was sent. Some of these can be identified because their ancient names are preserved in the modern. Armi certainly was important, undoubtedly identical as I have said with the Armanum of Sargon and Naram-Sin, and possibly in fact an ancient name of Aleppo. Very rarely mentioned are Alalakh, Ugarit, and Qatna. It is interesting that Homs should already be found in the Ebla Archives under the name of Emissa, an echo of the classical Emesa, and Damascus already in the form of Dimashqi. The mentions of cities in the Palestine area are very uncertain, although in this region identifications on the ground will be easier once the readings are certain. Urusalima certainly seems an ancient name of Jerusalem. Megiddo is vouched for with certainty, and Lachish seems sure enough, but from the phonetic rendering we cannot be at all confident of the presence of Hazor or, in the extreme south, of Gaza.

Though we can be sure from the size of the Archives in Room 2769 that the production of cloth and the cloth trade formed a very important base element in Ebla's economic prosperity during the Mardikh IIB1 phase, other similar activities were probably also characteristic. One of these must have been a flourishing trade in high-quality furniture. An adequate idea of Ebla furniture, carved in relief, or open work with figures in the round, is given by the finds in Room L.2601 in the North-West Wing of Royal Palace G. Some part of this very fine production, probably a considerable part, was destined for export. We know this for certain from some economic texts of Nippur in the Third Dynasty of Ur, contemporary that is with Mardikh IIB2, in which is recorded the arrival of precious furniture from Ebla.

We can guess from the Archives at other productive activities, especially in the field of metallurgy, the manufacture of tools and weapons or of ornamental objects. Certainly workshops must have

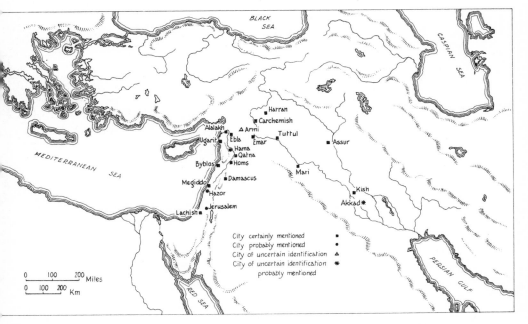

Figure 48   Ebla's Commercial Relations in the Period of the State Archives

been functioning near the Palace for gold and silver smithing and the casting of bronze. The frequent mention of objects of very great value in metal in the Archive texts reveals that there must have been, directly at Ebla, an intense activity organised under Palace control. Huge quantities of gold and silver received in tribute or in payment for merchandise were converted into finished goods and a part of them certainly re-exported in trade.

The economic structure of Mature Protosyrian Ebla must certainly have been extremely complex and highly developed. It was no doubt the result of a long process of economic evolution. To elucidate the details will require intensive study of the texts when they have all been published. Only then shall we be able to bring together the Ebla of Mardikh IIB1 as reconstructed archaeologically on the site with that revealed by the documents.

5. Features of the organisation of the state

It is no easier to define in concrete terms of institutions the character of Ebla's government during the Mature Protosyrian Period than it is with our present knowledge to trace the exact geographical extent of its political power. Some essential elements already seem clear, however, from the first readings of the Archive texts, and it is hard to see how they could in any radical way be altered by future studies.

The highest institution of Ebla was represented by the king. He was officially designated by the Sumerian title e n, to which corresponded in Eblaite, as we know for certain from the bilingual vocabularies, *malikum*, a specifically West Semitic word, contrasting with the Akkadian *šarrum*, quite unknown in the language of Ebla. As is well known, e n in Sumerian is properly speaking the equivalent of 'lord' and not 'king', while *malikum* in all the West Semitic languages is the specific term for 'king'. It is thus of special importance that according to firmly-established tradition at Ebla there was an exact and unvarying equivalence between the Sumerian e n and the Eblaite *malikum*. All the more so when we find that the specific Sumerian word for 'king', l u g a l, is not at all unknown in the Eblaite texts, where it means merely a very high official. Moreover, although it is not yet clear what Eblaite term corresponded to the Sumerian l u g a l, it is certain that at Ebla, in some cases at least, l u g a l, alternated with the other Sumerian term u g u l a 'superintendents', while l u g a l denoted a dignity which could be held by several persons of high rank in the court at the same time.

The qualification for kingship at Ebla is not known, but it can be said that though we do not know the relationship of the first four kings of the city to one another, both Ar-Ennum and Ibrium appear quite frequently as high officials in documents of their predecessors. It must be inferred that the kings, even if not always chosen from the royal family, came none the less from a restricted circle. They may perhaps be defined quite conventionally as a city aristocracy. It is however certain that in the time of Ibrium and Ibbi-Sipish some form of co-regency was adopted at Ebla, because in several documents of these two kings the royal title appears associated with the name of the heir-apparent in a fixed formula. With Ibrium there constantly appears Ibbi-Sipish, who succeeded him on the throne. With Ibbi-Sipish it is always Dubukhu-Ada, who was evidently the successor-designate.

In the business of government the king must have made extensive use of the royal family and especially his sons. This is shown quite clearly by the high official positions held by the princes and the active parts they played. Thus a 'king of Raeak' is explicitly defined in one Archive text as 'son of the king'. 'Sons of the king' are quite often governors of cities. Ibbi-Sipish during the reign of Ibrium visited A.EN.GA.DU^{ki}, evidently on political business.

The active government of Ebla seems to have been carried on always by the king and by a group of dignitaries, whose names frequently recur in the Archive texts of the different reigns and who were probably given the collective title of 'judges' or 'fathers'. But it is still difficult to establish with certainty if this referred simply to the group or if it had a more individual significance. From several texts we learn that the totality of the central administration of Ebla, that is of the organs of government of that city, was called by the collective term é-MI+ŠITA^{ki}, that is 'house of MI+ŠITA^{ki}', where this last title must have denoted a very ancient civic dignity.

A document of particular importance, which must date from the reign of Ar-Ennum, under the description 'staff of the é-MI+ŠITA^{ki}' lists thirteen court personages, each with a number of subordinates of his own, varying between four hundred and eight hundred. In addition 4,700 persons are registered as staff employed specifically by the é-MI+ŠITA^{ki}. The total of direct employees of the dignitaries and the administration is 11,700 men. It is interesting to note that one of the first dignitaries in this document is Ibrium, but that Ibbi-Sipish is already there as well. We cannot be certain, however, if this one was really the son of Ibrium and the future king of Ebla. The total of almost twelve thousand for the aggregate of staff employed in the administration seems astonishingly high. For one thing it would have been very difficult for such a multitude of individuals each to do his own job in the administrative buildings of the city Acropolis. It must therefore be supposed that the document in question indicates the comprehensive total of staff in the central administration, including those not personally engaged on duties at Ebla. But it is impossible to decide whether the dignitaries listed in the document had precise and specialised administrative functions or whether they were not more of a corporate college of government.

Another text of particular interest which records the deliveries of amounts of barley to the staff of the city administration throws special light on the municipal administrative units and the offices of government. The total built-up area of the city was subdivided into two great zones, the one called é-MI+ŠITAᵏⁱ, the other simply Ebla, evidently in a strict sense. From the administrative reality illustrated by this document and the archaeological facts of Tell Mardikh it can be clearly inferred that the term é-MI+ŠITAᵏⁱ meant the Acropolis, while Ebla could either mean, obviously, the whole city taken together, or also the Lower City alone. From the Archive document we learn that the Lower City was subdivided into four 'wards', designated indifferently by the Sumerian technical term for 'village' or 'rural district' or by that which properly means 'gate' but also 'quarter'.

The four wards had well-defined administrations. The 'first quarter' had twenty superintendents and a hundred subordinates; the 'second quarter' twenty superintendents and ninety-eight subordinates; the 'third quarter' ten superintendents and thirty subordinates; the 'fourth quarter' twenty-one superintendents and fifty subordinates. The superintendents were arranged in groups of five for each ward. In addition, the fifty superintendents of the first three wards and the twenty superintendents of the fourth were subordinated to two high officials known generically as 'inspectors', but of whom the first was one of the highest functionaries of Ebla, the i l z i, while the second is listed only by name. It is of particular interest that the wards of Ebla were four and that they were called by the names of the city gates, these being generally the names of deities — the 'Dagan Gate', 'Rasap Gate', 'Sipish Gate' — so that there is an exact correspondence with what is known of the city lay-out of Ebla from archaeology. In fact it is evident that the four city gates of Mardikh IIIA must have been put up at the beginning of Middle Bronze Age I on the sites of the earlier gates of the Mardikh IIB1 city and, since it is known that the temples of the Old Syrian city were situated for the most part in the Lower City at the foot of the Acropolis, and at least in one case were built on Mardikh IIB1 foundations, it is very probable that gates and 'quarters', or wards, took their name from the greatest temple of the ward. Owing to the way the city was planned the bulk of the temple must have immediately appeared to a traveller against the background of the Acropolis the moment he entered the city area.

For the Acropolis itself three palaces are listed — the 'Palace of the King', the 'Palace of the Council (of Elders)'?, a third palace difficult to interpret — and then the 'Stables'. The administrative staff was distributed as follows: for the 'Palace of the King' ten superintendents and sixty subordinates; for the 'Palace of the Council' ten superintendents and fifty-five subordinates; for the third Palace twenty superintendents and thirty-five subordinates. In the 'Stables' were sixty superintendents and sixty subordinates.

In the case of the Acropolis too it is interesting to contrast the administrative reality given by the texts with the planning reality given by the archaeology. Too little has yet been excavated of Royal Palace G for a general interpretation of it to be possible. But the building undoubtedly has not the organic structure of a single, unified, comprehensive palace building. Evidently it was only one of the official residential buildings of the Ebla Acropolis, with a well-defined role, and did not, as was already normal in Mesopotamia from the Proto-dynastic Period onward, discharge all the functions of government.

It seems probable that the staff listed in this document both for the Lower City and for the Acropolis is to be understood as the total of employees engaged in the management of the city wards and the day-to-day business of the palace buildings, in the precise sense of clerks of a properly local, that is, municipal, administration. The larger number of officials and clerks, however, mentioned in the other document, enumerating the staff of the é-MI+ŚITA^{ki}, should be understood as a comprehensive total of employees of the whole state administration.

If it is undoubtedly difficult, and perhaps altogether impossible, to indicate the boundaries of what could be called the State of Ebla, it is also probable that the territorial limits, in the political thinking of the time, would have been much less important than is generally supposed. For this reason it seems more opportune, at least provisionally, to consider the form of control which Ebla exercised over its territories. In this assessment it at once appears that the political instruments operated by the government of Ebla were quite sophisticated. In the first place, there was a form of direct control exercised over non-distant regions. Here the cities must have been in complete subordination to Ebla, being governed by an u g u l a, that is, a 'prefect', often a 'king's son' or a 'judge', at any rate a high dignitary of Ebla. This was the case with a series of minor centres, pre-eminent among them Armi, which as we have seen may have been Aleppo, perhaps the first city in the kingdom after Ebla. In several texts the governor of Armi appears in first place among the high officials of the kingdom itself, immediately after the members of the royal family. Moreover if the equivalence of the two titles u g u l and l u g a l, which seems typical of the Ebla chancellery, extended also to the administration of the cities, we should have to infer that in some cases this title was borne also by governors

of far distant cities of importance. Thus Shura-Damu bore the title
l u g a l of Mari. But this may be because the local title for 'king' at
Mari was in fact the traditional Mesopotamian title of l u g a l and not
e n as at Ebla, and it was only Enna-Dagan who some years before
Shura-Damu had assumed the title of e n of Mari on the Eblaite model.
So perhaps when Shura-Damu reverted to the title l u g a l of Mari it
was in conscious deference to local tradition.

In the second place, there was a particular form of strict though
indirect subordination imposed when, probably in consequence of
military campaigns, as in the case of Mari in the time of Ar-Ennum, a
dignitary of Ebla assumed the title of 'king' of a city which evidently had
a culture and traditions different from those of Ebla. There are traces in
the Archives of other cases of e n of cities in which the king's proper
name is followed by an indication of his degree of kinship with the king
of Ebla. It is thus possible that this was government practice limited to
those cases in which a regime of strict subordination was imposed on a
defeated territory.

In the third place, a regime of indirect subordination, based on
juridical rather than political grounds, was that of cities also fairly
distant, and apparently completely independent, ruled by local
e n, but bound to Ebla by treaties. This was the case with Assur and
perhaps with Hama. In such cases the tangible expression of partial
subordination was probably the payment of a tribute. This may have
been the case with Kanesh in Anatolia, which would explain the formula used by the scribes of the chancellery of Ebla for a list of cities,
including Kanesh, 'cities which are in the hand of the king of Ebla'.

6. Aspects of religious Life

The State Archive texts on the whole, being in the great majority
essentially administrative documents, do not deal with the city's
religious life. Nevertheless, there is information of great value on the
religion of the Mardikh IIB1 period to be derived from a number of
particular tablets of the Hall of Archives L.2769 and also from the
documents taken all together. The information is all the more important for referring to markedly different levels of religious feeling. First,
definite light is thrown on the official religion and its regular cult by
some few lists of offerings to the deities of Ebla by the king and the
court. Secondly, there are the beginnings of an insight into the religion
of educated people in the literary texts included among the lexical or
more generally instructional tablets from the northern rack of the Main
Archives, among which some myths are to be found. Thirdly, aspects of
popular religious feeling, or at any rate reflections of a more personal

religion are brought to light by the abundance of proper names of the period, representing the generations, five at least, to which the texts belong.

The Ebla pantheon was markedly polytheist. Some five hundred divinities are mentioned in the texts. The principal god of the city seems to have been Dagan. His name appears also under the formula 'Lord of the Land', an appellation which in Mesopotamia is traditional for Enlil and the deities equivalent to him. Actually it seems that the abbreviation 'Lord' to indicate Dagan was even more frequent at Ebla than the proper name of the god. Certainly many forms of Dagan were worshipped there, and these must have been the local gods of definite major cities. Thus in the list of offerings we have 'Dagan of Tuttul', 'Dagan of Bulanu', 'Dagan of Irim', 'Dagan of Sumad', 'Dagan of Ziwidu'. It is very difficult to interpret the name Dagan *kananaum*, which has been taken to mean 'Dagan of Canaan'. But there are phonetic difficulties in the way of this suggestion which must be explained before it can be considered. Quite frequent in the texts is a particularly interesting formula which it seems can be indifferently substituted for Dagan. This is the appellation 'lord of the gods', or as an alternative 'lord of the stars'. All this goes to show that Dagan was regarded as head of the Ebla pantheon.

Other important deities were Rasap, who in later tradition usually appears as Resheph; Sipish, corresponding to the Ugaritic Shapash; Eshtar, a very important goddess; Ada, the equivalent of Adad; and Kamish, certainly an archaic form of Kemosh. Lesser but well-attested deities were Ashtartu and Ashera, who several centuries later were to become two great goddesses of the coastal city pantheon; Malik, whose particular nature must have had something to do with royalty; and Kashalu, corresponding probably to Kathir of Ugaritic documents.

The peculiar attributes of the deities of Ebla are difficult to deduce from the evidence of the Archives, in the very nature of the texts. They can only be very broadly indicated on the basis of contemporary Mesopotamian documentation and comparison with later cultures of Syria. Nevertheless there are some important indications from the correspondences between Eblaite and Sumerian deities in the bilingual vocabularies of the Archive Room L.2769. Some of these are deceptive because purely phonetic, as with the great Sumerian god Enlil whose Eblaite equivalent is Illilu. But most of these 'translations' are illuminating and confirm the interpretations based on tradition. Thus Rasap is defined as equivalent to Nerga, the god of war and pestilence, and Sipish to Utu, the sun god.

The role of Dagan, whose traditional equivalent in Mesopotamia is the great Enlil, though he is related also to An, is difficult to define exactly. In Mesopotamia, from the beginning of the documentary evidence, in the Akkadian era, he is presented as a typical god of the Euphrates cities, from Terqa to Tuttul, and later he seems to have been worshipped especially at Puzrish-Dagan during the Third Dynasty of Ur and at Isin in the time of the Amorite dynasty from Mari. It is very probable that he was a great vegetation god, and his physiognomy is probably to be related to the aspect of the corn god known in more recent times. His role as the greatest chthonian deity of the North Mesopotamian and North Syrian areas may be the original reason for his having been equated with Enlil.

Of the other major deities, Eshtar was probably a typical great goddess and mother goddess, which would explain her equivalence with the Sumerian Inanna in the bilingual vocabularies of Ebla. Sipish is simply the North-West Semitic form, and probably archaic at that, of Shamash, and is certainly the sun god. Rasap is an atmospheric god connected with war and pestilence and therefore with the underworld. It is possible also that he has aspects, no doubt secondary, typical of a storm god. These are exclusively aspects of the great North Syrian storm god, Ada, already well attested at Ebla, though not yet in a role of pre-eminence. Ada was probably also considered at Ebla as son of Dagan, an identification attested for the North Mesopotamian area as early as the Old Babylonian era.

In the sphere of personal religion an important part seems to have been played by Damu, a divinity not much mentioned in the lists of offerings but very conspicuous in the sphere of personal names, especially in the circle of the royal family at the end of the Ebla dynasty. His presence is so overwhelming among the personal names that it might well be suggested that Damu had some specific link with the dynasty of Ibrium. Perhaps he was the dynastic god or simply the personal god of Ibrium and Ibbi-Sipish. In any case the very character of Damu specially lends itself to a position of this kind. In a Mesopotamian context he appears as a divinity connected with health and medicine and for that reason also with magic and exorcism. Moreover Damu, who in Mesopotamia was the son of Nininsina, appears in the Mesopotamian lists and in cult in close connection with Dumuzi, which shows his relations with the underworld, and with the goddess Gula, one of the most ancient Mesopotamian deities of birth. It is also interesting to note that, while Dagan does not appear very much in proper names, other gods, like Ada, whose role may have emerged into importance only in the Mature Protosyrian Period, or like Malik, for his probable relations with royalty, seem much less rare in court and chancellery circles of Ebla in the time of the Archives.

As for cult, the most detailed indications can be gleaned from the lists of offerings. These are extensive documents which enumerate the offerings, mostly animal, to the gods, always against the names of the donors, that is the king, the queen, the princes, other members of the royal family, and high dignitaries of the city. They are monthly accounts of offerings to the city divinities, and generally list the donors in order of rank. There are not many references to the organisation of cult. Those there are occur in administrative Archive texts and describe the categories of priests or temples of particular deities. Thus we learn that besides the temples of Dagan, Rasap, Eshtar, and Kamish, there were also at Ebla temples or perhaps chapels for the cult of gods of other cities, as was the case with the temple of 'Dagan of Sumad'. In the Archive texts, besides the offers of animals, drinks and bread for the deities, to be regarded as daily or at any rate ordinary ritual, there are records of dedications of objects of great value, mostly offerings from the Palace, or more frequently deliveries of a certain quantity of precious material, mostly gold or silver, for the production of furniture or votive objects of great value. For instance, ten minas of silver for a statue of Dagan *kananaum*, of nine minas and thirty-six shekels of silver for a chariot with two wheels for Dagan of Tuttul, or an unspecified quantity of gold for the decoration of a table and for a gold vase, gifts of Ibrium, for Dagan of Tuttul.

The literary Archive texts, among which are some quite long myths, fragments of hymns, and exorcisms, offer cultivated versions of two different levels of religious feeling. The exorcisms for example against harmful animals preserve in the canonical forms of a literary kind a level of very ancient traditional and popular belief, while the myths seem to be the fruit of theological speculation by an educated priesthood, at least in the versions that have come down to us. Both genres are of course Sumerian in origin but the most interesting point at Ebla is that the leading characters in the myths are Sumerian great gods rather than Eblaite, from Enki to Enlil, from Utu to Inanna. This indicates that in Mature Protosyrian Ebla a North-West Semitic literary tradition had not yet been formed to build up mythical cycles around the great figures of the local pantheon. The myths recorded at Ebla are translations into Eblaite of Sumerian myths.

Our findings are thus often extremely sketchy. They tend to give an undoubtedly compressed image of the religious life of the city. Yet even in the sphere of religion these Archive documents do constitute an extraordinary revelation. From a previous condition of almost total obscurity they bring our knowledge of this most ancient North-West Semitic culture up to a level of documentary parity, more or less, with the contemporary Mesopotamian world of the Dynasty of Akkad.

6
The Eblaite Culture and the Foundations of Artistic and Architectural Civilisation in Prehellenistic Syria

Any attempt to assess the historical development of a Syrian culture before the Hellenistic Age has until recently come up against one great difficulty. There was no concrete evidence, except in fragmentary form, from the centres of that culture. The exploration of one of the major cities of the Archaic Old Syrian Period, which was also the capital city of Yamhad during the Mature Old Syrian Period, is still impossible as it lies buried beneath the modern city of Aleppo. Of yet earlier cultures in the Syrian area, back through the third millennium, very little is known. The systematic exploration of Tell Mardikh and the rediscovery of Ebla has changed this picture. The decisive phases, if not the actual formative ones, of city civilisation in North Syria are the very ones on which we are now best informed. Some new information of a very partial kind about the first centuries of the second millennium has come in recently from other sites, but Ebla is at present unique in complementing these and in providing a solid historical foundation for elucidating the continuity of cultures in Syria.

Hitherto the cultures of the Early Bronze Age in Syria were known only from soundings, not often very extensive, and in any case only of stratigraphic value, of Hama, Ugarit, and sites in the Amuq. For the Middle Bronze nothing is known of the fundamental centre Aleppo and almost nothing of the other cities of some political importance, from Carchemish to Qatna. Also serious is the almost total lack of information for this period of the places situated on the Euphrates highway, from Terqa to Tuttul to Emar. For the Late Bronze Ages, the Middle Syrian centre of Aleppo is also completely unknown. So especially is that of Carchemish, seat of a Hittite viceroy over the Syrian domains of the Great King of Hattusas. Very little again is known, among the seats of Egyptian governors, of Simira, while some facts are beginning to trickle in about Qumidi. Finally, for the Iron Age, though the state of the evidence is already quite impressive, we must remember that we are denied any direct information about the greatest of the Aramaean kingdoms, Damascus, while too little is yet known of Arpad, the capital of the second kingdom in the region, Bit Agushi — always supposing that Arpad has been correctly identified with Tell Rifaat.

Thus though the culture of Protosyrian and Old Syrian Ebla is beginning to emerge with features of some richness and complexity, its exact place in history is undoubtedly still hard to assess. The surrounding background picture is still too shadowy and characterised by often tenacious prejudices in historical considerations. It will be possible to fill the gaps only by an intensive programme of combined research. But it still seems desirable to indicate now the areas in which our new knowledge about Protosyrian and Old Syrian Ebla has significantly contributed to an understanding of the complex problems of the origin, formation, and development of the artistic and architectural culture of Syria.

1. The art of Protosyrian Ebla and the Early Dynastic culture of Mesopotamia

Within the chronology of Mardikh IIB1 the relative datings of the Court of Audience of Royal Palace G, which is all we yet know of Mature Protosyrian architecture, and the assemblage of figurative works found in the rubble of the destroyed Palace do not necessarily correspond. The Court itself must in all probability have been built for special needs of prestige at the beginning of the succession of kings documented by the Archives, which as we know were found in the rooms under one of the colonnades of the Court. Its date would therefore be in the first years of Mardikh IIB1, probably in the time of King Igrish-Khalam of Ebla. Among the figurative works a relative dating within the span of Mardikh IIB1 can be suggested with some confidence for the Palace seals known from impressions surviving on bullae found in the Palace store rooms. Among the cylinders of which we have been able to reconstruct the figurative patterns almost completely, there are three with the names of officials, Reina-Ada and Iptura, known from Archive documents as dignitaries of Ibbi-Sipish, the last king of Ebla. We may undoubtedly suppose that these cylinders, in use during the last years of Mardikh IIB1, were carved during the reign of Ibbi-Sipish himself. When we come to the wooden carvings, there is nothing to tell us when in the Mardikh IIB1 period they were made. The extraordinary value of the furniture to which they belonged would only suggest that having once been made and taken into the Palace they may well have been kept there a long time. But it is certainly possible that they were made during one of the last two reigns of the dynasty, that is, in the second half of the Mardikh IIB1 period. It is even more difficult to determine the age of the remains of composite sculpture. The surviving fragments are in too bad a condition to be dated on their own and there are no other indications whether they belonged to the beginning or end of the period. All we can say is that the intrinsic value of all these objects was such as to make it likely that some of them had been kept for that as well as for artistic reasons. In any case it is clear that within the span of Mardikh IIB1 no particular date can be suggested for any of them.

Having assigned relative datings to the Court and its art treasures, though in necessarily vague terms, the fundamental problem remains of relating these to the art work of the Protodynastic Period and the age of Akkad in Mesopotamia. Clearly this requires that the absolute chronology of Mardikh IIB1 must first be determined. As I have repeatedly indicated, the dating suggested and adopted for Royal Palace G of Ebla at this stage is c. 2400–2250 B.C., based on a comprehensive assessment of the evidence, archaeological and epigraphic, so far available. A comparison with the evidence from written Mesopotamian sources suggests that Mardikh IIB1 with the five kings vouched for by the Archives corresponded with the last fifty or sixty years of the Early Dynastic Period and the first three reigns of the Dynasty of Akkad up to the early years of Naram-Sin of Akkad. The major difficulty about this estimate is palaeographic, since the documents of the Ebla Archives do have some archaising tendencies. But these tendencies do not all point one way. The Ebla texts have some palaeographic features in common also with the latest Early Dynastic texts and the early phases of the Akkadian, in any case earlier than Naram-Sin. So it seems probable that the archaising tendencies are due to Ebla's remoteness from the major centres of Sumer and Akkad.

Until final readings of the Archive documents have provided conclusive evidence of absolute chronology, no possibility of dating them should be neglected. There seem then to be three suppositions for consideration regarding the destruction of Royal Palace G, since all the evidence combines to rule out any date later than Naram-Sin of Akkad.

The suppositions are: first, that the Palace was destroyed by an unknown king late in the Early Dynastic Period of Mesopotamia; secondly, that it was destroyed by Sargon of Akkad; thirdly, that it was destroyed by Naram-Sin of Akkad. Taking the evidence all together, there is almost nothing to be said for the first supposition, which can therefore be rejected. The second cannot be completely ruled out but is exceedingly improbable in the light of the archaeological evidence. The third is far the most likely. Not only is it clearly indicated by the general archaeological horizon of Mardikh IIB1, but it also agrees very well with a series of topographical and stratigraphical features of the occupation history of Tell Mardikh. It is moreover in keeping with the most satisfactory chronological interpretation of the references to Ebla by Mesopotamian written sources together with the general archaeological evidence of the expansion of Akkad in Western Asia. Finally, certain palaeographical objections lose their force when we remember that the Ebla documents must have a span of 150 years, and that the remote geographical situation of Tell Mardikh may have been responsible for some backwardness in the evolution of its written tradition.

The artistic civilisation of Protosyrian Ebla must be differently assessed according to which of the last two suppositions we choose. In absolute terms the choice between the destruction of Royal Palace G by Sargon or by Naram-Sin, a difference of about fifty years, may seem inconsiderable. But the problem of Ebla's relations with the Early Dynastic culture of Mesopotamia takes on a very different aspect in either case. It is the role of Ebla and Syria in face of this Akkadian culture which must be analysed.

Architecturally Royal Palace G has not yet been explored completely enough to make a full assessment possible. But it is so far clear that it is a unique monument not only of the architecture of Near Western Asia in the third millennium as a whole, but also of the architectural tradition of Syria. A real judgment must await better knowledge of its ground plan and structure. But some general features which can be considered peculiar to this palace building are already apparent. In the first place the Palace of Ebla is not the realisation of a single project but the result of a series of works which must have slowly and progressively shaped the appearance of the administrative and residential area of the Acropolis. In the second place this absence of a thoroughgoing pre-established design is connected with a tendency of the Palace architects to adapt their building developments to the irregularities of the Acropolis terrain due to the piling up of the ruins of earlier settlements. In the third place the Palace seems to have been built up from specialised units separating and isolating different administrative functions without reference to a predetermined plan.

From these considerations it seems clear that the Protosyrian architects of Ebla were largely strangers to the Mesopotamian tradition of organic planning on a linear method, such as we already see operating in the most ancient Early Dynastic palace buildings of Kish. Similarly Protosyrian taste seems not to favour the employment of identical solutions of spatial problems for different functional needs. The use of standard treatments regardless of circumstance which remains characteristic of Mesopotamian architecture even after the Early Dynastic Period is not found at Ebla. Instead, by contrast with the unifying and levelling activities of Mesopotamian Early Dynastic architects, the attitudes of Protosyrian architects were more strongly rooted in history, owing to their respect for the environments in which their work was placed. Yet this sense of the pre-existing environment, at least in the Palace of Ebla, does not have a stultifying effect but is simply an original way of confronting the past with the demands of a new personal taste, and without any idea of annihilating the evidence of the past.

The design of the Court of Audience is exemplary in this sense. It is conceived with specific functional and representational needs in view, as a central node not only for the Palace area but very probably for the whole pattern of the city. There is a meeting of meanings and values in this open square, external to the Palace proper and backed by a panoramic vista of its great colonnaded façades. The variety of different doorways opening on the Court shows without any doubt that the Palace area of the Acropolis extended into the private residential area of the Lower City. The demands of political ostentation were met with splendour by these Palace façades. They were not only the back-cloth for the piazza scene but joined up the separate buildings of the Acropolis into one administrative and residential complex.

At Ebla the internal quarters of the Palaces seem to have been differentiated into places of varying rank, emphasised by occasional upper levels or storeys. Here was another element of contrast with the massive uniformity of Mesopotamian Early Dynastic and Akkadian Palaces and their linear development of repeated rooms centred round courtyards. In the Palaces of Kish and the Store Palace of Tell Brak, and still more conspicuously in the Old Palace of Assur, of uncertain date, the Mesopotamian palace was already a closed architectural organism. It was based on a repetition of fixed ground-plan elements, and its unity in isolation from the rest of the settlement was emphasised by perimeter walls usually entered only by a single passage. The Mesopotamian palace is by definition self-sufficient, an interruption in the city texture clustering thickly around it. In Protosyrian Ebla by contrast even the presence of the Acropolis, which could easily have been employed to break the city texture, has been interpreted in such a way as to recreate a general homogeneity of the whole settlement. Elements which could almost have been fated to become breaking points have been turned into hinges of attachment.

Of the figurative culture of Mature Protosyrian Ebla the wooden carvings, the cylinder sealings, the remains of small sculpture and the fragments of inlay already give a very suggestive picture of contacts between Ebla and the Early Dynastic and Akkadian world. The seal work and the inlays of Mature Protosyrian Ebla not only bear obvious signs of Mesopotamian inspiration, but in their function and subject matter closely resemble similar work of that period in Mesopotamia. As we have seen in the preceding pages, a number of figurative elements in the seal work are undoubtedly Protosyrian inventions and some of these, like the goddess dominating the wild animals, profoundly affect the figurative meaning of the friezes. But the very manner of understanding the cylinder as a vehicle of artistic expression in a definite religious sphere, and indeed the grammar of this whole figurative language are indubitably Early Dynastic Mesopotamian. In a similar fashion the inlays have functions and contents identical with those of Early Dynastic Mesopotamia in its later phases, although here too the narrative methods of representing the activities of war reveal an attitude which is, without much doubt, specifically Protosyrian. Events are shown in evolution, in contrast with the Old Sumerian practice of illustrating with figures only the effects of the destinies established on high, with the calm and solemn rhythms of triumphal processions.

The remains of small sculpture give a rather different picture. Here the techniques, characterised by the use of several materials, seem to reflect the Mesopotamian experiments in the principles of composite work, but the plentiful use of wood is a peculiarly Protosyrian adaptation. The concrete applications of this principle in Syria, which must have its historical roots in the composite works of the Jemdet Nasr Period, take some remarkably original forms at Ebla. We need only recall the precious plaques, perhaps of votive character, with figures in tufted wool costumes. In these very special reliefs, such as the bull-man figurine, the iconography is clearly derived from Early Dynastic Mesopotamia. In such cases there can be no doubt that Mesopotamian models existed or, even more likely perhaps, that some at least of the Eblaite workshops were so thoroughly impregnated with Early Dynastic imagery in its later phase that its themes were in constant use there.

The carved furniture with openwork decoration must be a speciality of Eblaite craftsmanship, probably altogether unknown in Early Dynastic Mesopotamia. It does seem possible, however, that this craftsmanship in wood at Ebla was sometimes associated with ivory work, such as we do know in Mesopotamia from Assur to Mari. But in the case of the wood carvings we have a typically Protosyrian technique used to create splendid furniture of exquisite artistic richness. Here the subjects are indeed partly derived from Early Dynastic Mesopotamia, but the formulae according to which the scenes are composed, with combats between heroic or mythical beings and wild animals interspersed with battle subjects of soldiers transfixing one another, are Protosyrian inventions. Again, those composite designs in which attacks of wild animals on grazing cattle are naturalistically rendered seem not to depend on Mesopotamian traditions. By contrast the giving of a human look to animal figures does seem a typically Old Sumerian idea. The single combats of warriors are harder to assess. They appear alien to the Early Dynastic tradition, but indisputably close to the heroic ideas of the Akkad Dynasty, with its esteem for the individual and his works, so far removed from the Old Sumerian mentality.

There is thus an undoubted connection between the artistic culture of

Mature Protosyrian Ebla and Early Dynastic Mesopotamia. Speaking technically, and iconographically, it seems possible to define this connection by saying roundly that Ebla formed part of the last phase of the Early Dynastic world, or rather took part in it. It did so in the most significant aspects of its artistic expression, so that they seem actually to depend on that Early Dynastic tradition. The earliest chronological references seem in no case to go back beyond the so-called Early Dynastic Period IIIB of Mesopotamia, in the phase defined as the First Dynasty of Ur. This is the case with the inlays found out of context and, in the final phases of the period, the seal work. In the general conception of their figurative designs these last must be regarded as very close to the Mesopotamian seals of the so-called 'Mesanepada and Lugalanda phase', though even so there must clearly have been at Ebla a local Palace workshop with a court style of its own. The remains of small sculpture still reflect advanced phases of the First Dynasty of Ur, up to the early experiments of the age of Akkad, and it is also to this period that the wooden carvings correspond.

The most complicated problem in the assessment of the art works discovered in the ruins of Royal Palace G concerns their style. The fragments of small sculpture and the inlays so far found are too scanty to justify any opinion but the wooden carvings and the cylinder sealings have a great deal more to say.

Formally speaking, the carvings reveal a sober and vigorous sculptural taste. The tense modulations of the faces, framed with fine, tight curls, are punctiliously rendered, without recourse to purely decorative formulae. In the thick precise textures of the flounced costumes the body masses show clearly through the network of fine shading. In the animal bodies too and the wild beasts' manes and fur there is a naturalistic feeling for line. It is all strictly concrete, without abstract geometry of outline. A lively interest in the individual seems to characterise this Mature Protosyrian art. In places, clearly, the quality is uneven, indicative of experiments leading up to mature achievement. In some of the fragments the bodies of naked heroes or the torsos of warriors are rather roughly drawn. In remains of bull-man figures these ancient mythical images may become conventionally evocative and stereotyped.

But in the full, severe modelling of the faces of the carved figures the naturalism of this art comes into its own. In this formal conception there are undoubted resemblances with the synthetic naturalism of this great art of Akkad, as it first begins to appear with the reign of Manishtusu and is fully realised in Naram-Sin's time. It is often said that a real artistic revolution occurred during the reign of Sargon of Akkad and the foundation of his Semitic dynasty. Or again, on the contrary, it is said that in Akkadian sculpture the fruitful search for naturalism launched during the Early Dynastic III Period reached fulfilment. Yet it was only in the time of Manishtusu that, on the basis of a new ideology in which the individual was regarded as the protagonist in human actions, even though the religious atmosphere perhaps was not profoundly changed, a new conception of space was put forward as a historically real place where earthly events occur. Perhaps the fundamental transition from the analytic naturalism of the Sumerian sculpture of the Early Dynastic III Period to the synthetic naturalism of the Royal School of Akkad had already begun in the time of Rimush. But the dating of many significant but fragmentary Akkadian works is still too uncertain. What is sure, at least from such evidence as we have, is that even in a straightforward line of development there is a gap between the meticulous productions of the Sumerian artists of the individual city workshops and those of the masters of the school of Akkad. The Sumerians had shattered the whole geometric unity of the works in 'Mesilim style' based on the delineation of volumes by rigid planes and straight lines, while those of Akkad working in depth instead of at the surface, liked to treat the human body as an organic unit rather than as a bundle of disjointed elements.

For the wide range of results achieved in the sphere of artistic expression and the novelty of the conceptions on which the quest to achieve them was based, Akkadian art is certainly revolutionary. But the roots of this revolution are still obscure. In the material from Mature Protosyrian Ebla there is not yet any monument which in point of sheer invention could challenge comparison with the great Akkadian masterpieces of Naram-Sin's time. But undoubtedly the Eblaite wood carvings of Royal Palace G in their line of formal search do come very close to the work of the masters of the royal workshop of Akkad. It is difficult to be sure about the historical connections that may have existed between the workshops of the Protosyrian Eblaite craftsmen and the school of Akkadian artists. But undoubtedly they must have been connected, if not by direct relations between their leading members, then by a general community of interests. In the first case, though we obviously cannot be specific, we can imagine movements of artists from the Akkad country to the Ebla country or the reverse. These may have occurred as a result of contacts already existing between the two areas. The references to Kish, infrequent though they are, and even if the mention of Akkad itself should not be confirmed, are sure evidence of such contacts. But still closer relations may have resulted from the destruction of Ebla, assuming that it was definitely Naram-Sin of Akkad who captured the Palace. If so, it must be supposed that after the Mardikh IIB1 phase Ebla had entered into such intimate and continuous relations with the Mesopotamian world as to share naturally in the latest tendencies of Akkadian artistic civilisation.

This last suggestion, however, might conflict with the evidence both of Eblaite seal work, which really cannot be considered as a provincial offshoot of the Akkadian, and of the other minor art work from Palace G. These in combination with local techniques which only remotely derive from Mesopotamia suggest that the Early Dynastic experiments, on reaching Ebla, may have been worked out there in an original way.

But the fundamental core of this whole problem of relations between the two artistic cultures is obviously the determination of a chronology for Royal Palace G. Of the two possible solutions, if we take the high dating, according to which Sargon was responsible for the destruction of the Palace, then it is obvious that the art of Mature Protosyrian Ebla must have been one of the most decisive sources of inspiration for the formation of the Akkadian style in the late second and the third generation of Akkad. If however we take the low dating, the more probable one, according to which it was Naram-Sin of Akkad who conquered and destroyed Palace G, it seems clear that however rich or original Ebla's own figurative ideas may have been, its formal experiments were parallel with those of contemporary Akkad. The first assumption, which would make Ebla the fulcrum of the Akkadian artistic revolution, is undoubtedly too bold in the present state of our knowledge. It would be anti-historical, contrary to a picture of general cultural development which in the light of the Ebla discoveries themselves must be correct in many points and cannot in any case be completely overthrown. The second assumption recognizes the complete historical actuality of the art of Ebla and singles out in it points of stylistic ferment which fully correspond to the tendencies of the time, and agree with the primary political and economic role of Ebla.

This then is how the artistic civilisation of Mature Protosyrian Ebla should be historically viewed. It was the collective expression of a refined culture, in no sense provincial or remote compared with the Early Dynastic or Akkadian worlds. Deeply rooted in the Old Sumerian culture of the Late Protohistoric Period and under its direct influence, it went its own way in the succeeding Early Dynastic Period and elaborated independently of Sumer special architectural and artistic modes and forms in correspondence with its own social development. But such independence lasting through the whole first half of the third millennium B.C. did not mean isolation. The architecture and art of Royal Palace G, while manifesting expressions of a peculiarly Syrian higher culture, distinct from the contemporary Mesopotamian culture, shared in a more general unity which still had its great traditional centres in the cities of Sumer and Akkad.

2. The Old Syrian architecture of Ebla and the tradition of Aramaean Syria

The architecture of Mardikh IIIA-B is exemplary and typical of a great city of the Old Syrian period. All the tendencies of architectural expression of Middle Bronze Age Syria meet in an original language of taste with its own range of technical elements in Old Syrian Ebla. In discussing the wonderful architectural and artistic remains of the Protosyrian culture of Ebla we found that the city's undoubted independence was only to be understood as rooted in an initial unity. The same developments, in Mesopotamia and Syria, of the Early Dynastic and Protosyrian cultures respectively, tended despite ever increasing differentiation to preserve their mutual ties. There must have been a constant circulation of experiences. In the Old Syrian world, by contrast, it is impossible to speak of any kind of artistic unity between Mesopotamia, Syria and Anatolia. And yet there is good evidence for the relations between different areas of Western Asia, at least here and there. We have only to recall the Old Assyrian trading operations in Cappadocia and the frequent contacts between Syria and Mesopotamia in the time of Shamshi-Adad I of Assyria and Hammurabi of Babylon. But in the specific field of architecture in fact the Mesopotamian and Syrian worlds were now quite distinct. Old Babylonian Mesopotamia went on elaborating the classical Neo-Sumerian conceptions with a complex spatial vision already apparent in some of the restorations to the precinct of Nanna at Ur and, after that, above all in the Tell Rimah temple in Assyria. In Syria and Palestine, however, we can by now distinguish without difficulty a realm of architecture effectively 'Western' and independent of Mesopotamia.

The earthwork fortifications of Ebla are perhaps the most imposing example of a type of city wall, well attested and much discussed, known to archaeological literature as 'Hyksos'. It was so called in consequence of having first been noted in a dubious Egyptian example which was exactly of the Hyksos age, and then frequently observed in cities, even minor ones, of the so-called 'Hyksos culture' of Palestine, during the Middle Bronze IIB-C period of this southern area, dated from 1750 to 1580 or 1550 B.C. This city wall consisted of ramparts dressed with plaster to protect the core of beaten earth from the elements and with stone (at least at the base to begin with) to contain the mass of soil and make it more difficult to scale. It was certainly characteristic of the cities of Syria and Palestine in the Middle Bronze Age. The origin of this kind of fortification, the exact purpose and function of which has been much discussed, has been interpreted in several ways. It has been maintained that it was, in Palestine, an innovation of Middle Bronze IIB-C, probably Northern in origin, that is from the North Syrian area, where the same type seems to have appeared at the same time. Against this, very recently, it has been held that the rampart of the Palestine area was to be regarded simply as a natural local development of the city wall of the Early Bronze Age and that its presumed appearance at the same time also in the north was nothing but a secondary chronological development.

But, disregarding doubtful cases where in unexcavated sites there is no convincing evidence of date, as with Tell Safinat Nuah, it is a fact that several important tells of Northern Syria had fortifications like these during the Middle Bronze on a particularly grand scale. It was certainly the case with Qatna to the south and Carchemish to the north, to name only two of the big cities in which owing to their large surface area the circuit of ramparts on the surface remains very obvious. But in many small cities the same defensive system must have been used. The date of the ramparts of Ebla, which, as we have seen, must have been erected about 1950 B.C., is a sure indication that fortifications of this type were characteristic of the first emergence of the great urban culture of the Archaic Old Syrian Period.

It must have been particularly in the great traditional centres of Upper Syria that the Old Syrian culture established itself, Qatna, Ebla, Aleppo, Carchemish, perhaps Emar and Tuttul. It was in these larger cities, first probably under the leadership of Ebla, then almost certainly under that of Aleppo and Carchemish, that the great artistic civilisation of the Mature Old Syrian culture developed. The intensive exploration of the Palestine area has revealed also many lesser sites of the Middle Bronze Age, apart from the very few great cities like Hazor in Galilee which could rival those of North Syria in cultural importance. In these, by a process still difficult to be sure about in detail, from 1850 B.C. onward or a little earlier, began the spread of a culture very close to that already flourishing in Upper Syria not many years after the catastrophe which overwhelmed the Protosyrian civilisation. This movement towards a substantial unity of culture in the Syro-Palestinian area of the Old Syrian Period is the context in which the use of ramparts in city perimeters must be viewed. The phenomenon itself still needs detailed study of its local features and occasional backward spots. Undoubtedly these typically colossal perimeters were characteristic of the town planning of the cities of Northern Syria from the Archaic Old Syrian Period onward. With technical improvements, which have been noted especially from the fringes of the Palestine area in the Middle Bronze IIC phase (revetments entirely of stone for instance), they remained a highly typical element of the Old Syrian cities of the Syro-Palestinian area, until the destruction of the northern cities by the Old Hittite kings and of the southern cities by the first pharaohs of the XVIIIth Dynasty.

The religious architecture of Old Syrian Ebla with its single-chambered temples was characterised by the independence and unity of the sacred building. The temples were isolated in the city fabric by open spaces all round them. The massiveness of their main external walls themselves rigidly emphasised their compactness. The sheer volume of solid material in the sanctuaries of Ebla was a distinctive feature of Old Syrian architecture. Though examples are not yet known from North Syria as it has been so little explored archaeologically, there is nevertheless evidence in the Palestine region for the most recent phase of the Old Syrian Period. Two late monumental versions of the temple type of Middle Bronze II derived from this Old Syrian tradition are the so-called 'Temple-Fortress' of Tell Balata (the ancient Sikem) and Temple 2048 of Megiddo VII. In both these buildings the problem of access to the sacred precinct, in some way unsolved in the archaic temples of Ebla, finds a coherent solution in the arrangement of two towers standing out as buttresses from the façade. In conformity with the Old Syrian vision of the solid unity of the architectural structure, these buttress-towers neither break nor modify the compactness of the mass of masonry. In the same search for solidarity one of the temples of Hazor, in Phase 3, attributed to the years around 1700 B.C., has the antae of the façade thickened.

The typological design of Great Temple D of the Acropolis of Ebla is conceived according to the three fundamental principles: tripartite division of internal space, axial arrangement of ground-plan units, and long main axis of the principal chamber of the cella. Although razed to the foundations, it is possible that one of the Byblos temples, the so-called 'Syrian Temple', or 'Building II', may have been constructed on a very similar plan. The interpretation of the foundation traces of 'Building II' is still controversial, but it is possible that it consisted of an axial succession of vestibule, antecella, and cella, the cella almost square and flanked by two long side chambers. If we disregard these 'aisies' as an innovation peculiar to Byblos, such a construction would be remarkably similar to the Great Temple D of Ebla: the constant width of the three axial chambers, about 7.50 metres; the transverse main axis of vestibule and antecella, both equally 'narrow' on this view; the thickness (about 2 metres) of the main external walls, identical with that of the internal cross walls; the long main axis of the probably better lit cella contrasting with the narrowness and probable obscurity of the antecella.

It is also possible that the tripartite, axial structure of Great Temple D of Tell Mardikh was a standard type of palace sanctuary. That this was in some way characteristic, though not exclusively so, of the great sacred buildings connected with palace residences in Old Syria may be indicated by the remarkable Temple of Alalakh VII. This has the cella placed crosswise and the antecella broad and not very deep, and may thus be a special version of the axially and longitudinally tripartite temple which was later to be more completely realised on this same site, at the Alalakh IV level. The preference accorded in the same architectural sphere of the Old Syrian culture, and after that again in the Middle Syrian, to a cella developed sometimes in length and sometimes in breadth, however it is regarded from the point of view of its use of internal space, is a phenomenon which cannot yet be convincingly assigned to a definite period or environment. Neverthelesss, there is an organic coherence of architectural vision fundamental to all the sanctuaries of Old Syrian Ebla — Great Temple D, Temple B1, Temple N, and the possible Temple C. It indicates clearly that any choice between the two types most widespread in Syria and Palestine had nothing to do with the Assyrian preference for a long cella or the standardisation of the broad cella in Babylonian temples. Indeed, both the Assyrian temples and the complex temple buildings of Southern Mesopotamia were completely different from the Old Syrian in their use of space and far from the traditions of Syria altogether. The former long preserved the Archaic tradition of entrance at the side rather than axially from the front, while the latter took over from the Neo-Sumerian culture the architectural plan based on a central courtyard.

The singular ground plan of Sanctuary B2, if we are correct in supposing that it was related to a particular function of the building rather than to be understood simply as a 'house' of a deity, must be regarded historically as an example of a rare aspect of sacred architecture in Syria. Some features, like the presence of a court of entrance and a probable second courtyard behind the central cella, might suggest some similarity with Mesopotamian temples of the Babylonian type. But these are only marginally and obliquely echoed in Syria, and there is not in the Ebla Sanctuary a single precise point of reference to the Old Babylonian sanctuaries, which were indeed pivoted on a courtyard but uncompromisingly axial in their symmetry. Sanctuary B2 has no axis of symmetry. On the contrary, several independent pathways could be followed inside the building owing to an arrangement of spaces which was the negation of the rational, linear Old Babylonian planning method. If any rule can be discovered in this sanctuary of Sector B of Tell Mardikh it consists certainly of the courtyard surrounded by long chambers of rectangular ground plan and small chambers of square ground plan. This type of scheme, based on a courtyard with rooms placed all round it and no main axis, seems to be basic also to the Temple on the Amman citadel and the so-called Double Temple of Hazor. Thus it seems very probable that Sanctuary B2 of Ebla is not an isolated building but is to be placed at the beginning of an Old Syrian tradition productive also in the Palestine area. Here it gave rise to buildings of the Mature Old Syrian Period which some centuries later (though still in the Late Bronze Age) were taken as models but with interesting innovations, such as the doubling of the ground plan.

The technique of the North Wing of Royal Palace E, with its packed core walls and diminutive orthostats, is typical of the Palace of Alalakh VII and that of Tilmen Hüyük, which must be regarded as two minor residential palaces of the Mature Old Syrian Period. The exploration of Royal Palace E is not far enough advanced for much to be said about the plan of the building. There is no doubt, however, that it must have been far more elaborate and complicated than the two minor palaces of North-West Syria just mentioned. It is possible that the Syrian architects had a feeling for placing their rooms to exploit the features and existing structures of a site which gave free play to particular solutions of problems in the individual centres of power in the Old Syrian cities, but did not lead to the establishment of fixed canons for residential palaces. In these perhaps the elementary plans of the simplest private houses merely repeated themselves on a larger scale and in multiple units.

Indeed a scheme of this type has been followed in the North Wing of the Old Syrian Palace of Ebla. The houses of Sector B, although inserted in a particularly uneven area of the Lower City, are centred on a courtyard preceded by a vestibule and followed by two rooms opening on the side of the courtyard opposite the entrance, and are exactly similar to contemporary houses at Kültepe, the ancient Kanesh in Anatolia. There are enlargements of this elementary scheme both in some houses of the same sector of Mardikh IIIB and at Alalakh VII, with rooms arranged on two or three sides of the courtyard, sometimes up to a total of five or six. The simplest type seems characteristic of the Old Syrian Period, while the extensions of the ground plan, already in evidence in Late Old Syrian Ebla, spread more widely in the Middle Syrian Period. The correspondences between Ebla and Kanesh suggest something more than mere contacts, perhaps some sort of unity between the North Syrian and Central Anatolia areas and this may have been responsible for a number of elements common to the seal work of the two regions. It is probable that in the Old Syrian Period the political and commercial situation favoured the spread of some common features in parts of the Syro-Anatolian area, and that the great North Syrian cities played a very active part in this spread. During the Middle Syrian Period, by contrast, a greater regional differentiation took place, until finally the political events of the beginning of Late Bronze II brought the Hittites to the domination of North Syria, from the Euphrates to the sea.

One of the most imposing monuments of Old Syrian Ebla, the South-West Gate, is conceived on a ground plan very characteristic of the Middle Bronze Age in North Syria. Matched only by the North-West Gate, it must have been the main city entrance of the Old Syrian city. Its central core consisted of a massive building with ground plan *à tenaille*, finished with orthostats on the east side, and fortified with a high square tower. The general defensive scheme, based on a long straight passageway leading axially through two successive gates, which has been realised so imposingly in the Ebla Gate, is identical with that of one of the gates of Alalakh VII. There is an exactly similar gate also at Qatna, and another at Carchemish which may go back to the Old Syrian Period. As we have already seen in discussing the ramparts of the city perimeter, this type of city entrance too is well attested in Middle Bronze II Palestine, at Sikem, Megiddo, and at Gezer.

It is interesting that in all the Old Syrian city gates not only the general ground plan, but also the general size of the complex of structures and the relative proportions of the different parts of the building show very precise similarities from one city to another. Thus we have a fixed typology standardised in all its elements, and there must have been rigid rules for its application, dictated no doubt by strategical requirements. Thus the South-West Gate of Ebla is fortified on the east side, that is, to the right of anyone entering the city. Similarly the North-West Gate must have been fortified on the west side, also to the right of anyone entering, as would be suggested by the fact that the north-western extremity of the ramparts emerges on to the open country. It was no doubt a rule that the best fortified section of the city gates should be that to the right of anyone entering the city, the right of the besiegers and left of the defence being notoriously the weakest against incursions from outside.

Obviously we cannot yet say that the city gates of Mardikh IIIA played any special part in the creation of this monumental type. But there is no doubt that the South-West Gate of Old Syrian Ebla was one of the earliest of the whole Period because the first paving attested there belongs to Middle Bronze I and thus to the Archaic phase of the Old Syrian culture, when also the political importance of Ebla in North Syria must have been at its height. Nor is there any evidence to indicate that the ground plan *à tenaille* of the Old Syrian gate is based on Protosyrian models. It has not yet been possible to explore the perimeter and the gates of Mardikh IIB1-2. Nor have any fortifications of Protosyrian cities yet been brought to light during regular excavations. There are some indications that since the Protosyrian fortifications must have been turreted perimeter walls with bastions emerging at regular intervals, the gates cannot have been extended in very great depth. Very probably the emphatic lengthening, or extension in depth, of the Old Syrian city gates *à tenaille* must be connected with the massive thickness of the great beaten earth ramparts, which made it necessary to lengthen and strengthen the defences along the axis of the gates.

Yet there can be no doubt that Middle Bronze Age Ebla does share a common architectural tradition with the Syrian and Palestine area. This is apparent not only in some aspects of the architectural culture of Mardikh IIIA-B but from all its monuments taken together. The points of correspondence are many. We have seen how exact and close they are between Ebla and Alalakh both in the simpler kinds of building and in the more important monumental styles. There are similarities also of settlement structure and of some major monuments linking Ebla, Carchemish, and Qatna. (In these last two cities, however, the archaeological exploration of Middle Bronze levels, though certainly of great importance, has not gone very far.) Lesser cities, like Tilmen Hüyük, are closely related with these major ones but again the limited amount of excavation done gives a rather limited impression of the relations. The other great city of the Middle Bronze Age with which Ebla has precise and extensive affinities is undoubtedly Hazor to the south, in the North Palestine area. Those with Kanesh, in central Anatolia, are confined to particular sectors, and with Byblos, on the Mediterranean coast, rather limited.

Taking this evidence altogether, fragmentary as it still is, we have an evident picture of a unified Old Syrian architectural ambience. Contrary to the usual view of the Old Syrian world's indebtedness first to Egypt — the Middle Kingdom — and then to Old Babylonian Mesopotamia, from Mardikh IIIA-B we now have unequivocal evidence that in architecture at least the Old Syrian culture was independent. Its unity still needs definition within geographical limits, and it is still poorly documented, but in this field, as in its other artistic manifestations, the Old Syrian culture expressed a political situation in keeping with the emergence of the Amorite dynasties over the whole Syrian area.

In the early (Archaic Old Syrian) phases this culture must have had one of its creative centres in Ebla, when there must have been more intensive relations with Anatolia owing to the lively activity of the Old Assyrian trading colonies. When Ebla began to decline in consequence of the hegemony of Aleppo, established by the kingdom of Yamhad in the time of Shamshi-Adad I, the lead must have been taken by Aleppo and Carchemish in carrying on the artistic experiments initiated by the workshops of Ebla. It is certain that even some minor kingdoms of the northern area, undoubtedly in the Aleppo sphere of predominance, such as Alalakh and Tuba, contributed to the development of the Mature Old Syrian culture in the time of Yamhad hegemony. It is thus probable that this more advanced phase of the Middle Bronze Age saw a spread of the Old Syrian culture.

The process in Syria was perhaps parallel to that in Mesopotamia, with the multiplication of Amorite principalities during the time of the

Isin and Larsa dynasties. In Syria as in Mesopotamia there was some
sort of crisis in the development of city civilisation. It led, towards the
end of the Archaic Old Syrian Period, to an intensification of settlement in the North Syrian area and an extension of the Old Syrian
culture to border regions. It must have been in consequence of this that
the Old Syrian architectural tradition escapes total dispersion after the
Old Hittite destructions in the northern regions and the New Egyptian
destructions in the southern. In the great upheavals of the Middle
Syrian Period over the great plain of Northern Syria many important
cities suffered the fate of Ebla and were never rebuilt. Yet in the border
regions of this central area even the few Middle Syrian settlements so
far excavated had clearly retained the classical Old Syrian architectural
tradition. Thus in the Euphrates area, at Emar, at Tell Fray, and at Tell
Mumbaqat, in the Late Bronze II temples, there was an obvious
persistence of the longitudinal, axial, and sometimes tripartite conception of the sacred building. At Tell Fray, it is true, there were also
important Middle Assyrian influences deriving from the particular
political position of this city on the frontier between the Hittite and
Assyrian spheres of influence. Several northern cities of the Palestine
area, from Hazor to Sikem and Megiddo, in the Late Bronze Age were
renewing the buildings of Middle Bronze IIB-C with alterations
especially to the façades and the proportional width of the rooms, so as
to adapt them to new functional and aesthetic needs.

Certainly during the Middle Syrian Period, in the panorama of
architectural achievements of the Syrian area, there must have been
innovations which were perhaps not in the direct line of development of
the Old Syrian tradition. A typical problem of this kind is that of the
origin of the so called *bit hilani* which has been convincingly
recognised in the palace buildings of Alalakh IV and Ugarit. There is no
doubt that in the Aramaean age there was a regular standardisation of
this ground plan, which had not even been hinted at in the palaces of
Ugarit and Alalakh. There had indeed been a specialised use of the
porch there but only in relation to a definite arrangement of the ground
plan. It is also true that in the Old Syrian world there are no obvious
forerunners of the Middle Syrian types. A gallery in the Palace of
Alalakh VII in fact merely demonstrates that the use of columns was
customary in Old Syrian architecture. There is no connection with the
bit hilani. But undoubtedly the scenic taste for colonnaded
elevations and side screens in Royal Palace G of Protosyrian Ebla, even
though in the context of a different architectural vision, does reveal a
sensitivity to problems exactly of the *bit hilani* order.

By the beginning of the first millennium B.C., in the Aramaean age,
we have architectural evidence of sufficient range and from a wide
enough selection of important cities to attempt some critical discussion

of the origins of the tradition on which the architecture is based. This is all the more needed because the usual perfunctory scheme of values is so unsatisfactory. It sees in the development of the so-called 'Neo-Hittite' culture a succession of two or three phases, in which the supposed original inspiration of the Anatolian monuments of the imperial Hittite age is gradually overlaid by Neo-Assyrian influences. Even in terms of 'Neo-Hittite' artistic civilisation this line of reasoning is weak enough. Many of the features attributed to Assyrian influence are simply stylistic, of no particular artistic significance but merely a fashion of the day. They have no application to the architectural reality of Aramaean Syria. The only monuments there of Assyrian character are those built by the Assyrians themselves in the period following the Assyrian conquest, whether at Tell Halaf, Arslan Tash, or Tell Ahmar.

In fact, the North Syrian architecture of the Aramaean age clearly expresses a profoundly unitary architectural culture. It must have been formed historically, the mature result of a complex process, not of a meeting or superposition of heterogeneous influences. Its origins must go right back to the Protosyrian age and its formation carry the authentic stamp of the Old Syrian. It is possible, as I have hinted and as Palace G at Ebla suggests, that Syrian architecture was addicted to colonnades and galleries from the start, with appropriate differences from one period to the next. In this same Protosyrian culture the complex of the palace buildings would then be the forerunner of a circular city plan with the complex of palace buildings at its centre. The remarkable regularity of the circular city of Samal would then derive from an illustrious and very ancient tradition, going back to Protosyrian Ebla with its concept of the city as a world in miniature, a microcosm.

The axial structure, the longitudinal development and the tripartite division of space are definite elements of sacred buildings in the Aramaean age. The Temple of Tell Taynat exhibits these characters in the form closest to Old Syrian models. Then, also in the same area of the Amuq, there is a probable temple at Tell Judaida and a more doubtful example from the citadel of Hama. Moreover the Tell Taynat building is certainly a palace temple like Great Temple D at Ebla. Thus in the Syria of the first millennium B.C. all the spatial features most typical of the Old Syrian sanctuaries are still preserved, revealing a continuity of architectural tradition which cannot be limited to particular types of building method. Nor did the great Old Syrian tradition have followers only in Aramaean Syria. There can be no doubt that Solomon's temple at Jerusalem, which also is a palace sanctuary, derives from these models of the classical Old Syrian Period.

Similar considerations apply to the city gates in Aramaean Syria, though here there are possibilities that the tradition's line of descent is less straight. The standard type has two axial compartments developed laterally. Yet the earliest examples. like the 'Fountain Gate' of Tell Halaf, are extended longitudinally, while in one of the gates of Samal we find the arrangement of defence extended in depth with two gateways, one advanced and a courtyard dividing it from the inner gateway. In both these cases there are evident similarities with the city gates *à tenaille* of Old Syrian architecture and the South-West Gate of Mardikh IIIA-B. But it is also clear that the same ground plan of the Aramaean gates with two axial compartments and development in breadth is itself a natural evolution from the ancient Old Syrian type. The need for longitudinal extension, due to the massive thickness of the enceinte with ramparts, becomes less pressing with the return to curtain fortifications of masonry. The reduction of the enceinte thickness must involve a corresponding reduction in the thickness of the buttresses separating the compartments, which must undoubtedly also have occurred in the Middle Syrian Period.

The exact relationship between the Protosyrian and Old Syrian cultures in architecture cannot yet be determined from the Ebla evidence. Ebla does, however, provide some indications of the links connecting the earliest tradition, and certainly the Old Syrian experience as a whole, with the architecture of the Aramaean age. The Old Syrian tradition can thus be taken as a classical point of reference for the historical development of architecture in this area, the internal unity of which we are now able to understand.

3. The artistic civilisation of Ebla and the problem of the transmission of the Syrian figurative legacy

Considered in the most general framework of events in the ancient Near East the history of Ebla can be represented schematically so as to take account of the peculiar features of the individual periods, in three major phases.

The first, of which we have as yet no concrete evidence, goes from the Late Protohistoric Period to the end of the Early Protosyrian Period, extending through the obscure period of Final Mardikh I and Mardikh IIA. The second, which corresponds with Mardikh IIB1-2, is the age of the Mature and Late Protosyrian Period, of the great Ebla of the State Archives. The third, attested by the city of Mardikh IIIA-B, extends throughout the Archaic and Mature Old Syrian Periods. The first phase we identify as the period of formation of the city culture of North Syria. The second phase represents the great flowering of the Protosyrian culture. The third phase sees the progressive affirmation of the Old Syrian culture.

After its contacts, probably intensive, during the Late Protohistoric Period with the culture of Uruk, around 3000 B.C., Ebla became one of the centres of the North Syrian area in which the Protosyrian culture was formed. It is probable that Ebla did not assume a position of importance among the western cities until the later phases of the Early Protosyrian Period, around 2500 B.C. and almost certain that these cities up to that time were of small economic and political power. During the whole of this phase the small, perhaps only sparsely distributed, western cities must have kept up essentially commercial relations with Sumer and Akkad, the cultural influence of which must have been considerable. In the compass of artistic achievement the Mesopotamian techniques and genres of the Mature Early Dynastic Period, that is mostly of Early Dynastic IIIA and B, provided the means of expression for a predominantly Syrian ideology and style.

What Royal Palace G of Mardikh IIB1 reveals, during the first part of the second phase just referred to, is the full flowering of this Protosyrian culture. It was a splendid maturity, in parallel with that of Early Dynastic Mesopotamia, and reaching a peak of political power in the Ebla first of Ar-Ennum and then of Ibbi-Sipish. It may have been the emergence of Ebla in Northern Syria that first prompted some of the great kings of Sumer and Akkad to take an actual military interest in the more westerly of the Sumero-Akkadian cities. This was the case with Eannatum of Lagash, who, after taking some powerful northern cities such as Kish and Akshak, conquered Mari. By the end of the Early Dynastic Period warlike intervention in the West had become a necessity no longer to be postponed, as when Lugalzagesi of Uruk boasted of having pacified and made safe the roads 'from the Lower Sea to the Upper Sea'. But in the earlier period, after the expedition of Eannatum of Lagash along the Euphrates, followed, it seems, by the victory of Enshakushanna of Uruk over Inbi-Ishtar of Kish and the sack of Kish, Ebla developed its trade and its hegemony both together, in a time of expansion begun probably by the reign of Igrish-Khalam.

Deeply affected by the Sumerian culture, Ebla in this Mature Protosyrian Period borrowed its forms from Early Dynastic Mesopotamia. But the content was its own and it seems to have worked out in substantial independence the methods of expressing it. The originality of planning and architectural vision of the city that resulted was matched by the output of Ebla's workshops seeking their own formal solutions and taking part in the most fruitful artistic experiments of the time. Scanty though the evidence of Mature Protosyrian art still is, we can say that this was the phase in which a native store of images must have been formed, which was not the endless process of borrowing figurative themes from abroad so long imagined by scholars.

Of course such a tradition and such a heritage cannot have been built in entire independence from the Mesopotamian world. On the contrary, as we have seen, the Ebla environment was vigorously adapting the stock of Early Dynastic iconographic themes to its own religious use. This adaptation no doubt involved changes in the meanings originally attached to the individual images. But the most interesting aspect for us of the whole process is that it did in fact go back to the Protosyrian period.

In this sense the case of the bull-man standing frontally is very significant. This figure is an Early Dynastic invention regularly included in the chains of figures on cylinder seal friezes in the Mesilim period. This mythical being was adopted in the figurative parts of the Palace seals of Mardikh IIB1 with a function similar to that known from Mesopotamian seals. But the context of meanings was more explicit in Syria than in Mesopotamia. In the Protodynastic seal work there are no divine figures to whose sphere these nature spirits must be assigned. But in the Protosyrian it is evident that both the traditional bull-man figures and also the male and female figures belong to the retinue of the great goddess of nature, ruler of wild animals and protectress of flocks and herds. The Early Dynastic seals, it seems, seek to represent a world of mysterious and indefinite forces animating wild nature, in face of which humanity must establish the order preordained by the gods. But the friezes of the Mature Protosyrian seals evidently illustrate the rule of the Great Mother and her control over the natural world. In passing from one to the other it is clear that a rationalisation has taken place.

It was certainly from the Protosyrian seals that the figure of the bull-man was later taken over on to the cult basins of the Archaic Old Syrian Period. In at least two of these the bull-man appears like a guardian image over the ritual banquets which were their principal theme. His significance may have changed with time. On the basins perhaps he may still have figured as being connected with the fertility of nature, which it was probably the function of the ritual banquets to ensure. But the bull-men confonting one another in pairs on the four faces of a basalt base in Temple N must have had a different meaning. Already on Akkadian seals the bull-men have really become retainers of Shamash, the great sun god particularly venerated at the time of the Akkad dynasty. They see to the opening of the gates of heaven at dawn and cause the sun to rise from the mountains of the east. The presence of the two bull-men flanking the base of Temple N, which incidentally was the only temple of Mardikh IIIA-B with its entry to the east, indicates that at Ebla too, in the last years of the Archaic Old Syrian Period or at the beginning of the Mature phase, this being had a specific relationship with the sun god.

The bull-man figure, rare in Mature Old Syrian seal work, reappears in the 'Neo-Hittite' monumental art, above all at Carchemish but also in lesser cities such as Karatepe. From the Aramaean age onward their function as guardian spirits, custodians of the sun's celestial residence, became standardised. The occurrence of the theme in 'Neo-Hittite' reliefs is therefore not due to a constant repetition in the course of history of influences from Mesopotamia on North Syrian workshops, but simply the transfer into Protosyrian culture of elements from the Early Dynastic figurative legacy. So the history of these elements is that of the changes in meaning and modifications of the theme in the cultures of Syria. The question why these images appeared at definite moments of artistic history in Syria is not answered by putting it down to external influences. It is simply one aspect of the history of figurative tradition in Syria.

One creation of the Protosyrian repertory which does not derive from the Early Dynastic world but has found its way into the Palace seal friezes of Mardikh IIB1 because of its affinity with other composite figures of nature spirits is the lion-headed hero. This image too, a very rare one, was passed on from the Protosyrian repertoire to the Old Syrian. There again it was used in contexts with wild animals, as for instance on the side of the limestone basin of Great Temple D of Mardikh IIIA and in a very few sealings of about 1700 B.C.

This same basin, however, also carries examples of iconography which did originate in Early Dynastic Mesopotamia but which reached the Old Syrian culture only by way of its Protosyrian ancestor. This must be the case with the composition on the principal face of the basin, with a banquet scene in the upper register and passing flocks in the lower. This has exact precedents in Early Dynastic seals from Ur, just as the composite dragon on the side of the same monument is an innovation clearly from the Akkadian repertoire. The first, the two registers with banquets and flocks, must be of Mesopotamian origin, since it is also well attested on Early Dynastic votive plaques. It must refer to a rite of an important ceremony connected with fertility cults. As for the second, the dragon spouting jets of fertilising water, from the very fact that apparently it is an innovation from Akkad and has some connection with a dyad of great storm-raising deities indicates that neither monster nor dyad are original creations of the Akkadian artist. Rather, it suggests that the Akkadian seal carvers had absorbed in Mesopotamia a mythical image which had been transplanted there from the West. Probably it was linked with the iconography of Dagan and Ishtar in some part of the north-west Semitic area between Tuttul and Ebla. The status of this iconography in the Protosyrian Period is still unknown. But both these images, the banquet with the flocks and the dragon, must have reached the Archaic Old Syrian culture through the legacy of the Mature Protosyrian world. This is clear enough from yet another figure, again on the limestone basin of Mardikh IIIA, the naked hero with curled locks and radiate beard.

The Mature Protosyrian Period thus appears to have been the formative age for the artistic tradition of Syria, to judge merely from the limited direct evidence and such other indications as there are. In the establishment of this tradition the part played by Ebla must have been fundamental. In Ebla it must have been the Court workshops with their craftsmen which were responsible for creating or adopting the images subsequently transmitted to later cultures of Northern Syria. The destruction of Royal Palace G and the annihilation for the time being at least of the political power of Ebla need not have meant the loss of this legacy of images. There need be no surprise that this did not happen in Ebla itself. As we have seen there was no serious break in cultural development in consequence of the destruction of Mardikh IIB1. Whether Ebla, apart from the almost certain loss of political power indicated by the inscription of Gudea of Lagash, continued to play a leading part in cultural elaboration we do not know. Certainly it remained a very important city in the Late Protosyrian Period. It may even be that the culture of Mardikh IIB2 spread still more widely in the North Syrian interior than in the past and it is possible therefore that in this final phase, just because of its political fragmentation, cultural growth was less intense but more widely diffused.

What must be clearly emphasised is that the Late Protosyrian Period was still an age of great cultural prosperity and intensive urbanisation in the North Syrian area. Connected perhaps with the increase in city civilisation during this phase is the reappearance of fragments of goblets of 'Painted Simple Ware' as far as Palmyra. Sherds of this same pottery have been found very recently in the city area of Aleppo itself. The crisis of the Protosyrian culture was caused at Ebla by the destruction of Mardikh IIB2, to be dated about 2000 B.C. But nothing is known of the circumstances which caused this crisis. The coincidence, broad enough, but most probably not casual, between this date, which must be somewhere between 2050 and 1950 B.C., and the collapse of the Neo-Sumerian monarchy, the end of the Third Dynasty of Ur and the capture and sack of Ur itself, suggests that the two events were due to not dissimilar causes.

Though it is a pure supposition, it seems probable that the origin of the collapse which overwhelmed the Late Protosyrian culture was in disorders created by Amorites in the Protosyrian social texture. The Amorites are already mentioned as such in the texts of the Mardikh IIB1 State Archives, at the same time as in the inscriptions of the last kings of Akkad. And it may be significant that apart from a peculiar type of 'Amorite dagger' this ethnic designation is used for one or more settlements. This would indicate on the one hand that for the people of

Ebla Amurru was also a place name, and on the other that the Eblaites knew of Amorites established in settlements and also of typical products of their craftsmanship in metal work. The Neo-Sumerian texts show an ever-increasing presence of Amorites employed as a labour force during the Third Dynasty of Ur. Thus it is possible that a similar pressure was slowly applied inside the Syrian organs of state in the last two centuries of the second millennium B.C. There may thus have occurred a disintegration of the economic and social bases of the Late Protosyrian kingdoms which finally caused the destruction of the centres of the ancient culture. And the destruction of Mardikh IIB2 does indeed mark the end of the Protosyrian culture.

In the total lack of written documentation, we may hazard a supposition that even though other forces, as happened in Ur, may have occasioned the actual destruction of Ebla, it was the upheavals provoked by the Amorites which started the internal crisis and may have caused the collapse of the Protosyrian culture. It is also probable that, as certainly happened in the West, at least to Byblos late in the Old Assyrian Period, and as is documented by the diplomatic archives of Mari for Aleppo, Carchemish, Qatna, and Hazor in the years around 1800 B.C., in Ebla too the Amorites played a leading part in the reconstruction and were the creators the Old Syrian culture.

The culture of Middle Bronze I-II in inland Syria must in fact have been the product of a profoundly changed economic and social situation. This is reflected in the material culture of Mardikh IIIA and Hama H which was radically innovatory towards the past. Never the less several elements of continuity can be observed in the transition from Mardikh IIB2 to Mardikh IIIA. The general city pattern was preserved. On the perimeter of the ancient curtain of the city walls the great rampart was erected according to a new technique introduced probably by the new rulers. The sites of the ancient gates were preserved and new city gates built there, sometimes monumental, on models which were probably innovations. The temples for the most part were built on the same foundations as the ancient sanctuaries. Royal Palace E was rebuilt on the thick rubble deposits which probably covered the remains of the Palace of Mardikh IIB2. The perimeter, probably circular, of the ancient brickwork city walls was altered to an approximately straight-line figure, so that the girdle of ramparts took on a vaguely trapezoidal outline. On the intellectual assumptions of the circular perimeter of Protosyrian Ebla were imposed the strategic needs of Old Syrian Ebla.

The greater importance attached to the South-West and North-West Gates is also probably to be seen as an important innovation. The monumental aspect assumed by the two western gates in the Old Syrian Period suggests that the city, more than in the preceding centuries, was gravitating towards a south-north axis of privileged communications, of which the poles would have been in Aleppo and Carchemish to the north and Qatna and perhaps already Damascus in the south. In Early Bronze IV A-B by contrast it is very probable that the main city gate was the North-East Gate, the one from which the road must have set out towards the great loop in the Euphrates and towards Mesopotamia.

The evidences of continuity in the transition from the Protosyrian to the Old Syrian culture are thus of two kinds, those based on the city planning of Ebla, and those suggested by the persistence of the Protosyrian artistic legacy in the art of the age of the Amorite dynasties. A continuity between the two great cultures of Ebla may thus be asserted. But it is still a question on what level it operated. As with the indications from planning, religion and iconography we may suppose there were other cultivated features of the Protosyrian civil order which were not so much rejected by the Amorite environment of the Old Syrian Period as reinterpreted and sometimes even distorted by the prevailing new values. Something of Protosyrian Ebla was thus saved and, with whatever reconsideration, absorbed by the Old Syrian culture of the Middle Bronze Age and handed on to the latest cultures of Pre-Hellenistic Syria. But what happened then, whether the Old Syrian legacy was handed on in its turn, this is a fascinating subject for Syrian archaeology to which Tell Mardikh is unable to contribute. It can only be illuminated by an intensification of research in the North Syrian area.

7

The Significance of Tell Mardikh-Ebla for the History of Civilisation in the Ancient Near East

As has been repeatedly and authoritatively stated, the rediscovery of the Protosyrian culture of Ebla through the systematic archaeological exploration of Tell Mardikh is revolutionising our historical knowledge of Western Asia in the third millennium B.C. Ideas hitherto firmly accepted about the most ancient development of urban civilisation in the Near East are being radically changed. The sensational aspects of the discovery of Royal Palace G of Protosyrian Ebla are now well known. Its architectural remains survive to an imposing height, and its State Archive, in sheer numbers of tablets found, rivals the most celebrated epigraphic discoveries of the nineteenth century. But the question must now be put as to the real significance of these finds from a properly historical point of view. Obviously at any given point a complete estimate will not be possible. But as the studies develop, we may expect that the themes and problems arising from the archaeological and epigraphic material of Palace G will gradually deepen. In their present state we can only suggest those which seem most interesting for the moment in the light of the most recent discoveries by the University of Rome at Tell Mardikh. The subject matter is complex and a historical assessment of Ebla and its significance makes little or no sense if we pick out just a few aspects, apparently the most sensational, from the entire culture of the city at a definite period, or if we ignore the development of events over the whole span of its history.

1. Urban culture from Sumer to Ebla

In any account of the development of city civilisation in Western Asia from its historical beginnings, two different approaches may be used. It occurred, we may say first — and this is the line which is becoming more and more popular — independently in different regions because of like economic circumstances. Or secondly, the same causes may be regarded as having operated in socially distinct conditions and through different political institutions, almost contemporaneously in Mesopotamia and Egypt, with secondary diffusion effects in neighbouring areas. Whichever approach we choose, there is no doubt that in Sumer the growth of city civilisation was a historical process. Its actual coming about can be observed, so to speak, vertically in the stratigraphy of Uruk and horizontally in the territory of Uruk. The stratigraphic sequence in the sacred precinct of Eanna, which was completed for recent phases of the Protohistoric Period by that of the ziggurat of An, tells the story of the progress in technology and urban planning and, more comprehensively, of the corresponding cultural development that contributed to form an actual city of Uruk. A surface examination of the terrain identified Eanna and Kullab, the two centres from whose fusion Uruk emerged. It showed up the changes in lay-out of late prehistoric villages associated with their concentration into a city. In the decline and abandonment of many agricultural holdings it confirmed the characteristic changes in economic and social structure characteristic of the Proto-Urban phase.

In the formation of city civilisation it is clear that Uruk played a special part. It was at Uruk, in distinction from all other centres of Sumer, that urban development in early times happened. Uruk was the city where all the external aspects of urban organisation assumed their most distinctive forms. Again, it was at Uruk that, in response to the demands of an emerging civic administration, the cuneiform script was first developed. The urban phenomenon at Uruk was in fact so early in time, so complete in its achievements and so wide-ranging in its results as to make it probable that it functioned as a model in Sumer and even more probably also in Akkad. Here, as recent studies at Kish seem to show, this type of development may have occurred with some delay and in a different manner from that at Uruk in the transition from Proto-historic villages to a real city.

It was already apparent in the years before the Second World War that the Uruk culture had had a very marked capacity for expansion and that the influence of the Old Sumerian model of the late Protohistoric Period had been largely influential in the establishment of city culture all over the Near East. The themes represented in its architecture and the highly individual iconography of its seals in the Late Period of Uruk or the Jemdet Nasr Period were widely diffused, as far as late Pre-Dynastic and Early Dynastic Egypt. But until the world war years there was no real evidence of the routes actually followed by the Uruk culture in this expansion, with the sole exception of Tell Brak in the Khabur area. With its 'Eye Temple' of the Jemdet Nasr Period this site proved to have been a centre of Upper Mesopotamia, extraordinarily close in its cultural horizon to the larger contemporary cities of Sumer. It was still difficult to understand the true historical significance of this apparently isolated and far-flung 'out-station' of the Jemdet Nasr Period. The sole importance of its situation seemed to be that of a cross-roads between the area of Assyria, Anatolia, and North Syria. It is only in the most recent years that the puzzle has begun to resolve itself. For the first time we have precise and unequivocal evidence of the route and manner of diffusion of the Old Sumerian culture of the Protohistoric Period towards the north and west. It has come from the archaeological exploration of the single great city comprising the two

sites Habuba Kebira and Tell Kannas and the smaller settlement of
Jebel Aruda, in the Euphrates valley in the region of Lake Assad. Both
these centres in their architecture, in the imagery of their seals, and in
their pottery are so closely similar to the late Uruk culture that they can
only be considered as actual colonies of that culture in the Upper
Euphrates valley.

The very fact that in the region of Meskene we have well-attested
outposts of the Uruk culture allows us to bring into the full light of
history the difficult question of the origins of the Ebla civilisation. It
depends on the further question whether the Protosyrian culture of
Ebla contains traces of the Archaic Old Sumerian tradition of the Uruk
and Jemdet Nasr Periods, and this can only be answered if the foundation of the settlements of Habuba, Kannas and Aruda can be
correctly understood as evidence of the diffusion of the Uruk culture
northward from Sumer. All this must be deeply studied in the years to
come. It is, however, already certain that in the very institutions of
Mature Protosyrian Ebla there were elements not attributable to
influences or developments then recent, datable that is to the Early
Dynastic Period in Mesopotamia. On the contrary they relate to much
earlier and apparently close connections between the environment and
tradition of archaic Uruk and the culture of Ebla. The title of king of
Ebla, for instance, as we have seen, rendered in Eblaite by the West
Semitic term *m a l i k u m*, 'king', is regularly represented logographically by e n, 'lord'. And this is the most ancient Sumerian royal
title, which certainly had some connection with the dignity of the head
of the archaic community of Uruk and was undoubtedly also a traditional title of the Early Dynastic kings of Uruk. Moreover the title
e n was in common use to indicate also the kings of other cities. Thus in
the Ebla Archive texts the king of Mari is designated the e n of Mari,
while it is well known from contemporary inscriptions of Mari itself that
the king of Mari bore the title of lugal.

This apparently odd circumstance is of the greatest interest for the
problem of the origins of Ebla. It seems obviously to exclude a close tie
between Ebla and Uruk in Early Dynastic times, all the more so as the
same Archive documents seem not even to mention Uruk, except in
word lists. Doubtless it was too far south. But they do mention Kish,
which was the great centre of Akkad in the middle and late phases of the
Early Dynastic Period. It is therefore very probable that contacts
between Uruk and Ebla were of a very early date, perhaps going back
actually to the latter phase of the Uruk or even to the Jemdet Nasr
Periods. Evidence that these or something like them were the periods
of contact between Uruk and Ebla comes from cylinder seals. Alongside the splendid seals of court dignitaries constituting the majority of
those used in Royal Palace G there are some rarer seals with more

schematic designs and with figures recalling those of the Late Uruk or Jemdet Nasr Periods. For instance there is the personage with a long smooth bell-shaped skirt in a field of rather spaced out figures and large schematic animal or vegetable ornaments, but without trace of the banded frieze of figures typical of Early Dynastic work. It is very probable that cylinders of this kind were already ancient, having been kept in use for reasons we can only guess. They undoubtedly show an extraordinary familiarity with Archaic Old Sumerian themes. Another aspect of the artistic culture of Mature Protosyrian Ebla which as a tradition depends on the Mesopotamia of the Late Protohistoric Period is composite sculpture. This is known to us at Ebla from fragments of miniaturistic sculpture, but there are also remains of larger statuary. The complexity of technical structure in a wonderful fragment of a female headpiece, perhaps divine, and the fine workmanship of the plaited tresses indicate that this piece was an image of a goddess, no doubt of sumptuous richness in its original form and very near in its conception and composite structure to the celebrated Uruk head.

Thus if the points of kinship with the archaic world of Uruk enshrined in the traditions of Protosyrian Ebla are to be found both in its fundamental institutions and in its primary store of artistic imagery, it seems fair to guess that the growth of Ebla into a city originated in a graft of the great Archaic Old Sumerian culture either of the Uruk Period or more probably perhaps of the Jemdet Nasr on a stock of local village culture. It is thus possible that a real qualitative leap occurred in the Tell Mardikh settlement, probably in the years of the Jemdet Nasr period, about 3000 B.C. Then a further expansion westward must have occurred in those outposts of the Uruk culture already known to have existed for some decades on the Euphrates in the Meskene area. It is obviously impossible even to guess at the exact form taken by this expansion, though the most probable supposition is that just about 3000 B.C. there was a real penetration by Sumerian colonists. If so, it was very probably on a small scale, and in those regions east and south of Aleppo where the ecological conditions would be favourable to the development of urban centres on the models worked out in Sumer. Now that the cultural complex of Habuba, Kannas, and Aruda has turned out to be of such obviously Archaic Old Sumerian character as to leave no doubt either of its culture or even perhaps of its ethnic composition, it seems very probable that Tell Brak is to be interpreted as a frontier post of the same culture, founded perhaps to control the routes of penetration into Anatolia. In the same way it would not be strange if other urban centres, initially perhaps of more modest size, had also been planted in the North Syrian area. There need be no doubt of their economic significance in view of the need to secure access to those regions of Syria rich in timber.

The uniqueness of the geographical position of Tell Mardikh compared with the earliest city settlements of Mesopotamia is merely
apparent. The present-day aridity of the Ebla region is certainly not as
it was in antiquity. This needs further investigation, but we can already
say that the Tell Mardikh country, whose gently rolling landscape
hardly breaks the flat perspectives of the North Syrian plateau (about
400 metres above sea level), slopes insensibly towards the depression of
the ancient Madkh swamp. This small marshy basin, which was still full
of water at the beginning of this century but is today completely dried
up, was fed by the small river of Aleppo, the Nahr Quweyq. This too in
our day is almost completely dry, but once upon a time was assuredly of
far greater capacity, to judge from the Arab medieval geographer
who compared its flow, no doubt with some exaggeration, with the
Euphrates. The Nahr Quweyq spent itself in the Madkh basin, the
western banks of which were a little more than 10 kilometres from Tell
Mardikh.

The Madikh region was quite densely inhabited in the Early Bronze
Age, especially in its final phases, the remains of which have perhaps
partly hidden the debris of earlier occupations. This was established
beyond doubt through a surface exploration by members of the Tell
Mardikh Expedition. It seems likely that the Madkh swamp at the
beginning of the Protohistoric Period offered an environmental image
and an ecological situation not unlike that which originally induced the
inhabitants of the villages of the Uruk Period in Sumer to group
together in the first great city concentrations. This creative event, as we
know, was prompted essentially by the irrigated agriculture of the
marsh lands on the lower course of the Euphrates. The Madkh, though
more concentrated and on a smaller scale than the Euphrates marshes,
was perhaps not the only attraction of its kind. Other particularly fertile
swamp lands further west, such as the Ghab, the Rug, and to the north,
the Amuq, may have been settled for similar reasons. This is not to say,
of course, that in the subsequent development of the Protosyrian
culture during the third millennium these other centres played parts as
important as Ebla.

While some cities which had become important at least during the
Old Syrian Period, but also perhaps as early as the Late Protosyrian,
were situated on the shores of the Madkh marshes, Tell Mardikh arose
rather far from what even in ancient times must have been the banks of
the swamp. It is difficult to explain the distance, not at all insignificant,
of the Ebla site from the Madkh region. A variety of reasons can be
suggested for an apparently singular choice but the most likely seems
the dominant position of the tell in this rolling country. In that case the
decision would have been strategic. From the Tell Mardikh region it is
possible to control also the access to the Idlib region, which is rich in

mountain springs and today green with tree plantations, especially olives.

The strategic value of the Ebla site is very probably also emphasised by the very name of the city. Its etymology is undoubtedly difficult and can be variously interpreted. It does however seem very probable that the name Ebla in the West Semitic region both north and south means a site of rock emerging from a natural limestone hillock and gleaming white in the sun. At Tell Mardikh it is certain that the rock slab does rise under the ruins of the site towards the Acropolis, because at its foot, both north and west, the rock level is higher than that of the surrounding plain. It is thus very probable that the characteristic feature of the site where Ebla arose was a hillock of naked limestone caught by the sun's glare as it emerged from the rolling landscape of the North Syrian plateau.

2. Value and originality of the Eblaite culture of the third millennium

We have isolated those fundamental aspects of the artistic civilisation of Protosyrian Ebla which characterise its independence of the Early Dynastic Mesopotamian world. We have laid down the chronological limits between which original formative relations between Proto-historic Sumer and the Ebla region must be placed. We may be asked in what light the Tell Mardikh culture now appears, taking as a whole its known manifestations.

As a premise for any consideration of this kind it must be borne in mind that probably the very foundation of city civilisation in North Syria was due to the expansion of the Sumerian civilisation, or rather to the grafting of the higher city culture of Old Sumer on a local cultural stock of which too little is yet known for us to be able to say how it happened. But it is significant, by contrast with what has been observed in the Euphrates settlements of the Lake Assad region, that there is yet no trace, either at Tell Mardikh or in other sites of inland North Syria of a massive, organic presence of cultural elements attributable to the Mesopotamia of the Uruk Period. It is therefore probable that from the very beginnings of the phenomenon of urbanisation there was no real colonisation, even limited to a few centres. Rather, there was a process of adoption of individual features of the Old Sumerian culture and imitation of an extraordinarily attractive model of settlement. In the concrete reality of the phenomenon, the base of the population must have remained the local one and the society, while no doubt undergoing structural transformations, cannot have been sensibly altered in its composition by acquiring a number of technological features from outside.

The social composition of Mature Protosyrian Ebla at the outset of the second half of the third millennium was very homogeneous. It was substantially free of ethnic elements other than of local origin. The personal names of Ebla are for the most part characteristically North-West Semitic. They are clearly distinct, in a striking majority of cases, from contemporary Akkadian and Amorite names attested by documents of the Neosumerian Age some decades later. In the Ebla Archives themselves the names of persons from cities of Akkad, rare though they are, are easily identifiable as Akkadian, in evident contrast with the Eblaite names. The fact that the proper names of Protosyrian Ebla, at least in the Royal Palace G phase, are quite distinct from the Amorite names of Mesopotamia and Syria in the Old Babylonian Period is moreoever a clear indication that the ethnic base of the Protosyrian city culture was different from that which became dominant in the North Syrian area itself after 2000 B.C.

In the light of what has been said it seems a likely hypothesis that the Eblaite proper names in the Protosyrian Period were representative of the population established permanently in the city settlements. This must await verification, of course, by analytic study of the personal names occurring in the texts of the Ebla Archives, with reference to the origin, sometimes specified explicitly, of the individuals named. Personal names of Amorite type would then be typical of the semi-nomad groups which emerged towards the end of the third millennium and pressed so hard on the great state organisations of Mesopotamia and Syria as finally to break them up.

The North-West Semitic environment of the Ebla population is clearly revealed in the language of the city as used in the Archive texts. This can probably be regarded as typical of the linguistic type of the urban culture in the Syrian area in the second half of the third millennium. The copious occurrence in the State Archives of lexical lists, that is encyclopedic registers, in the Sumerian language is clear evidence of the importance of Sumerian in the culture of Ebla of the time as an educated, administrative, and literary language. No doubt this is due primarily to the fact that the system of writing used at Ebla was invented by the Sumerians for their own language, and that in this system many words were written logographically, by single word signs rather than by phonetic letter signs. This meant that to write a text in Eblaite it was necessary to be deeply versed in Sumerian. The knowledge of Sumerian must have been combined in Ebla court circles with an assimilation of the more important features of the Sumerian culture. This is confirmed by the literary Archive texts, which are probably translations into

Eblaite of Sumerian literary works of mythological character, or else local reworkings of Sumerian myths.

One very noteworthy contribution to the historical definition of the culture of Protosyrian Ebla is provided by what the Archives have to say about religion. The divinities of Ebla are typical of the Syrian environment. Several of the great gods and goddesses of the city of the Protosyrian Period remained principal deities of some of the remoter cultures of the West Semitic area in the first millennium B.C. This was the case with Dagan, the great god of Ebla, and of Kamish, one of the greatest gods of the city and protector of the important settlement of Carchemish, in the very name of which the god's name is enshrined. The great gods of Sumer were completely foreign to the religious feeling of Ebla. Both at official and private levels the cult was of local gods. Even the divine types had their own peculiar characters distinct from those of Mesopotamia, as we see in the peculiar iconography of the Mature Protosyrian palace seals. The great goddess who tamed the wild beasts and protected the flocks was a dominant figure of this typically North-West Semitic iconography and was to have a long and complicated history in the later traditions of Syria.

Thus what is affirmed by the language and proper names of Ebla is borne out also by the religion of the Mature Protosyrian culture. Ebla was steeped in the pre-Sargonic Old Sumerian culture but that of Ebla was neither mixed up nor confluent with it. It kept itself distinct with its own means of linguistic and religious expression. In both spheres the local component played an active part and the whole culture is seen to have evolved in historical independence though not in isolation. In language and religion the relations of the Protosyrian culture first with the Early Dynastic Old Sumerian and then with the Akkadian culture seem to have operated at a certain social level. It was the educated class of the palace bureaucracy which was so well versed in the Sumerian language. The members of the same class, though they sacrificed to the gods of Ebla, were formed intellectually on Eblaite versions of Old Sumerian myths.

We have seen that the very nature of the State Archives, with their essentially bookkeeping function, prevents them from giving exhaustive information about the political institutions of Ebla. The title used at Ebla for 'king', we noted, whether in a Sumerian logogram or in the corresponding Eblaite word, proves that the institution of kingship at Ebla, and indeed generally the whole Protosyrian culture, had an independent historical origin distinct from that of the Mesopotamian kingship. It is possible that, while in the Sumerian ideology the image of the king as 'vicar of god' was dominant, so that in the Akkadian tradition the kings of that Semitic dynasty were to assume the title of 'God of Akkad', in the culture of Ebla the figure of the king was fitted into a framework which had to accommodate also the 'fathers' or 'judges'. It therefore seems probable that at Ebla in the core of traditions animating their conception of kingship special weight was given to the idea of the tribal group. The terminology of tribal life, in an established urban civilisation, was transferred to the orbit of the city.

The very plan of the Protosyrian city, with its broad open space (the Court of Audience) outside the Acropolis, seems to refer to a social situation profoundly different from that of contemporary Mesopotamia. The rigid separation there observed between the political power that emanated from the gods and the business of daily life was here denied. The open conception of the Court as the central node of the city organisation undoubtedly points to a social and institutional reality more open and with more participation than in the Sumerian and Akkadian world, though it cannot yet be specified in greater detail. In Sumer and Akkad traditionally the Palace was indeed an emergent unit but was also closed and isolated from the city fabric.

In connection with Ebla's ideology of kingship an interesting suggestion can be made. We remember that Naram-Sin of Akkad was the first in Mesopotamian history to assume the title 'king of the four regions'. The reference was intended cosmologically rather than geographically, to the four quarters of the world rather than to four particular countries as it was later to be interpreted. There is no precedent for such a title in Mesopotamian tradition before Naram-Sin, and there are no allusions there to the quadripartite conception of the world. So it seems pertinent to ask whether precedents are to be found in the culture of Ebla, which was destroyed by Naram-Sin. In fact, they are. Two significant bits of evidence suggest that the quadripartite conception of the world was peculiarly native to Ebla. First, in the palace seals of Mardikh IIB1 there is that frequently recurring figure of the naked hero kneeling and supporting on his head with raised arms the circular symbol composed of four heads, two of lions, two of 'humans' or perhaps 'monkeys'. Secondly, in the topography of Protosyrian Ebla both the Archive texts and archaeological exploration show that the city was quadripartite, essentially subdivided into four quarters arranged approximately like the quadrants of a circle, with the Acropolis at its centre. The quadripartite symbol upheld by an Atlas figure is obviously of cosmic significance, and indeed the naked hero in Mesopotamian iconography is a follower of the god Enki, connected with the primordial waters and destined to raise up the earth. The regular division into four of the city inscribed in an approximately circular perimeter wall is connected with the notion of the city as microcosm, by which the image of the world is reflected in that of the city, understood as centre of the universe.

If the idea of the division of the world into four was really typical of the conception of Ebla, it would then be quite understandable that Naram-Sin, after the destruction of his great western rival, should have assumed the title of 'king of the four regions'. At one blow he would have appropriated from the Eblaite culture the concept foreign to the Mesopotamian world of the division of the cosmos into four, signified by it the re-gathering into one of the civilised world, and symbolised the universality of his political power, henceforth without a rival. While it seems certain from these considerations that Naram-Sin of Akkad got this cosmological idea from Ebla, it still has to be shown, however probable it may seem, that in assuming a title which was to be one of the most exalted in the long tradition of Mesopotamian kingship he was revenging himself on the universalistic ideology of power built up at Ebla. Obviously the Mesopotamian title has not been found in the Archive texts. But the fact that Ebla, the capital of the kingdom, was conceived as a microcosm and therefore as the centre of the universe, indicates that this universalistic ideology was a characteristic feature of the idea of royalty there.

We have already seen in the architectural achievements of Mardikh IIB1 the independent working out of a body of experience shared in common with Sumer, no doubt originally derived from there, and going back in time to the Late Protohistoric Period. The art of Ebla got the main part of its techniques and imagery from Mesopotamia. Its style reflects the tendencies of the earliest decades of the Akkadian age. But its works, in which we find Protosyrian and Old Sumerian themes side by side, are a refinement of local taste. In the architecture the peculiarly Eblaite vision is even more in evidence, and the Mesopotamian influences become seemingly less important in Protosyrian planning and design. Instead, the topographical conditions are interpreted functionally, and the Palace buildings are structured according to specific functional needs. Faceless schemes based on 'modules' are avoided, and the whole complex is unified, with typically panoramic effects, by monumental colonnaded elevations.

Taking the Protosyrian culture as a whole, two periods and two levels can be picked out at which Mesopotamian influence operated. In the first phase, during the Late Protohistoric Period, the influence must have been decisive. It stimulated the formation of the Protohistoric higher city culture in the North Syrian area, in regions ecologically similar to the marshlands of the Lower Euphrates. The legacy of these first intense and fertile contacts between the late North Syrian city culture and the Mesopotamian Protohistoric culture remained alive in the institutions and political organisation of Ebla, and in the preservation of certain artistic techniques. In the second phase, which probably had no salient features but lasted throughout the Protodynastic Period, contacts remained frequent. But the society and culture of Ebla being now fully formed in institutions, ideology and economic activities, their fundamental structure was no longer affected. The impact of Mesopotamia on the culture of Ebla was perhaps confined now to individual groups of people, at an educated level. It is possible also that in this second phase there were return influences of Ebla on Mesopotamia. The most important thing received by Ebla, at a point of time which cannot be definitely determined, was undoubtedly the cuneiform script. It was adopted almost certainly in the Early Dynastic Period, a gift from the Old Sumerian culture to the Protosyrian. The major return export, from Ebla to Akkad, must have concerned the notion of kingship as a cosmic thing built into the universe itself.

The fundamental value of the rediscovery of Ebla lies certainly in a realisation of the substantial independence of the Protosyrian culture, not in its origins but in its development. Independent in its institutional, ideological and economic structure, Ebla was the centre of the most ancient great culture of Western Asia yet to enter historical record. The written documents and archaeological remains from Ebla are so abundant in quantity and significant in quality as to give a complete picture of the city and its remarkable skill in building on the foundations of city civilisation from the Old Sumerian age.

The originality of the Protosyrian culture must be understood in terms of its time. Ebla was a centre of busy commercial activity. From its active relations with centres still more ancient, it was stimulated to absorb cultural elements from the Sumerian and Akkadian worlds. It thus participated in a larger historical unity, where local individualities not only remained intact but interacted mutually with others. In the panorama of cultures in Western Asia in the third millennium B.C. the position of Ebla must have been of extraordinary vitality and fundamental importance. Its contribution to the diffusion of urban civilisation in the Near East was undoubtedly exceptional and intensely original in form.

3. The rebirth of Ebla and its meaning for the history of Ancient Western Asia

From a viewpoint that has long been dominant in the modern historiography of Western Asia its civilisations have been seen antihistorically, as if everything in them were uniform and fixed. It has been thought legitimate to use the archaeological material of any period, written or other, to put together a unified account of a region's culture. The region is thus presumed to be culturally homogeneous. Similar attitudes have determined the occasional sorting into categories of

Sumerian and Babylonian literature. Old Sumerian, Old Babylonian, and Neo-Assyrian royal inscriptions have been used at random to identify the salient characteristics of 'Mesopotamian' kingship. Anatolian architecture has been reconstructed by reference to a rigid classification of plans. Such research methods may be described as 'philology gone mad'. Works of literature, ideological theories, architectural achievements are treated, not in strict relation to the taste of their time, but so as to ignore the historical reality of cultures as they are most meaningfully expressed and can actually help to define the real essence of a historical period. A process of abstraction, instead of choosing what is significant from a series of individual realities, distorts them into mere outline sketches. These, besides being of course overgeneralised and indistinct, falsify the historical substance. They substitute for the works themselves, alive with a depth of meanings perceptible only in their own time, a range of pale abstractions — genres, schemes, types — which never existed in history and are divorced from every context.

A method so profoundly antihistorical has its roots in an uncritical approach to history. It is fundamentally negative and tends to depreciate in advance the cultures it claims to investigate. The ancient Near Eastern civilisations are valued not for their original contributions to the historical development of mankind but merely as preparatory for other civilisations. These others are on the 'positive' side of the line, and those on the 'negative'. Two different and partly opposed attitudes meet in this view. The classicist values the ancient east simply as the forerunner-without-history of Greece and Rome. The Bible student sees nothing there but the local environment in which revelation operates. Both viewpoints, if only because they are opposed to one another, subordinate the realistic analysis of the cultures of the ancient Near East, in the one case to Hellenic rationalism, in the other to Hebrew religiosity. In either case they are degraded to a mere scenic background, lacking the dimension of time. In either the historical development of cultures is denied.

But cultures do develop in history, and only by giving the greatest possible consideration to their change with time as well as to their location in space can they be properly understood. For the antihistorical viewpoint the rediscovery of the Protosyrian and Old Syrian civilisation of Ebla is nothing but a single tessera of the great mosaic of historic cultures of Prehellenistic Western Asia, apparently all one but really a tangle of random lines and discordant colours. It may be added that Ebla, being an unexpected tessera, only increases the disorganisation and discordance.

For a historically conscious view, by contrast, Ebla has a different meaning. It has been revealed first of all as one of the critical, early turning points in the spread of city civilisation to the West. But it acquires also a special force from the light it throws on other disputed points of ancient Near Eastern history. The discoveries at Ebla answer certain questions but those they ask are just as fundamental. They are all connected with the question of the origins of the Protosyrian and Old Syrian cultures of Ebla, and some decisive answers will certainly be contributed by interpretations of the archaeological and epigraphic material of Tell Mardikh as they accumulate in the years to come. First, in what environment did the Protosyrian culture originate, what were its components, and how did it form? Secondly, how did the Protosyrian culture develop in terms of the actual connections of the Protodynastic and Akkadian world with Ebla? Thirdly, what identified the Old Syrian culture in the tangle of relations characterising the age of the Amorite dynasties? Fourthly, what was the succession, continuous or otherwise, of the pre-classical cultures of Syria from their remote origins, which are now beginning to be identified, up to the threshold of the classical age?

Merely to ask these questions represents an overthrow of the previous conclusions of modern historiography of the cultures of Syria. Instead of a perfunctory sketch of development attributed entirely to influences from outside we have today a solid array of evidence to be sorted into cultural assemblages for judgment each as a whole. The new thinking required by archaeological exploration however wide in scope or complete in its coverage of long periods of time, is neither more nor less than a demand for homogeneity in the grouping of material for study and the avoidance of judgments based on chance objects divorced from a precise text.

Any assessment of the culture of Syria in the third millennium had been made virtually impossible by the obliteration or sparseness of the material evidence. In place of this blank canvas the Ebla discoveries have provided a picture, still to be filled out in detail but already drawn in general outline, of a North-West Semitic high urban culture, with which we are becoming acquainted at the centre of its political power and in the time of its greatest prosperity. Its Protohistoric Old Sumerian component is grafted on a vigorous local stock from which its religion and ways of thinking largely derive. The result was the formation of a high urban culture of the Late Protohistoric Period in North Syria. Uniform and homogeneous in its development, the Protosyrian culture certainly had its biggest centre in Ebla up to about 2250 B.C. After that date and up to the final catastrophe, to be dated about 2000 B.C., it is possible that Urshu became the most important Protosyrian centre. The economic structure of the Protosyrian culture must have been based largely on the trade in finished goods, from cloth to works of fine craftsmanship.

For what followed, in the second millennium, the old picture was one of a succession of outside influences, Egyptian and Babylonian. It was based on the occurrence in Syria of certain art works, indicating contacts at a high level, mostly diplomatic, and on doubtful, often false, derivations of iconographic themes. This picture has now been replaced. Instead, the Ebla excavations have supplied detailed and abundant evidence of what was certainly among the oldest and most important centres of Middle Bronze Age Syria. The Protosyrian decline had no doubt been partly economic, not unconnected perhaps with the rigid control of the whole of Mesopotamia by the kings of the Third Dynasty of Ur. After the regime's collapse there was an interregnum, a prolonged crisis provoked by the absorption of the Amorites. Out of these population changes the Old Syrian culture emerged. It is a striking circumstance that this culture played a similar part in Syria to that played by the Old Babylonian age in the formation of a Babylonian culture. It was in the Old Syrian Period, especially its mature phase, that the foundations were laid of later Syrian traditions. It was an age when, over the whole Fertile Crescent, Amorite dynasties were installed in the larger cities of Mesopotamia and Syria. As a consequence, the special features of the Old Babylonian, Old Assyrian and Old Anatolian cultures were finally established. The age of the Amorite dynasties was decidedly that in which the greatest development of city civilisation in Syria and the formation of its literary and artistic traditions occurred. In the mature phase of the Old Syrian Period this development seems to have given rise to a remarkable diffusion of the Middle Bronze culture in the Palestine area, with features of a predominantly provincial type.

The break in the history of the Tell Mardikh settlement and also in the general transition from the Protosyrian to the Old Syrian culture is irrefutably attested by the archaeological evidence. There is no doubt however that the roots of the Old Syrian were in the Protosyrian. Profound changes in the economic and social base must have given rise at the outset of the Middle Bronze Age to an evolution of religious feeling or perhaps of the ideological foundations of institutions. There seems however to be no doubt that the Protosyrian culture was the origin of at least some of the concepts which had a long history, not only in the pre-classical and classical East but in the West as well. Among these was the image of the great goddess, ruler of wild beasts and protectress of flocks; and the ideology of universal kingship, which had such a long and significant resonance from the Hellenistic age to the Roman, and from the Roman to the Medieval West. These are only two aspects of the extraordinary creativity of the Protosyrian culture, and the contribution of Ebla, which went far beyond the development of the historical cultures of the ancient Near East.

The definition of Ebla's contribution in historically valid terms is the aim of the studies now under way, occasioned by the archaeological discoveries and written records of Tell Mardikh. It has already become a focus of critical reflection on the most ancient phases of Near-Eastern history. The assessment of this contribution will be progressive, an outcome of the dialogue now beginning and continually to be renewed among archaeologists, philologists and historians on the great Protosyrian culture revealed by Ebla.

8

Bibliographical Note

The preliminary excavation reports of the Expeditions working in Syria before the Second World War are generally to be found in the major technical journals of the archaeological institutes of the individual countries. Specially important among these is *Syria* (Paris) published by the French Institute in Beirut. In the years since the war the excavation reports have been appearing in the *Annales Archéologiques Arabes Syriennes* (Damascus).

On Ebla in the Old Syrian Period, besides the author's preliminary reports, reference may be made in general to P. Matthiae, 'Les fouilles à Tell Mardikh de la Mission Archéologique en Syrie de l'Université de Rome', in *Rivista degli Studi Orientali*, 42 (1967), pp. 19–26; P. Matthiae, 'Tell Mardikh, Origine et développement de la grande culture urbaine de la Syrie du Nord à l'époque des royaumes amorrhéens', in *Archeologia*, 69 (1974), pp. 16–31; P. Matthiae, 'Ebla nel periodo delle dinastie amorree e della dinastia di Akkad. Scoperte archeologiche recenti a Tell Mardikh', in *Orientalia*, 44 (1975), pp. 337–60. On the architecture, M. Liverani, 'Il Settore B', in *Missione Archeologica Italiana in Siria, 1965 (MAIS 1965)*, Rome 1966, pp. 31–58; M. Floriani Squarciapino, 'Il Settore D', in *MAIS 1965*, pp. 59–79; M. Floriani Squarciapino, 'Il Settore D', in *Missione Archeologica Italiana in Siria, 1966 (MAIS 1966)*, Rome 1967, pp. 63–77; P. Matthiae, 'Unité et développement du temple dans la Syrie du Bronze Moyen', in *Compte Rendu de la XXe Rencontre Assyriologique Internationale, Leiden 1972*, Leiden, 1975, pp. 43–72. On the art in general, P. Matthiae, 'Syrische Kunst', in W. Orthmann, *Propyläen Kunstgeschichte, XIV, Der Alte Orient*, Berlin 1975, pp. 466–93. On the sculpture, P. Matthiae, 'Le sculture di Tell Mardikh', in *Rendiconti della Pontificia Accademia Romana di Archeologia*, 38 (1965–1966), pp. 19–59; P. Matthiae, 'Le sculture in basalto', in *Missione Archeologica Italiana in Siria, 1964 (MAIS 1964)*, Rome 1965, pp. 61–80; P. Matthiae, 'Le sculture in pietra', in *MAIS 1966*, pp. 103–42; P. Matthiae, 'I frammenti di sculture in pietra', in *MAIS 1965*, pp. 111–38. On the glyptics, P. Matthiae, 'Empreintes d'un cylindre paléosyrien de Tell Mardikh', in *Syria*, 46 (1969), pp. 1–43; S. Mazzoni, 'Tell Mardikh e una classe glittica siroanatolica del periodo di Larsa', in *Annali dell'Istituto Universitario Orientale di Napoli*, 25 (1975), pp. 21–43. On other finds, P. Matthiae, 'Le figurine in terracotta', in *MAIS 1964*, pp. 81–103; P. Fronzaroli–G. Matthiae Scandone, 'Le figurine in terracotta', in *MAIS 1966*, pp. 139–52; A. de Maigret, 'Due lance iscritte da Tell Mardikh-Ebla', in *Rivista degli Studi Orientali*, 50 (1976), pp. 22–35.

On the identification of Ebla see P. Matthiae, 'Tell Mardikh, Excavations in the campaigns 1967 and 1968', in *Archaeology*, 24 (1971), pp. 55–61; P. Matthiae–G. Pettinato, *Il torso di Ibbit-Lim, re di Ebla*, Rome 1972. On the Tell Mardikh region see M. Liverani, 'I tell preclassici', in *MAIS 1964*, pp. 107–33; A. de Maigret, 'Tell Munbatah. Un nuovo sito nordsiriano del periodo caliciforme', in *Oriens Antiquus*, 13 (1974), pp. 249–98.

On Ebla in the Protosyrian Period see P. Matthiae, 'Ebla. Fouilles de Tell Mardikh', in *Encyclopaedia Universalis, Universalia 75*, Paris 1976, pp. 193–96; P. Matthiae, 'La scoperta del Palazzo Reale G e degli Archivi di Ebla (c. 2400–2250 B.C.)', in *La Parola del Passato*, 168 (1976), pp. 233–66; P. Matthiae, 'Ibla, B. Archäologisch', *Reallexikon der Assyriologie*, 5, Berlin 1976, pp. 13–20; P. Matthiae, 'Preliminary Remarks on the Royal Palace G of Early Syrian Ebla', in *Syro-Mesopotamian Studies*, in the press; P. Matthiae, 'Le palais royal protosyrien d'Ebla: nouvelles recherches archéoligiques à Tell Mardikh en 1976', in *Académie des Inscriptions et Belles-Lettres, Compte Rendus*, 1977, pp. 148–72; P. Matthiae, 'A Fragment of a "Second Transition Period" Statuette from Tell Mardikh', in *Baghdader Mitteilungen* (= Festschrift A. Moortgat), 7 (1974), pp. 125–37; R. Dolce, 'Su alcuni resti di intarsi del periodo protodinastico da Tell Mardikh-Ebla', in *Oriens Antiquus*, 16 (1977), pp. 1–24; P. Matthiae, 'Impronte di cilindri del Periodo Protosiriano IIA dal Palazzo Reale di Tell Mardikh-Ebla', in *Archiv für Orientforschung*, in the press; P. Matthiae, 'Les intailles en bois du palais royal G d'Ebla et l'art syrien du IIIe milléniare av.J.-C.', which will appear in *Syria*.

On the State Archives of the Protosyrian Period see P. Matthiae, 'La biblioteca reale di Ebla (2400–2250 B.C.). Risultati della Missione Archeologica Italiana in Siria, 1975', in *Rendiconti della Pontificia Accademia Romana di Archeologia*, 48 (1976), pp. 19–45; P. Matthiae, 'Le Palais Royal et les Archives d'Etat d'Ebla protosyrienne', in *Akkadica* 2 (1977), pp. 2–19; G. Pettinato, 'I testi cuneiformi della biblioteca reale di Tell Mardikh. Notizia preliminare sulla scuola di Ebla', in *Rendiconti della Pontificia Accademia Romana di Archeologia*, 48 (1976), pp. 46–58; G. Pettinato, 'Ibla. A. Philologisch', in *Reallexikon der Assyriologie*, 5 (1976), pp. 9–13; G. Pettinato, 'The Royal Archives of Tell Mardikh-Ebla', in *Biblical Archaeologist*, 39 (1976), pp. 44–52. On the language of Protosyrian Ebla see G. Pettinato, 'Testi cuneiformi del 3. millennio in paleo-cananeo rinvenuti nella campagna 1974 a Tell Mardikh-Ebla', in *Orientalia*, 44 (1975), pp. 361–74; P. Fronzaroli, 'West Semitic Toponymy in Northern Syria in the Third Millennium B.C.' in *Journal of Semitic Studies*, 22 (1977), pp. 145–66; I. J. Gelb, 'Thoughts about Ibla', in *Syro-Mesopotamian Studies*, I/1 (1977), pp. 1–28. On the history, administration, and religion of Protosyrian Ebla see P. Matthiae, 'Ebla à l'époque d'Akkad: archéologie et histoire', in *Académie des Inscriptions et Belles-Lettres, Comptes Rendus*, 1976, pp. 190–215; G. Pettinato, 'Carchemish-Kar-Kamish. Le prime attestazioni del III millennio', in *Oriens Antiquus*, 15 (1976), pp. 11–15; P. Matthiae– G. Pettinato, 'Aspetti amministrativi e topografici di Ebla nel III millennio a.C.', in *Rivista degli Studi Orientali*, 50 (1976), pp. 1–30; G. Pettinato, 'Il calendario di Ebla al tempo del re Ibbi-Sipish sulla base di TM.75.G.427', in *Archiv für Orientforschung*, 25 (1977), pp. 1–36; P. Matthiae, 'Ebla in the Late Early Syrian Period: the Royal Palace and the State Archives', in *Biblical Archaeologist*, 39 (1976), pp. 94–113; G. Pettinato, 'Relations entre les royaumes d'Ebla et de Mari au IIIe millénaire d'après les Archives Royales de Tell Mardikh-Ebla', in *Akkadica*, 2 (1977), pp. 20–28; G. Pettinato, 'Dagan e il suo culto ad Ebla. Un primo bilancio', in a forthcoming volume of the Oriental Seminary at Heidelberg; G. Pettinato, 'Gli Archivi Reali di Tell-Mardikh-Ebla, Riflessioni e prospettive', in *Rivista Biblica Italiana*.

Index

Note to the Index

Entries for Tell Mardikh are grouped according to the author's chapter headings, which correspond to phases in the city's development and rediscovery. There is also a section dealing with specific buildings and structures. Entries for pottery, sculpture, etc., which appear here in their appropriate periods (e.g. Mardikh IIB1), may also be found elsewhere in the index as independent collective entries.

Tell Mardikh, the Tell, from the South-East.

The Lower City and the West Rampart, from the South.

The Acropolis, from the South-West.

The East Rampart, from the South.

Royal Palace G, the east façade of the Court of Audience, from the South.

Royal Palace G, the Royal Dais in the Court of Audience, from the East.

Royal Palace G, the first flight of the Ceremonial Stairway, from above.

Royal Palace G, entrance to the Ceremonial Stairway, from inside.

Royal Palace G, the Monumental Gateway, from the West.

Royal Palace G, the steps of the Monumental Gateway, from the South-East.

Royal Palace G, Store Room L.2712, detail of north wall.

Royal Palace G, Vestibule
L.2875, from the East.

Royal Palace G, door to Vestibule L.2875, detail of the
inlaid steps.

Royal Palace G, Archive Room L.2769, from the South.

Royal Palace G, Room L.2834 of the Guard House, from above.

Royal Palace G, Room L.2834, detail of the door.

Royal Palace G, Room L.2764 of the Administrative Quarters from the West.

Royal Palace G, Room L.2866 of the
Administrative Quarters from the
East.

Royal Palace G, Archive Room
L.2769, from the West.

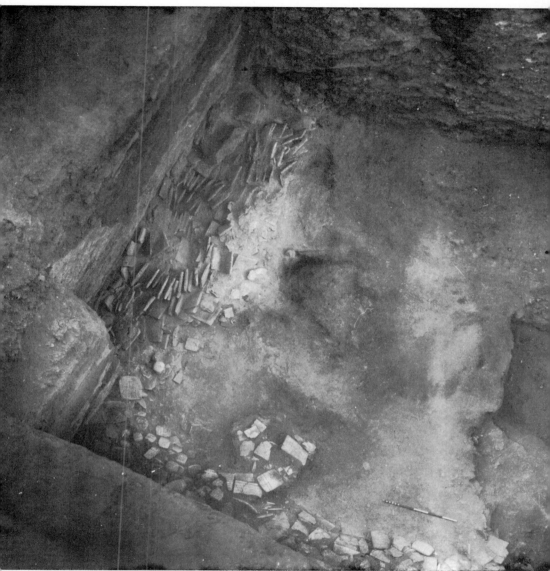

Royal Palace G, tablets *in situ* along the north and east walls of Archive Room L.2769.

Royal Palace G, tablets *in situ* along the north wall of Archive Room L.2769.

Royal Palace G, tablets *in situ* along the east wall of Archive Room L.2769.

Royal Palace G, tablets *in situ* on the floor against the north wall of Archive Room L.2769.

Relief with heads of dignitaries (TM.76.G.3000), wood, from Room L.2764 of Royal Palace G.

Bull-man figurine (TM.76.G.850), gold and soapstone, from Room L.2764 of Royal Palace G. (Aleppo Archaeological Museum)

Arm of chair with openwork carving and inlay, wood, from Room L.2601 of
Palace G.

Relief of lion sinking his teeth into a caprid (TM.74.G.1010), wood, from
Room L.2601 of Palace G.
(Aleppo Archaeological Museum)

Relief with figure of king with axe (TM.74.G.1000), wood, from Room L.2601
of Palace G.
(Aleppo Archaeological Museum)

Relief with figures of warriors (TM.74.G.1011), wood, from Room L.2601 of Palace G.

Relief with lion attacking a bull (TM.74.G.1012 and 1013), wood, from Room L.2601 of Palace G.
(Aleppo Archaeological Museum)

Top. Fragments of a composite plaque with procession scene, limestone and lapis-lazuli from Room L.2866 of Palace G.

Left. Turban of a royal statuette (TM.76.G.830), limestone, from Room L.2764 of Palace G.

Right. Gold foil with incised decoration (TM.76.G.851), from Room L.2764 of Palace G.
(Aleppo Archaeological Museum)

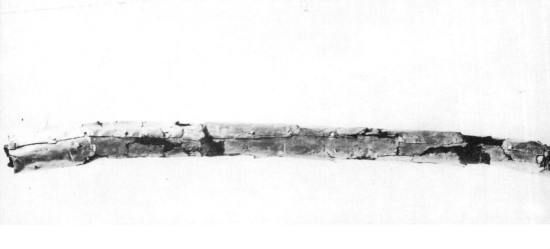

Above. Sceptre (TM.74.G.604), wood and gold, from Room L.2601 of Palace G.

Below, left. Fragment of inlay with prisoners' heads (TM.72.B.335), limestone, from Sector B.

Below, right. Fragment of skirt of statuette (TM.70.B.113), limestone, from Sector B.
(Aleppo Archaeological Museum)

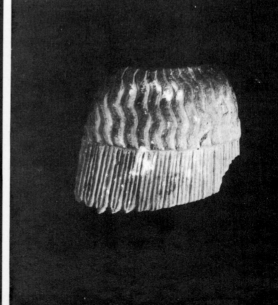

Bullae with cylinder seal impressions (TM.75.G.630 and 588), clay, from
Room L.2716 of Palace G.
(Aleppo Archaeological Museum)

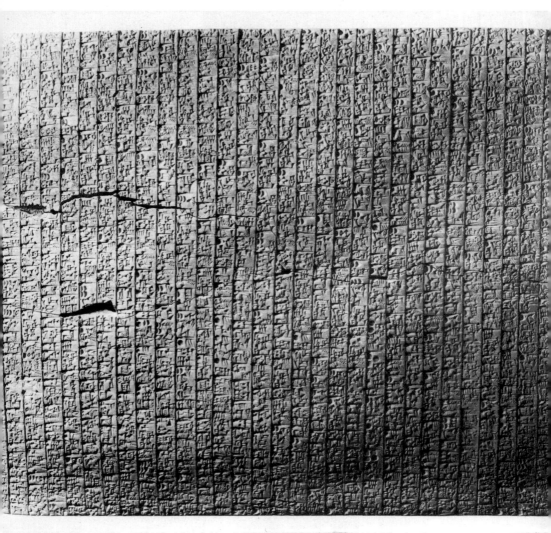

Cuneiform tablet with economic text (TM.75.G.2429), clay, from Room
L.2769 of Palace G.
(Aleppo Archaeological Museum)

Cuneiform tablets with economic texts (TM.75.G.1559 and
1527), clay, from Room L.2769 of Palace G.
(Aleppo Archaeological Museum)

Cuneiform tablet with lexical lists
(TM.75.G.2422), clay, from Room
L.2769 of Palace G.

Cuneiform tablet (TM.75.G.1713),
clay, from Room L.2769 of Palace G.
(Aleppo Archaeological Museum)

Cuneiform tablet with economic text (TM.75.G.2115), clay, from Room L.2769 of Palace G.

Cuneiform tablet with lexical lists (TM.75.G.1415), clay, from Room L.2769 of Palace G.
(Aleppo Archaeological Museum)

Cuneiform tablet with economic text (TM.75.G.1781), clay, from Room
L.2769 of Palace G.
(Aleppo Archaeological Museum)

Cuneiform tablet with historical text (TM.75.G.2367), clay, from Room
L.2769 of Palace G.
(Aleppo Archaeological Museum)

Sector G, the stone stairway
towards Great Temple D,
from the South.

Great Temple D, the sounding
in the Cella L.204, from the
East.

Sector H, filling at the top of the West Rampart, from the
South.

Sector A, trench on the exterior of the South-West Rampart,
from the South.

Torso of statue with the inscription of Ibbit-Lim (TM.68.G.61), basalt.
(Aleppo Archaeological Museum)

City Gate A, from the North.

City Gate A, detail of the first
pier on the east side.

City Gate A, detail of the
second pier on the east side.

Left. City Gate A, detail of the pivot stones of the inner gateway.

Right. City Gate A, detail with the original east wall of the outer courtyard.

City Gate A, outer gateway, from the North.

City Gate A, detail of west walls, from the East.

Great Temple D, Cella L.204,
from the South.

Great Temple D, detail of
offering table and baetyl in
Cella L.204.

Temple B1, the Cella, from the North and from the South.

Temple N, the Cella,
from the East and
from the West.

Sector B, private houses, from the East.

Sanctuary B2, general view, from the South.

Sanctuary B2, detail of the offering tables in the south corner of Room L.2113.

Sanctuary B2, the central room L.2124, with the dais, from the West.

Sector B, private houses, from the South.

Royal Palace E, rooms on the east side of the courtyard, from the East and from the South.

Royal Palace E, detail of tne south-west area.

Excavated area of Fortress M on the east rampart, from the South.

Fortress M, one of the rooms from the North.

Royal statue (TM.65.A.234), basalt, from Sector A.
(Damascus National Museum)

Relief with warriors' and lions' heads, side of basin, basalt, from Sector B.
(Aleppo Archaeological Museum)

Ritual basin (TM.65.D.226), limestone, from the south-west corner of the
Cella of Temple D.
(Aleppo Archaeological Museum)

Fragment of relief with warrior's head (TM.65.D.227), basalt, from the Cella of Great Temple D.

Fragment of basin wall with bull-man (TM.65.B.230), basalt, from Sector B.
(Aleppo Archaeological Museum)

Ritual basin (TM.72.N.468), limestone, from the Cella of Temple N.
(Aleppo Archaeological Museum)

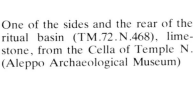

One of the sides and the rear of the ritual basin (TM.72.N.468), limestone, from the Cella of Temple N. (Aleppo Archaeological Museum)

Side face of the ritual basin: detail with heads of goddesses (TM.72.N.468), limestone, from the Cella of Temple N.

Fragment of wall of basin with bull-man's head (TM.64.B.23), basalt, from Sector B.
(Aleppo Archaeological Museum)

Base of statue with bull-man figures (TM.72.N.565), basalt, from Temple N.
(Aleppo Archaeological Museum)

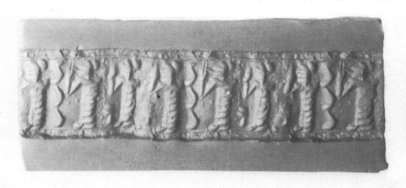

Top and middle. Cylinder seals of the Archaic Old Syrian Period (TM.70.B.232 and TM.70.E.505).

Above. Cylinder seal of hykos type (TM.70.B.231).

Left. Incised plaque with three goddesses (TM.66.E.144).
(Aleppo Archaeological Museum)

Spear heads (TM.71.M.842 and 841), bronze, from Fortress M.

Bulla with cylinder seal impression of Mature Old Syrian Period (TM.71.M.843), clay, from Fortress M.
(Aleppo Archaeological Museum)

Fragments of jars with cylinder seal impressions
(TM.66.B.207 and TM.65.B.843), clay, from Sector B.
(Aleppo Archaeological Museum)

Small pot with female head (TM.70.B.930), vitreous paste, from Sector B.

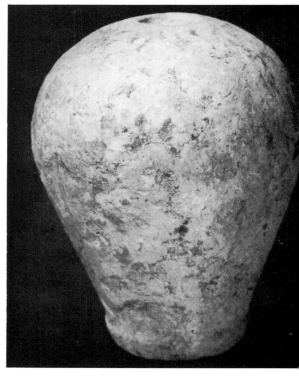

Left. Handle of ritual knife (TM.72.N.409), bone, from the Cella of Temple N.

Right. Mace head (TM.71.M.737), whitish stone, from Fortress M. (Aleppo Archaeological Museum)

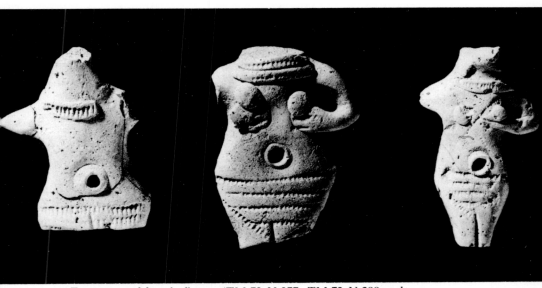

Fragments of female figures (TM.72.N.277, TM.72.N.299 and
TM.72.N.307), clay.
(Aleppo Archaeological Museum)

Sector E, entrance to the Persian building, from the West and from the South.

Female figurines (TM.71.E.453 and TM.70.E.516), clay, from Sector E.
(Aleppo Archaeological Museum)

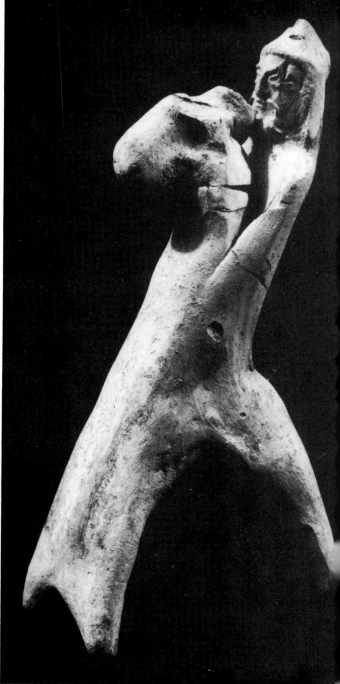

Heads of female figurines
(TM.71.E.220 and TM.65.S.50),
clay, from Sector E.

Figurine of horseman (TM.65.E.153),
clay, from Sector E.
(Aleppo Archaeological Museum)